URBAN DEPRIVATION AND THE INNER CITY

URBAN DEPRIVATION AND THE INNER CITY

EDITED BY COLIN JONES

CROOM HELM LONDON

©1979 Colin Jones
Croom Helm Ltd, 2-10 St John's Road, London SW11
ISBN 0-85664-713-6

British Library Cataloguing in Publication Data

Urban deprivation and the inner city
   1. Cities and towns – Great Britain
   2. Great Britain – Social conditions – 1945 –
   I. Jones, Colin, b. 1929
   362'.042' 0941   HT133

Printed in Great Britain by offset lithography by
Billing & Sons Ltd, Guildford, London and Worcester

CONTENTS

ACKNOWLEDGEMENTS

The idea for this book was generated from a series of papers given to the SSRC Urban and Regional Economics Seminar Group.

My thanks are due to John Firn for his enthusiasm at the inception of the project and to John Parr not only for his encouragement throughout but also for his kindly forbearance at my innumerable requests for advice at vital stages of the editing. In addition I am indebted to Christine MacCallum who typed a large proportion of the final manuscript.

PREFACE

This book represents an attempt to study closely a topic of great policy importance. It is examined essentially through the medium of the case study, with contributors drawing on the experience of all the major conurbations of Britain. The contributors themselves come from a wide range of fields — economics, geography, public administration, social policy and sociology — to provide a comprehensive look at the question. An attempt is made by each contributor to pull together the policy implications of their analysis and many are critical of the government's strategy, some are very critical.

INTRODUCTION

Dereliction, high concentrations of unemployment, drab and vandalised council estates, low educational achievements by schoolchildren, factory closures, decaying neighbourhoods and population decline in our cities and conurbations can all be regarded as inner city problems. Some of these phenomena can also be described as aspects of urban deprivation. If there are differences between the two, they are partly in the breadth of definition: the inner city problem for instance relates not just to people and the areas they live in but also to firms; and partly in spatial location, since urban deprivation is not necessarily found in the inner city.

But where is the inner city? This question is not easily answered; indeed it is much easier to recognise an inner city problem than to define where the inner city itself is. The Lambeth Inner Area Study (Great Britain, 1977a), for example, defines its study area by reference to where the inner city problems are, not the other way round. Indeed it is possible to identify those areas of the city where the problems of employment loss, high unemployment, public and private housing problems,and population decline, etc. are each individually confined or at least predominate. Thus Dicken and Lloyd (chapter 2) consider just the contiguous central industrial zone immediately adjacent to the central business district; Karn (chapter 7) is concerned with the inner areas of nineteenth-century terraced housing; Bramley (chapter 3) and Jones (chapter 8) both focus on the nineteenth-century cores of our conurbations.

If we are to attempt to define the inner city it would be as a series of possibly overlapping zones or areas, one for each problem. These areas would not necessarily be coincident or even contiguous; there is for instance quite likely to be a band of local authority housing between the central industrial areas and the neighbourhoods of nineteenth-century housing still remaining. This no doubt long and tedious task would be something of a diversion and is not pursued here. A rough and ready guide perhaps would be the nineteenth-century urban areas and their subsequent redevelopment.

Urban deprivation, too, is not scattered at random; many of the concentrations of social problems associated with the concept are to be found in the inner parts of large towns and cities. They are, however,

11

not confined to these areas; and indeed the deprived estate, Ferguslie Park, whose problems are examined in chapters 4 and 5, is one such estate. The spatial definition in this respect is unimportant; the forces which fashion urban deprivation in the inner urban areas are not distinct from those which do so at the periphery.

The notion of urban deprivation is discussed in detail by Norris (chapter 1); he argues that it should not be seen as a state but as a process. The same logic applies to the concept of the inner city problem. Thus the inner city problem is useful not as a spatial description of where the problems exist but as a way of looking at the problems in our urban areas. It provides an umbrella for an examination of (and for the government to tackle) the interaction of urban economic decline, physical decay and the concentrations of the socially disadvantaged, particularly poor people. It is this approach which we follow in this book, as we attempt to explore the divergent processes and interactions within and between different sectors of the urban system, and the subsequent problems which arise.

A Perspective on the Problem

Since the early 1960s all Britain's major cities have experienced massive industrial decline, particularly in their inner parts. In Central Clydeside, for example, the numbers employed dropped from 808,000 to 704,000 between 1961 and 1971; this decrease of 8.4 per cent was the largest fall of all the conurbations outside London. At the same time there was an increase in employment in the rest of Great Britain outside the conurbations of 7.9 per cent (Great Britain, 1977b). It is generally accepted that the most significant decline in employment has been in manufacturing industry rather than services. Dicken and Lloyd (chapter 2) examine the components of this decline for manufacturing industry in Manchester between 1966 and 1975; they note significant differences between the experience of that city and Liverpool.

One major explanation for the decline in manufacturing industry is that the conurbations, and the core cities in particular, historically contain a high proportion of firms and industries that in recent years have become uncompetitive. But as the cities have lost a higher proportion of jobs than would be suggested by national trends and their industrial structure, this cannot describe the whole picture (Keeble, 1978). One factor in the process has been the restructuring of British industry and the consequent mergers and changes of ownership during this period. The extent and impact of these changes are also discussed by Dicken and Lloyd (chapter 2).

Meanwhile the development of factory lines has meant that production technologies have become more spatially extensive. Since the last war there has also been a revolution in communications, particularly with the general improvement in the roads network and the building of motorways but also in rail transport. These changes together with the greater locational freedom and flexibility of multi-plant firms has meant that the periphery of the conurbations or areas outside the conurbations have become more attractive to industry than the inner cities.

In addition the late 1960s saw a vast slum clearance programme which although mainly aimed at improving housing conditions also led indirectly to the displacement of industry. Often small firms just closed down while others moved out to modern premises on the edge of the city. In parts of Britain this compulsive movement from the nineteenth-century urban cores was exacerbated by the Government's regional policy through Industrial Development Certificates. The refusal of such a certificate meant that some firms who wished to expand were forced to move to the Development Regions of the country.

Other firms chose to move to the periphery in order to escape their cramped and possibly dated premises to facilitate growth. The overall impact of these various components of change has been the decentralisation of industry. Indeed Cameron and Evans (1973) note that between 1961 and 1966 this was true for nearly every individual industry in all conurbations.

Even more deep-rooted than the outward movement of jobs has been the suburban trek by the population; Jones (chapter 8) looks at the historical growth and decline of present-day cities and the processes which have shaped them. By reference to Glasgow and Liverpool he shows that the major factors in the decline of the cities' populations have been the reduction in suburban travel costs with the introduction of new modes of travel, slum clearance and overspill policy and the desire for better housing, in part the result of increased incomes.

The impact of population and economic decline in cities has often meant large areas of vacant and derelict land. In addition migration from the cities has been selective; more than half for instance of the householders rehoused under formal overspill agreements by Glasgow were foremen, supervisors and skilled manual workers. Similarly migrants also tended to be younger than the average for the population as a whole; 28 per cent of the net-migrants from Glasgow between 1966 and 1971 were aged between 25 and 34 years. The consequences are an increasing proportion of economically dependent people in core cities.

The loss of skilled and young members of the labour force from the core cities has important implications for the spatial distribution of unemployment. For as Bramley (chapter 3) and McGregor (chapter 4) note these are major factors which influence an individual's vulnerability to unemployment. The unskilled are generally much more prone to unemployment than other groups wherever they are living.

Overlaid on this has been the industrial decline and decentralisation which has led to a reduction in the demand for labour, particularly in the core cities of the conurbations. In addition the geographical, industrial and demographic features of the inner city create a distinctive labour market which leads to possible problems such as a mismatch of jobs and skills. Based mainly on evidence from London, Bramley (chapter 3) seeks to explain the relative importance of these factors in the determination of the high unemployment rates of inner city residents.

Whatever the precise nature of the process, Holtermann (1975) shows that in each conurbation at the time of the 1971 Census, the inner area normally defined by the core city contained a higher proportion of the worst unemployment enumeration districts (EDs) than its share. The contrast is most dramatic in South-East Lancashire where Manchester and Salford account for 29 per cent of all the conurbation's EDs and 73 per cent of the worst 5 per cent of male unemployment EDs.

Usually these EDs or pockets of high unemployment are either situated in neighbourhoods of cheap private housing or low-grade council estates. McGregor (chapter 4) looks at the labour market experiences of males living in one of these estates. In particular he examines the hypothesis that the spatial concentration of households who are unable to generate high or regular incomes compounds and reinforces their individual problems through stigmatisation in the labour market.

These low-grade housing estates tend to be either tenements built in the 1930s to rehouse families from slum clearance or new medium or high-rise housing dating from the mid-1960s or even later. English (chapter 5) considers the allocation of tenants to these estates and the policy implications. These estates invariably suffer from design faults and in the case of the older housing from consistent neglect with respect to maintenance and improvements.

A similar lack of investment and decay is found in the older areas of low-quality private housing. The low outlays on repairs and renovation come on top of the fact that most of these houses were built without basic amenities. The lack of investment in these older houses can be seen as a response to economic forces. One element has undoubtedly been the blight of these areas, particularly the apparently unending drive of urban renewal programmes, initially in the form of slum clearance and now taking the shape of improvement. (A review and critique of these policies is provided by Mason (chapter 6).) The consequent questions over the expected life or ownership of these properties has led to an acceleration of the physical deterioration.

Another factor in this process of physical decline is the (former) concentration of rented properties in these areas. The demise of the private landlord began at the turn of the century and was fuelled by the unfavourable tax position of housing relative to other investments and successive measures of rent control. Today many of these properties which were formerly rented are now owner-occupied but the legacy of disrepair and lack of maintenance remains.

Unfortunately the new occupants in these neighbourhoods also have their problems, not least of which as Karn (chapter 7) describes are their low incomes which seriously constrain the amounts they have available to spend on repairs and improvements. On top of this she shows how the reluctance of building societies and the local authority to give mortgages on houses in three typical areas of nineteenth-century houses in Birmingham serves to exacerbate the level of disinvestment in these neighbourhoods.

Summary

In this introduction we have attempted to provide an outline of the contents of the subsequent chapters within a broad overview of the subject. The emphasis of the book is on the analysis of the processes at work which create the problems in our urban areas. There is indisputably a wide range of forces which have helped fashion the urban problems of today and we can only claim to consider the more important. The processes examined can be seen to be sometimes independent, sometimes overlapping but always reinforcing.

Much of the interpretation of these processes, as you will read, questions the efficacy of the government's policies towards inner city regeneration. Part of the answer lies in additional money and a better use of the present resources. But is the inner city problem just a problem of markets or rather system failure? The development of the motor age and the beginnings of a new industrial revolution may well lead to fundamental changes in urban structure; just as there was a shift from a rural to an industrial and urban economy in the nineteenth century. If so, like Canute we are fighting against the tide.

References

Cameron, G.C. and Evans, A.W. (1973) 'The British Conurbation Centres', *Regional Studies*, vol. 7, pp. 47-55

Great Britain (1977a) Department of the Environment, 'Inner London: Policies for Dispersal and Balance,' Final Report of the Lambeth Inner Area Study, London: HMSO

Great Britain (1977b) Department of Employment, 'Employment in Metropolitan Areas.'

Holtermann, S' (1975) 'Areas of Urban Deprivation in Great Britain: An Analysis of 1971 Census Data,' *Social Trends*, no. 6, London: HMSO

Keeble, D. (1978) 'Industrial Decline in the Inner City and Conurbation,' *Transactions*, Institute of British Geographies, new series, vol. 3, no. 1, pp. 101-14

1 DEFINING URBAN DEPRIVATION

Geoff Norris

Towards the end of the 1960s the concept of deprivation entered the arena of academic and political discourse on the problems of economic and social inequality in Britain. Prior to the emergence of this concept, analysis of these issues had been carried out through the use of the concept of poverty (i.e. material poverty), the examination of poor housing (particularly the study of 'slum' areas), and to a lesser extent through research into the level of provision of services provided by central and local government. One of the reasons for the popularity of the concept of deprivation has been its attempt to bring together the issues raised by these problem areas under the umbrella of a more general approach. This very generality has raised a number of critical definitional issues, which it is the purpose of this chapter to explore.

The chapter, however, is not intended as a summary of the existing literature on deprivation. While there have been a number of interesting critical commentaries in the academic journals (for example Edwards, 1975; Hamnett, 1976) which provide accounts of the problems, much of the more important work, in terms of its practical consequences, has been carried out by researchers in central and local government who have been attempting to relate the concepts of deprivation, multiple deprivation and urban deprivation to the problems and policies of their political masters. There are a number of widely published accounts of this type of analysis (Great Britain, 1975a; Flynn et al., 1972) but it is probable that much that has been written has remained unpublished.

While it is not therefore possible to undertake a complete examination of this body of work as a whole there are grounds for suggesting that there is a tendency to adopt similar procedures and definitions in the analysis of the problem. Central and local government researchers face similar political and methodological difficulties for reasons which are explored later and consequently similar definitional approaches are likely to follow. It is a discussion of these definitional problems, and the consequences and pitfalls of the solutions adopted, which form the focus of this chapter.

An interest in definitional problems does not mean, however, that the aim here is to develop a set of concepts which can be used to derive an unambiguous definition of urban deprivation against which practice

17

can be measured. Rather our aim is initially to outline the definitions
which appear to have been implicit in much of this work; implicit for,
in fact, in many cases there was no attempt to rigorously define the
relevant concepts. The chapter will then argue that even within the
terms of these definitions actual empirical studies have committed a
number of methodological errors with practical consequences. Many
of these criticisms have been discussed elsewhere in some detail
particularly by Edwards (1975) but also Hamnett (1976), and
consequently the discussion here attempts to be brief but comprehensive.

A second aim of the chapter will be to understand the reasons which
lie behind these failures. The concluding discussion therefore extends
outside the narrow confines of the definitional framework in order to
examine those ways in which this framework itself predisposes analysts
towards a certain view of the problems and at the same time forecloses
discussion on other significant issues raised by the concept of deprivation.

Definitional Problems

Any attempt to come to grips with the notion of deprivation has to
tackle the issues raised by three separate concepts: deprivation,
multiple deprivation and urban deprivation. These three terms have
provided the major themes around which many students of the problem
of inequality in our society have played a number of variations. The
fact that 'the problem of inequality' is the overarching issue which has
been underlying much of this analysis should serve as a reminder of the
fact that much of the earlier work in this field was carried on under the
banner of the analysis of poverty itself.

It would appear to be the case that the interest in poverty in
advanced capitalist societies which burgeoned during the early and
middle 1960s has now been superseded by the concern with deprivation.
A useful way into the problem of defining deprivation lies therefore
through an examination of the way in which the concept constitutes a
development on this earlier work in poverty. Since shortly after the
Second World War with an early paper by Townsend (1954) poverty
has been seen as a problem of inequality in the distribution of resources;
that is the inadequacy of material resources relative to the living
standards of society as a whole.

The concept of deprivation would appear to introduce two features
to the analysis of inequality. First, deprivation is clearly an attempt to
bring into the arena of discussion features which lie outside a rather
narrow concern with purely material resources. The use of the word
displays an apparent sensitivity to problems of emotional and cultural

deprivation for example which the poverty analysts of the 1960s tended to ignore in their struggle to obtain official recognition for the continued existence of stark material inequality in an age of so-called affluence. While the poor were often seen as those lying at the bottom of an overall distribution the deprived can be interpreted as being those who fall below a certain well-defined line. It turns the examination away from a study of the overall structure to those who do not reach a certain level.

The introduction therefore of the problem of accessibility to non-material resources by the use of the notion of deprivation means that the issue is seen as multidimensional. Multiple deprivation as an issue emerges from this feature of deprivation as a concept. If deprivation means a relative lack of access to all kinds of resources, both material and non-material, then an immediate problem is the identification of the relationship between an individual's position and the whole range of dimensions to which the general notion is supposed to apply. The identification of the multiply deprived, those who appear at the bottom end of each of several dimensions of unequally distributed resources, and attempts to explain why such reinforcement occurs, have provided major research themes in recent years. One of the processes involved here, the fact that the unequal distribution of some resources in space 'explains' the incidence of multiple deprivation, has given rise in its turn to a further elaboration of the deprivation concept, urban deprivation.

It would be quite reasonable to maintain that the notion of urban deprivation merely refers to deprivation which occurs in urban areas and that therefore the concept has no special significance. This would, however, constitute an underestimation of its impact and the kind of analysis which it implies. As a result of obvious connections with urban economics the concept of urban deprivation has come to stand for the analysis of the relationship between deprivation and space in general.

In fact the relationship under consideration consists of two separate issues. The first is the purely descriptive question of the extent to which deprivation, and indeed multiple deprivation, is geographically concentrated, not only in certain regions or cities, but more crucially within a particular city. The mapping of the incidence of deprivation at the small-area level has of course raised questions about why this geographical concentration of the problem should occur. The second separate problem which urban deprivation concerns, however, is the more difficult, and politically more significant question, of whether the fact of spatial concentration itself constitutes at least some kind of partial explanation of the overall incidence of deprivation. The concern here then is with the explanatory relevance of space.

Empirical Research

Within the terms of the definitional approach described above attempts to analyse deprivation display three important methodological deficiencies. Faced with a plethora of relevant but not wholly adequate indicators the tendency has been to present deprivation as whatever can be easily measured. There is no critical assessment of the status of different indicators nor any attempt to relate various measures to some underlying explicitly formulated concept. In this sense all indicators are accorded the same validity as measures of deprivation. A second deficiency which follows from this extreme operationalism is that not only are certain dimensions of deprivation more adequately accounted for than others but also it is possible to suggest that identifiable 'errors' are being made. Certain facets of the problem are being ignored.

Third, while it is true that all indicators will in some sense bias the kinds of explanations and policies which are developed, one particular set of indicators appears to owe its importance more to prior assumptions about relevant policies and explanations for deprivation than to its direct relevance to the phenomenon itself. Specifically the emergence of explanations of deprivation in terms of the pathology of individuals (and a consequential recourse to policies based on improving methods of social control and management) is related clearly to the use of certain measures to assess the incidence of deprivation. It is to these latter measures that the chapter now turns for they illustrate not only this third deficiency of research on deprivation but also offer good examples of the first two methodological difficulties noted above.

A number of authors (for example Flynn *et al.*, 1972; Strathclyde Regional Council, 1976) have made use of statistics generated by official agencies whose functions consist in controlling and coping with the immediate problems of certain sections of the poor. Statistics such as crime rates, truancy levels, incidence of social work referrals, all come within this category and have been used to chart the incidence of deprivation in various areas. The deficiencies of these kind of measures even as accurate indicators of the reality they purport to measure have been well known for some time. They measure the incidence of a particular behaviour pattern or attribute as far as this is known to and recorded by the official agency in question.

They are just as much measures of the activities of a particular service or agency as an indicator of the behaviour the latter are attempting to modify or control. In this context comparisons between areas must be particularly suspect. It is well established for example that local authorities will vary in the extent of their provision of a wide range of services for the poor. Differences between areas on these indicators will contain an unknown element which will be accounted for by the different levels of provision between areas.

Secondly, although it is usually correct to argue that the adoption of particular behaviour patterns which cause people to come into contact with these various agencies is related to the experience of poverty and deprivation, what is rarely explicitly stated is that this relationship is rarely simple or the same for all the poor. Crime statistics offer a particularly good example here for it is known that recorded criminal activity is a young man's occupation. Poverty, however, is not infrequently an old woman's fate. Where statistics on crime are used therefore they will necessarily point only to poorer younger people and to the areas in which they live. The poverty of the old is not taken into account by such measures.

It is not sufficient to point to both the measurable and unmeasurable deficiencies of these statistics as indicators of deprivation. It is necessary to underline what they do measure: the recorded incidence of problems which certain, largely working-class poor, sections of the population pose for other, usually more affluent, members of our society. What are recorded are problems of management in the broadest sense. The question which needs to be raised here is whether the importance given to some of these indicators is solely a result of their assumed relationship to deprivation or because they actually measure real problems of social control. The point here is not that social control is necessarily to be rejected as a policy alternative but that it covers quite different issues and policies from those raised by deprivation.

Analytically social control as a problem immediately raises questions concerned with who is controlling whom in whose interests. The problems of power and interests immediately emerge. Secondly, improving social control mechanisms is not and never can be a solution to the problems of deprivation and poverty unless the view is being taken that the reason deprivation is a problem is *because* it leads to antisocial behaviour. However, the two issues, deprivation and antisocial behaviour, should not be confused. If social control is the real issue then this should be made clear, but a policy or a study which concentrates on such issues should not be allowed to masquerade as a policy for deprivation.

Research work which eschews measures based on the activities of various agencies of local and central government has to make considerable use of direct measures of characteristics of individuals obtained through censuses and surveys. The census of population, frequently used in this context, and other surveys were not specifically constructed to measure deprivation or poverty and consequently researchers using them are forced to rely on indicators of deprivation which they happen to include. Again such indicators are merely related, usually in an unknown fashion, to the incidence of deprivation rather than being direct attempts to measure the phenomenon. Locality-based data on money incomes and assets for example are particularly difficult to obtain although most researchers would probably see these as being central to any assessment of the distribution of material deprivation.

In the context of the identification of material poverty, measures such as the proportions of unemployed men, single-parent families, large families and old age pensioners in the population are often used without any attempt to assess the relative contribution each measure makes to the overall incidence of material poverty. What is particularly disturbing about this failure is that a certain amount is known about not only what proportions of these separate groups do have particularly low incomes but furthermore what proportion of all the poor consists of people in these categories.

This uncritical use of a variety of indicators lends itself to situations where certain dimensions of the problem receive more attention than others merely by virtue of the greater availability of quantifiable data concerning the former. Thus housing receives a considerable amount of attention as a result of the large amount of information available on certain aspects of inadequate housing, plumbing amenities and space in particular. A good example in this respect is provided by the Department of the Environment's analysis of census indicators of urban deprivation in Great Britain; of the 39 main indicators 18 relate to housing amenities or housing tenure (Great Britain, 1975a).

An understandable reliance on publicly available quantifiable data moreover leads to significant gaps in the empirical work on deprivation in precisely those areas where the concept is supposed to be an improvement on its predecessor, poverty. The recognition, implicit in the concept of deprivation, that the problem of inequality is more than merely the lack of access to material resources, remains largely un-explored by the empirical deprivation literature. Quantified measures of emotional and cultural deprivation (even assuming that the considerable definitional problems could be overcome) are virtually nonexistent and are likely to remain so. Secondly, while policies developed for tackling the problems of deprivation at the small area level have placed some emphasis on the social structure of deprived areas, such as the values and attitudes of residents and the way in which they relate to each other as individuals and groups, there is no doubt that empirical analysis of deprivation has been very little concerned with these less quantifiable but important aspects of the problem.

While British sociologists wrote extensively in the 1960s on the nature of interaction at the neighbourhood level amongst the working class as a whole very little is known about whether deprived areas display distinctive patterns of internal social relationships (i.e. whether they have distinctive locality-based social structures) or whether their residents adhere to a significantly different set of values, beliefs and attitudes. The single notable exception is Damer (1974). This tendency to ignore structure at the expense of a concentration on the attributes and characteristics of individuals is an important one because it is not just based on the problems of data availability, but derives from the way in which deprivation comes to be defined in terms of the position and situations of individuals. This individualistic bias is a significant feature of the definitional framework outlined earlier and has vital wider consequences which are examined later.

Problems with the empirical analysis of deprivation are incorporated into the examination of multiple deprivation. Attempts to assess the incidence of multiple deprivation will founder necessarily on the deficiencies of the measures of deprivation noted above. If the aim is to identify those individuals or groups who are deprived simultaneously on a number of dimensions then certain issues require prior clarification. A concern with correlations between different indicators implies the ability to weight these different indicators relative to each other. Such weighting is rarely attempted in practice even at the crudest level. The assumption is usually made that achieving a high score on four dimensions is 'worse' than a high score on three different dimensions. This is not necessarily the case. The very fact that we are dealing here with correlations rules out those aspects of deprivation which are either unmeasured or nonquantifiable.

The search for high intercorrelations of different measures over-simplifies a complex social reality to an extent that results from such an exercise are often meaningless. The identification of multiply deprived areas for example through correlation analysis ignores both the difficulties of ecological correlation and the possibility that it is more useful to think in terms of different types of multiply deprived

areas (Gittus, 1969; Edwards, 1975). Given the whole catalogue of
basic methodological sins being committed in this kind of exercise, the
end product — the identification of multiply deprived individuals or
areas — must be more of a statistical freak than an approximation to
social reality. What we have is the representation of an aspect of the
real world, the multiply deprived area or individual, whose homogeneity as a category we have good reason to doubt, through the
manipulation of unweighted interval measures which have been used to
describe a limited number of aspects of the problem, only some of
which can be appropriately categorised through the use of interval
measures.

What is possibly more disappointing here is that the search for the
Holy Grail of *the* deprived area has diverted attention away from some
of the more pertinent facts and questions about the relationship
between different dimensions of deprivation. While there has been
some work on the development of a typology of deprived areas which
could usefully be extended, the most fruitful issue for policy must
surely be the analysis of the social and political contexts in which the
expected correlations do *not* occur. In this respect the absence of
multiple deprivation in combination with some degree of deprivation
as measured on one particular indicator raises obvious policy issues.
An example is the variation in the correlation between high unemployment areas and high housing deprivation as noted by the Department
of the Environment's comparisons of conurbations (Great Britain,
1975b). There has been no attempt to explain why there is in
Glasgow a high correlation between these indices while in some other
cities, for example Newcastle, no such correlation occurs.

The problems of measuring multiple deprivation and the analysis of
urban deprivation are also inextricably entangled. This is hardly
surprising, for multiple deprivation is frequently identified by the use
of area-based indicators. Strictly speaking such analysis is usually
concerned with the listing of small-scale geographical areas which
contain relatively high proportions of people who are deprived on
different dimensions or indicators of deprivation. Whether these
individuals themselves are multiply deprived is rarely directly testable.

Although the use of the concept of urban deprivation does not
necessarily imply an assumption about (or even an interest in) the
explanatory role of space in the determination of the nature and extent
of deprivation there is no doubt, as was noted earlier, that this has
become a central problem for researchers in this field. While an assessment of the explanatory relevance of space constitutes an important

and researchable problem there are certain difficulties relating to the aspects of this issue which have been given emphasis in both the political and academic literature. Concern with the effects of the spatial distribution of the poor has a long history amongst both politicians and academics. Interest in recent years in this country has been sparked off in the political sphere at least by Sir Keith Joseph's notion of transmitted deprivation and Enoch Powell's fears over the acknowledged geographical concentration of immigrant communities. At the root of both these political concerns lies the alleged potential threat to social and political stability posed by geographical 'enclaves' of deprived groups whose very spatial concentration supposedly leads to the expanded reproduction of damaging and 'alien' life styles, values and attitudes.

For academics faced with a problem formulated in this way these concerns must have a certain 'déjà-vu' element, for analogous issues had been raised, discussed and, it was thought, discarded many years earlier under the rubric of the 'culture of poverty' debate. This thesis, had in fact undergone rigorous examination, albeit mainly in the United States, some time before its emergence into serious debate in the British context. A critical analysis of the concept can be found in Valentine (1968). There is no intention to reiterate here the arguments which formed the basis of that discussion but it is important to note that the analysis of this issue requires careful examination of those aspects of deprived areas which are frequently absent from many recent studies of deprivation, with their concentration on quantifiable aspects of deprivation. Indeed the culture of poverty problem is related precisely to those aspects of local social structure which are notably absent from most recent attempts to measure and analyse multiple deprivation.

Explanations of the geographical concentration of the poor in terms of the culture of poverty are not only highly partial but are also based on prior assumptions about the social reality of this concentration which are highly questionable. In fact the extent to which deprivation, or at least deprived groups, are concentrated spatially seems to vary between different dimensions of deprivation and different groups. Such variation implies that different sets of explanatory factors will affect these different dimensions. More crucially, however, the culture of poverty framework covers but one of the several mechanisms whereby spatial concentration may relate to the overall extent of deprivation. In particular this approach analyses purely the effects of concentration on the deprived themselves while ignoring what may be more relevant, its effects on the non-deprived and particularly on key groups, and also the institutions controlling access to resources. These are, however, discussed later in this volume by McGregor (chapter 4) and English (chapter 5), and also by Damer (1974).

Finally there is a very real danger here that a concern with the explanatory significance of the spatial distribution of deprivation becomes a substitute in terms of both research and policy for a more complete approach to the problems. There is no doubt that whatever the significance of spatial manifestations of the problem the geographical distribution of particular types of individuals can never be the prime determinant of the level and nature of deprivation in society as a whole. Consequently a policy which focuses on the spatial redistribution of the poor alone, leaving the actual level of deprivation untouched, cannot present itself as a complete solution to deprivation.

Dispersing the poor geographically, however, may reduce the impact of poverty on the remainder of society, the non-poor. As with the problem of social control what is critical is that the aims of policies must be clarified. Although threats to the established social and political order as a result of the collective action of the deprived themselves may seem remote, the questioning of the legitimacy of that order by others who become aware of the poor because of their visibility may be less so. For example an area which consists almost entirely of poor housing is more visible than a similar number of such houses spread individually throughout a city. Both kinds of threats will be reduced to the extent that the poor are geographically dispersed. Such a policy will do little to affect the overall level of deprivation, however.

The Position of Research Workers

Many of the methodological deficiencies of deprivation research have been in the previous section related quite properly to the methodological difficulties facing the research worker. Adequate data are limited in terms of their relevance to the underlying problem and it is indeed difficult, though not impossible, to assess the relative merits of the various indicators which are usually used. This is by no means the whole story, however. Research workers in local and central government have a particular occupational position in an established political structure and it is this which accounts for many of the difficulties noted above.

In general such researchers are being asked to produce what Eversley has called 'facts by which men may act' (Eversley, 1973, chapter 10). This requirement of much government research work, that it should produce evidence which can be incorporated into a programme of political action, is not specific to the problem of the analysis of deprivation but covers most of such work. Given this general context, discussion of definitional issues is clearly out of place and the attractions of the counts of individuals scoring on directly comprehensible indicators are obvious. The benefits of measures of the unemployed, the low paid, the old and single-parent families are that they offer an analysis, in terms which are immediately understandable, of separate minority groups for whom established policy frameworks already exist.

The existence of a predetermined policy framework has been particularly critical for the kind of research which has developed around the concept of deprivation. Although researchers have been apparently concerned with the issues relating to the extent to which deprivation can usefully be seen as an area-based problem it has generally been the case that its geographical concentration has been largely assumed by policy and the research problem has been to identify *which* areas are deprived. The existence of area-based policies and, indeed, their persistence as a solution to the problems of deprivation has been the established political framework within which most local and central government researchers have had to operate.

This political framework is particularly critical for local government researchers, for the position of local government in relation to this issue has not been one of initiating policy in the first instance but of reacting to central government initiative. This is not an unfamiliar position for local government but it has had obvious implications for research activity. Faced with central government programmes which distribute resources to *areas* according to a number of crude measures of deprivation in these areas the task of local government researchers has undoubtedly been to use research findings to press most effectively their particular claims for a share of this central government money. It has distinctly not been therefore the task of such researchers to question the basis of these policies by critically examining the definitional framework used to identify areas with high levels of deprivation.

One important and illuminating exception to this understandable tendency for local and central government research to accept the constraints on research of an established policy framework has been the work carried out by the Community Development Project (CDP) research teams. While largely accepting an area basis for the analysis of the incidence of deprivation the concern of some of the CDP teams has been to demonstrate the relevance and indeed the critical importance of causes of deprivation which are not area-specific. The concentration of deprivation in particular areas is seen merely as the spatial manifestation of the effects of more generalised processes characteristic of the operations of an advanced capitalist economy (for example, Coventry CDP, 1975).

This attempt to relate the problems of a particular area to the wider processes of capitalist development is interesting precisely because it is an exception and because its effects on concrete policy have been negligible. The implication of these particular CDP findings, that the causes of deprivation are not area-specific, would theoretically be that policy for deprivation should itself no longer be area-specific. Area-based policies for poverty continue to dominate, however, notably in the form of the inner city partnership initiatives and the Inner Urban Areas Act, 1978. The tenacity of the area-based approach to deprivation is now considerable and it is this apparent durability of this political framework which is an important determinant of the form taken by much of the research work on deprivation (see Mason, chapter 6 in this volume).

The Problem of the Definitional Framework

It has been argued that research work on deprivation has to a considerable extent been carried out within the definitional framework outlined earlier. While the methodological difficulties of the empirical studies have been discussed briefly what these studies also illustrate are the problems of the initial conceptualisation of the problem itself. The definitional framework outlined inhibits critical analysis in two ways: it focuses on consequences not causes and thinks in terms of individuals not structures. These two deficiencies are intimately related to each other.

Deprivation has been seen as a state or position occupied by particular individuals. Analysis in these terms tends to produce counts of different types of individuals, different minority groups, seen as separated subsets each of which faces a particular difficulty (e.g. unemployment, old age, low pay) for which as we have noted, there are appropriate established policy frameworks. An alternative logic to the problem of definition illustrates the extent to which this framework restricts analysis and forecloses discussion of certain key issues.

This alternative approach starts by noting that the word deprivation comes from an active verb, to deprive. Deprivation should be seen therefore as a *process* whereby groups or individuals are deprived. Immediately we are focusing on the systematic mechanisms whereby a process of deprivation occurs. The incidence and nature of particular deprived groups are the end result of this process. This approach does not exclude the possibility that one element within this process is the position, attributes and behaviour of the deprived themselves, but it does emphasise that these characteristics of the deprived are only relevant in the context of a more general process. The mechanisms which are relevant here are clearly not the unique and idiosyncratic biographies or circumstances of particular individuals but the regularised, indeed routinised, series of events and practices which reproduce deprivation. What is critical here is that we are not talking about particular individuals but structures understood as systematic relationships between groups and institutions.

What may be termed the individualistic approach to deprivation asks certain kinds of questions only: how many deprived people are there? where do they live? in what ways are they deprived? how can their situation as individuals be improved? An alternative which sees deprivation as a process whereby a structure of deprivation reproduces itself poses immediately an entirely different set of questions. An examination of the issues which are then posed illustrates the difference between this framework and the earlier one.

The individualistic approach looks at the situation of individuals and raises questions about how the position of these particular people can be improved within a stable and maintained structure. It does not raise the more critical issue of the ways in which that structure itself can be altered or indeed the ways in which policy can intervene in a process which reproduces deprivation. There is a considerable difference between examining the difficulties particular individuals have in competing in the labour market which lead to their own unemployment and analysing the operation of the labour market as a whole, in an attempt to understand the processes which generate and maintain high overall levels of unemployment. Retraining programmes for example can clearly offer solutions to the employment problems of particular individuals but their effects on the actual levels of unemployment are less obvious and less real.

Multiple deprivation as a process is not seen as the problem of the particular individual who happens to score highly on several dimensions of deprivation but as a feature of the relationships between formally independent systems of resource distribution. This raises questions not about why a particular family with low income has poor housing but concerning the processes that sustain a distribution of housing resources in favour of those groups who are also favoured by other resource distribution systems of society. A critical feature here for example would be the role played by significant public sectors in distributing resources which are normally seen as part of an overarching welfare state system; the distribution of health care facilities, educational resources, housing and income for those who are not employed are the important sectors here. While an individualistic approach to deprivation looks merely at the position of individuals and families in relation to these various sets of resources, deprivation viewed as a process looks at the way in which the whole of the society's resources are distributed in a particular field.

Part of such an analysis would necessarily cover the relationship between the relevant private and public sectors and the effect of private sector provision on the levels and type of resources available to the public sector. This should involve the discovery of those mechanisms by which distribution systems reinforce each other and, more pertinently, the analysis of the political forces at work which support and maintain these reinforcing mechanisms. The analysis moves from the study of the fortunes of particular individuals at the level of the small area to the study of relationships between structures.

What this alternative perspective serves to illustrate is a theme which has emerged in earlier sections of this chapter: the need to clarify the aims of particular policies and their relevance to the problem of deprivation. There is an important difference between policies which are directed towards altering the mobility of individuals between positions in an unequal structure and those which would aim towards the alteration of the mechanisms which underlie and reproduce that structure. The dominance of definitional frameworks based on an analysis of the positions of individuals will necessarily lead to a primary concern with the fates of those particular people and not to an attempt to understand and modify the processes which maintain the structure which they occupy.

References

Coventry Community Development Project (1975) Final Report, parts 1 and 2, Coventry
Damer, S. (1974) 'Wine Alley, The Sociology of a Dreadful Enclosure', *Sociological Review*, no. 3, pp. 221-48
Edwards, J. (1975) 'Social Indicators, Urban Deprivation and Positive Discrimination', *Journal of Social Policy*, no. 4, pp. 275-87
Eversley, D. (1973) *The Planner in Society: The Changing Role of a Profession*, London: Faber

Flynn, M., Flynn, P. and Mellor, N. (1972) 'Social Malaise Research: A Study in Liverpool', *Social Trends*, no. 3, pp. 42-52

Gittus, E. (1969) 'Sociological Aspects of Urban Decay', in *Urban Decay* (ed. Medhurst, F. and Parry Lewis, J.), London: Macmillan

Great Britain (1975a) Department of the Environment, 'Census Indicators of Urban Deprivation, Working Note 6, Great Britain', London: HMSO

Great Britain (1975b) Department of the Environment, 'Census Indicators of Urban Deprivation, Working Note 10, The Conurbations of Great Britain', London:

Hamnett, C. (1976) 'Patterns of Inequality, Unit 15: Multiple Deprivation and the Inner City', Milton Keynes: Open University

Strathclyde Regional Council (1976) *Urban Deprivation*, Glasgow: Strathclyde Regional Council

Townsend, P. (1954) 'The Concept of Poverty', *British Journal of Sociology*, no. 5, pp. 130-7

Valentine, C. (1968) *The Culture of Poverty: Critique and Counter Proposals*, Chicago: University of Chicago Press

2 THE CORPORATE DIMENSION OF EMPLOYMENT CHANGE IN THE INNER CITY

Peter Dicken and Peter E. Lloyd

In recent years a substantial body of research has come to hand to show that there has been a significant 'drift' of manufacturing industry away from the older conurbations in general and from the inner areas of the great cities in particular. Dennis (1978) and Gripaios (1977a, b) have reported this trend for London, Cameron (1973) for Glasgow and Fagg (1973) for Leicester. Our own work in the North West Industry Research Unit has closely documented the process for Manchester (Lloyd and Mason, 1978; Dicken and Lloyd, 1977) and for Merseyside (Lloyd, 1977, 1979; Dicken and Lloyd, 1977, 1978). In each case it has been shown that a substantial decline has occurred in the manufacturing employment stock of the inner areas, the bulk of which has been due to the physical closure of industrial establishments.

In response to the observed trends a battery of legislation nationally and a flurry of activity locally has sought to shore up this declining industrial base. Much of this effort has gone into the provision of premises and financial assistance, as for example in the seven inner city partnership areas; while almost every local authority has greatly expanded the activities of its industrial development office. Nationally, much emphasis has been given to the role which small industry will play in creating new jobs and a new wave of industrial enterprise (National Enterprise Board, 1977).

While the need to act quickly against such dramatic decline has brought a powerful response, there are still key questions to be answered about the causes of the observed decline and effective policy to attack the roots of the problem rather than its symptoms. In this chapter we explore, in the context of events in inner Manchester 1966-75, a substantial 'grey area' of knowledge about the inner city and its population of manufacturing establishments. Much of the theory inherited from the past has its relevance at the level of the plant — the physical unit of production. By contrast, much of the policy being applied is operationalised through the firm — the decision-making organisation. Where, as we shall show, is increasingly the case, the two are by no means coterminous the ramifications need clearly to be understood since the nature of this relationship is critical both to the

causes of the decline and to the ways in which active policy will relate
to it.

Manufacturing Plants in their Organisational Context

We begin with a brief discussion of the organisational setting of industry
in general, developing a conceptual framework which we subsequently
relate to the inner city in particular. In setting manufacturing plants in
their organisational context the most basic distinction would seem to
be between:

1. Those plants which belong to firms having only one plant, that is
to *single-plant firms*, and

2. Those plants which belong to firms operating more than one
plant, that is to *multi-plant firms*.

In each case we are concerned with the locus of ultimate control insofar
as this can be identified. This may well involve following a whole chain
of corporate links in which one firm is a subsidiary of another firm
which, in turn, is a subsidiary of another and so on. The question of
who owns or controls whom is often difficult to answer with any
certainty.

The main reasons for distinguishing between single-plant firms and
multi-plant firms are not only organisational, they are also explicitly
spatial and relate to a difference in the potential flexibility of their
operations. By definition, single-plant firms operate entirely at one
geographical location. As long as they remain as single-plant entities all
changes and adjustment must be accommodated at that site. Multi-
plant firms by contrast, operate at several locations (in the case of very
large firms at vast numbers of locations). They not only divide their
operations between these sites in ways determined by their own
organisational design and structure but also they can reallocate functions between their plants and cross-subsidise the loss-making operations
of one plant with the profit-making operations of another if this is
regarded as contributing towards the firm's overall interests.

Differences in potential flexibility, then, represent an important
distinction between single-plant and multi-plant firms. Thus if faced,
say, by local problems which interfere with production either
temporarily or even permanently, the response of the single-plant firm
must be either to adjust *in situ* or find an entirely new location. Faced
with similar problems the multi-plant firm may be able to solve them
by shifting resources to one of its other existing plants. In other words,
multi-plant firms — especially those with geographically dispersed
operations — tend to be less constrained by local economic conditions.

A further important difference should also be noted. On the one hand, the plant which belongs to a single plant firm possesses the entire package of the firm's operations, including its decision-making functions. On the other hand, a plant which is a unit within a multi-plant firm may have only a limited part of the firm's total functions. From the viewpoint of the community or region, therefore, a critical consideration relates to *which 'parts' of firms it possesses*. Does it, for example, consist mainly of 'low-level' production or fabrication units employing semi-skilled or unskilled workers at relatively low wage rates or does it have a large proportion of 'high-level' units offering well-paid employment for highly skilled workers?

At least as important as this would seem to be the location of the firm's decision-making functions: its headquarters. There is much current concern with the issue of 'external control' — with the extent to which headquarters units, particularly of very large business enterprises, tend to be concentrated in a small number of centres while many other parts of the country possess relatively few executive and decision-making functions (Westaway, 1974; Firn, 1975; Dicken, 1976). Many local economies, therefore, are especially open to additional external influences transmitted through those of their plants which belong to multi-plant firms controlled from elsewhere. The behaviour and viability of such plants may be determined more by changes occurring within the firm as a whole than by strictly local conditions.

In view of such considerations, multi-plant firms can be categorised further according to the geographical location of their headquarters in relation to a particular study area. In the present case we shall distinguish between:

(1) Multi-plant firms whose headquarters are located within Greater Manchester.

(2) Multi-plant firms whose headquarters are located outside Greater Manchester. These can be subdivided further into:
  (i) firms headquartered within the United Kingdom (*domestic firms*); and
  (ii) firms headquartered outside the United Kingdom (*foreign firms*).

Thus we have a fourfold firm typology as the basis for our discussion in this chapter. Each and every plant in inner Manchester can be assigned an *organisational* position which falls within one of the following sets:

(1) Single-plant firms

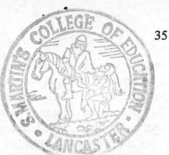

(2) Multi plant firms
   (i) locally headquartered
   (ii) externally headquartered
       (a) domestically owned
       (b) foreign owned.

A typology such as this permits us to examine the components of industrial change (births, deaths, survivors, etc.) for inner Manchester through the 'ownership lens'. It enables us to ask how far manufacturing change at the plant level is related to various types of business organisation. For example, do plants belonging to a particular organisational type have a greater or lesser propensity to close down, to expand or contract their employment than those belonging to other organisational types? To what extent is employment change associated with ownership change? These kinds of question tie in studies of small areas, such as inner Manchester, with broader changes in the national economy.

The pattern of change in the organisational structure of manufacturing industry at the national level is now well documented (see, for example, Prais, 1976; Hannah, 1976; Hannah and Kay, 1977). We need do little more here than note the salient characteristics of such change. In common with all industrial societies in capitalist and mixed economies manufacturing industry in Britain has become increasingly dominated by a small number of very large business enterprises. The relative importance of large enterprises has increased at the expense of smaller enterprises.[1] For example, Prais (1976) estimates that in 1970 the 100 largest manufacturing firms in Britain accounted for 41 per cent of net output in manufacturing compared with 16 per cent in 1909. Expressed rather differently, he claims that whereas in 1909 more than 2,000 firms were needed to produce one half of total manufacturing output in the United Kingdom, by 1970 a mere 140 firms were able to produce the same proportion. The corollary of such an increase in the relative importance of large firms is the decline in the importance of small firms. In 1935 there were approximately 136,000 manufacturing firms in Britain employing fewer than 200 workers. These accounted for more than one third (35 per cent) of total net output in manufacturing. By 1968 there were only 58,000 such firms and these produced just 16 per cent of net output (Bannock, 1976).

Recent research seems to suggest that such an increase in firm concentration is only partly, if at all, explained by increases in plant size stimulated by developments in production technology. Prais (1976) in particular argues that the giant enterprises of the modern economy operate not a few massive plants but rather a large number of plants. Though some of these may indeed be very large most tend to be medium- or small-sized. These comments refer to the 'giant' enterprises in the economy but it seems that in general there has been both a general overall increase in average plant size together with a tendency for more and more firms to become multi-plant in their operations.

This is not the place to try to explain these developments; indeed there is much debate about the primary variables underlying them. Clearly they are the outcome of a number of complex interacting forces. However, one of these does merit our attention: the process of *acquisition and merger*. Disregarding why mergers occur, there is little doubt that merging is one of the most important means by which many business enterprises have grown. In aggregate terms, mergers tend to occur in a series of intensive waves or peaks separated by periods of relative quiescence. In Britain, mergers were particularly prevalent in the periods 1919-20, 1926-9 and, more especially, in the middle and late 1960s (Hannah and Kay, 1977). During these periods very large numbers of firms 'disappeared' by merger. For example, between 1963 and 1968 more than 5,000 firms in Britain were acquired by other firms.

Although not all observers would agree, there are grounds for suggesting that the growth of at least the largest firms, and hence the overall increase in business concentration, has been produced very largely by merger activity. Certainly this is the view stated recently by Hannah and Kay (1977) in the case of Britain. This would seem to be borne out by experience in the United States. The US Federal Trade Commission asserts that almost the entire relative growth of the very largest corporations in the United States was produced by merger. The Commission estimates that if they had *not* been engaged in mergers the leading 200 corporations would have enlarged their share of total manufacturing assets from 42.4 per cent in 1947 to only 45.3 per cent in 1968. In fact, by very active merger activity they increased their share to 60.9 per cent.

The Inner Area of the Manchester Conurbation: Definition and Background

Changes at the national level then, form the broad context within which local changes can be observed. We now alter our focus to inner Manchester itself and examine the major features of its manufacturing change between 1966 and 1975. The whole subject of inner area definition is controversial. In the case of the present study we define the inner area of Manchester as a cluster of 30-kilometre grid squares focused on the city centre. It was selected by reference to the 1967 City of Manchester land-use map and was defined as the locus of the *contiguous* central industrial zone immediately peripheral to the central business district. Trafford Park, although relatively close to central Manchester and of critical importance to the city's economic base, was excluded since the purpose of the analysis is to examine the nature of the 'metropolitan' industries more typical of the inner urban core.

Essentially, the area is drawn from elements of the continuously built-up nineteenth-century urban core. It offers an environment to industry which is, above all, run-down and where the incidence of undeveloped open spaces paradoxically does little to reduce the high cost per unit site area. On the other hand, the core area still offers some of the centrality which was traditionally a prime asset of such locations but which, in a modern world, has become less attractive to manufacturing in particular.

The industrial structure of inner Manchester evolved in association with the growth of the city both as a regional commercial capital and more particularly as the focus of the cotton industry. It was essentially a manufacturing town with a strong labour-intensive base and was, of course, the archetypal manufacturing-industrial town of the nineteenth century. Its cotton industry associations gave it strong ties to the clothing industry and to many linked cotton trades like dyeing and finishing and fabric printing. Despite the post-1914 decline of the Lancashire cotton industry these ties remain in existence and they have been one means for the transmission of industrial decline to central Manchester. Printing and publishing was also strongly developed and this, together with textiles and clothing, forms the dominant group of industrial sectors in the contemporary industrial inner city. While Merseyside, consistently an area of high unemployment, has been a recipient of the full range of government industrial aid programmes and incentive schemes, Manchester has been a less conspicuous area of unemployment and only latterly (after 1972) did it receive any government assistance towards industrial development upon its designation as an intermediate area.

Manufacturing Change in Inner Manchester, 1966-75[2]

Before turning our attention to questions of ownership let us first

establish the broad characteristics of industrial change in inner
Manchester from the establishment or plant viewpoint. This aspect has
been covered in detail in two previous studies (Lloyd and Mason, 1977,
1978). In these, however, the time period for the analysis was 1966-72
and there is a need to update the aggregate picture to 1975 to suit our
present purpose. Not surprisingly, given the short space of time
between 1972 and 1975, there was little dramatic structural change so
we can content ourselves here with a brief summary of the 1975
position, encouraging the reader interested in greater detail to consult
the previous work.

Taking first the components of change accounting equation at the
establishment level of analysis, the following changes occurred over the
longer study period:

Manual   Manual   Entries   Exits   (Balance of change in
employment = employment + 1966-75 - 1966-75 + *in situ* survivors 1966-75)
in 1975   in 1966

51,757   =   91,523   + 11,808 - 45,994 +   (- 5580)

Even allowing for the fact that some 4,000 of the jobs recorded as 'exits'
were internal transfers, it is clear that for inner Manchester the dominant
contributor to the 43.4 per cent job loss was the *closure* of manufacturing
plants, rather than the shrinkage of employment in plants which survived. The basic closure figure represented some 45.9 per cent of the
1966 manual employment stock of the area. It is therefore no exaggera-
tion to say that the key component in the decline of manufacturing in
inner Manchester was the physical closure of industrial establishments.
The declining balance of workers in surviving plants was less evident. In
fact it was proportionately only half as important as a force for change
for Manchester as it was, for example, on Merseyside. A further point of
interest in comparing the two inner areas is that in the case of
Manchester the level of entry employment was more than sufficient to
counterbalance the losses through *in situ* shrinkage. For Merseyside this
was not so.

Looking at the components of change from the viewpoint of
industry *type* the most striking general feature of industrial events in
inner Manchester is that manufacturing industries of all kinds were in
decline (Table 2.1). No industrial order showed a significant net increase
in manual workforce and only some of those with very small absolute
numbers of workers could show declines of less than about 30 per cent
of their 1966 job stock. Against this background of widespread decline
some sectors — engineering, the metal industries, textiles, clothing and

the printing and publishing trades — suffered particularly heavy losses.

Table 2.1: Inner Manchester: Industry Types in Manufacturing

SIC order		Manual workers 1966	%	Manual workers 1975	%	Net change 1966-75 %
III	Food, drink and tobacco	3,030	3.31	1,876	3.62	-38.07
IV	Coal and petroleum products	79	.09	77	.15	- 2.50
V	Chemicals	2,921	3.19	1,913	3.70	-34.50
VI	Metal manufacture	2,501	2.73	1,502	2.90	-39.93
VII	Mechanical engineering	9,074	9.91	5,525	10.68	-39.11
VIII	Instrument engineering	1,695	1.85	547	1.06	-67.69
IX	Electrical engineering	9,434	10.31	6,305	12.18	-33.16
X	Shipbuilding	—	—	—	—	—
XI	Vehicles	1,047	1.14	685	1.32	-34.54
XII	Other metal goods	5,238	5.72	2,192	4.24	-58.14
XIII	Textiles	6,203	6.78	2,018	3.90	-67.46
XIV	Leather, etc.	955	1.04	810	1.57	-15.17
XV	Clothing and footwear	25,127	27.45	14,070	27.18	-44.00
XVI	Bricks, pottery, etc.	703	.77	335	.65	-52.27
XVII	Timber, furniture, etc.	3,845	4.20	1,845	3.56	-52.00
XVIII	Paper, printing, etc.	13,873	15.16	9,508	18.37	-31.46
XIX	Other manufacturing industries	5,798	6.34	2,549	4.93	-56.03
	Total	91,523		51,757		-43.45

For the most part these were derived from the weight of the closures component. Clothing and footwear alone lost over 15,000 jobs through closures. New openings offset this to a degree but the net fall in the manual workforce of these sectors was still of the order of 11,000. Though less extreme the story is the same for the other heavily declining sectors. Closures were dominant and *in situ* change, though uniformly downward, was relatively less significant.

From the *plant-size* viewpoint the pattern of decline was more distinctly distributed. The heaviest net losses by *number* of plants were among the small factories with which the area was particularly heavily endowed in 1966 (Table 2.2). Of the plants which actually closed down over the period (some were clearly replaced by new entries) around 90 per cent employed less than 49 workers. However, from the viewpoint of employment rather than numbers of establishments such small plants accounted for only half of the jobs lost. At the larger end of the size spectrum 20 per cent of the manual employment lost through closures was derived from only 11 factories. This compares with the

1,422 plants which contributed to the losses from the 1-49 group.

Table 2.2: Inner Manchester: Industrial Establishments by Size
1966 and 1975

Size class no. of workers	No. of establishments in 1966	No. of Establishments in 1975	Net loss
1 — 9	1,099	678	- 421
10 — 19	430	309	- 121
20 — 49	491	282	- 209
50 — 99	208	133	- 75
100 — 249	122	60	- 62
250 — 499	29	21	- 8
500 — 999	23	9	- 14
1,000 +	6	3	- 3

There is, therefore, a clearly distinct underlying pattern to the
industrial decline of inner Manchester looked at in terms of plant size
and industry type. The area both began and ended the study period,
as Figures 2.1 and 2.2 illustrate, with an industrial structure heavily
based on small and medium-sized factories in what might be called the
'classic' metropolitan industries — clothing, and the printing and
publishing trades, but with a significant sprinkling of larger plants
primarily in the electrical and mechanical engineering and metal goods
industries. Industry across the board was heavily affected by closures
between 1966 and 1975. Large numbers of small plants closed and
though there continued to be a trickle of incoming factories to replace
them the stock of small factories in the inner city was sharply reduced.
Among the larger establishments in the engineering and metal goods
trades there were also closures, smaller in number but with powerful
net effects on job totals. Survivors, too, declined — plants with more
than 500 workers which remained *in situ* lost over 4,000 workers
between them. Thus while there has been little structural shift in terms
of industry type, there is, as Figure 2.1 illustrates, a tendency for the
area to become more heavily dependent for its jobs on the smaller size
of plant ranges.

Manufacturing Change and Plant Ownership in Inner Manchester, 1966-75

The nature of manufacturing industry in the inner city — as in any
other area — is an amalgam of three distinct, though closely interrelated
dimensions: industry type, plant size and ownership (or enterprise)

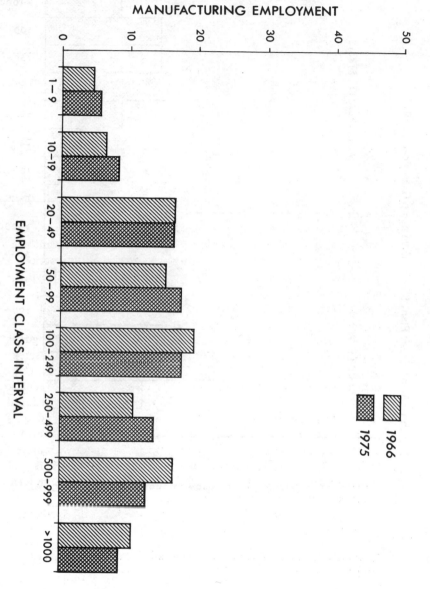

Figure 2.1 Plant Size in Manufacturing: Inner Manchester

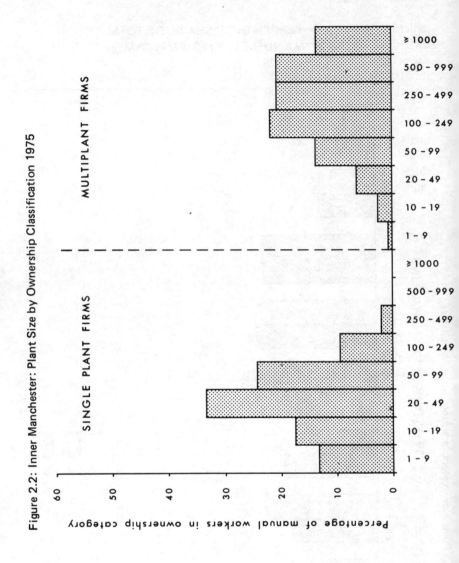

Figure 2.2: Inner Manchester: Plant Size by Ownership Classification 1975

structure. In the previous section we briefly discussed the first two of these dimensions. The third, as we suggested earlier, has been relatively neglected until recently. In what follows, therefore, we present the results of a preliminary analysis of the role of ownership structure in manufacturing employment change in inner Manchester.

Table 2.3 divides total manual employment in manufacturing in both 1966 and 1975 into the two major organisational categories: single-plant firms and multi-plant firms. At both dates, a little over one-third of total employment in manufacturing in inner Manchester was in single-plant firms and rather less than two jobs in every three were in multi-plant organisations. The stability between the two categories over the 1966 and 1975 period is striking, particularly in comparison with the situation in inner Merseyside (Lloyd, 1977, p. 8) where multi-plant firms in 1975 employed four workers out of every five. The rate of decline of employment in both single- and multi-plant firms was almost identical with the total decline of manufacturing employment in inner Manchester of 43.4 per cent. In other words, employment in both single- and multi-plant firms declined at a rate almost exactly proportional to each category's share of manufacturing employment in 1966.

Table 2.3: Manufacturing Employment in Inner Manchester: Share of Manual Employment in Single-plant and Multi-plant Firms, 1966 and 1975[3]

	Total inner city employment	Employment in single-plant firms		Employment in multi-plant firms	
		No.	%	No.	%
1966	91,523	33,827	37.0	57,696	63.0
1975	51,757	18,954	36.6	32,803	63.4
% change 1966-75	− 43.4		− 44.0		− 43.1

In discussing the organisational dimension of manufacturing industry earlier we suggested that the multi-plant category itself could be usefully subdivided further on the basis of the headquarters location of its firms. Table 2.4 provides this breakdown for inner Manchester in 1966 and 1975. The table shows that in 1966 multi-plant firms whose headquarters were based in Greater Manchester employed 35.5 per cent of all manufacturing employment in inner Manchester. In terms of the multi-plant category alone, locally-headquartered firms accounted for 56.2 per cent of the total. Employment in firms externally-headquartered accounted for a little over one-quarter of total 1966 manufacturing employment in inner Manchester. By 1975 the relative importance of locally headquartered and externally headquartered firms had changed very considerably. In fact the proportions were almost exactly the reverse of those prevailing in 1966. This reflects the very marked difference in employment change between the categories over the 1966 to 1975 period. Employment in the locally-headquartered category declined by almost 60 per cent while the job loss in those firms with headquarters elsewhere in the United Kingdom fell by 21.8 per cent.

Table 2.4: Employment in Multi-plant Firms as a Percentage of Total Employment, Inner Manchester, 1966 and 1975

	Firms with local HQ	Firms with HQ elsewhere in UK	Firms with HQ overseas
	%	%	%
1966	35.5	23.9	3.7
1975	25.3	33.0	5.1
% change 1966-75	− 59.6	− 21.8	−22.9

Table 2.5 demonstrates the result of such developments. It shows the extent to which the 'locus of control' of inner Manchester's manufacturing industry changed between 1966 and 1975. In 1966 almost three-quarters of total manufacturing employment was in firms headquartered locally (that is, in both single-plant and multi-plant local firms). By 1975 local control had shrunk quite considerably – by 10.5 percentage points in fact – so that by that date almost 40 per cent of total manufacturing employment in inner Manchester was controlled by firms located elsewhere. Although this is a considerable shift towards greater external control it is by no means as pronounced as in inner Merseyside. In fact, with 61.9 per cent of its manufacturing industry locally controlled in 1975 inner Manchester clearly remained an important haven for the independent, indigenous manufacturer whose plant and organisation coincided. The single-plant, single-owner firm was still an important part of the industrial scene in 1975.

These ownership characteristics in part reflect the industrial structure of inner Manchester. Some of the important industries in employment terms tend to be those in which single-plant firms are strongly represented at the national level. The most obvious example is the clothing industry which, as we have seen, is a dominant inner city employer. Almost two-thirds of the employment in the clothing and footwear order in 1975 was in single-plant firms. Further, those important industrial orders in inner Manchester which are less single-plant orientated — for example, mechanical engineering, electrical engineering and paper, printing and publishing — contain a significant proportion of locally-headquartered multi-plant firms. On the whole, therefore, the leading industrial sectors in inner Manchester display a good deal of *local* control. Eighty-eight per cent of all employment in clothing and footwear, 62 per cent in mechanical engineering, 46 per cent in electrical engineering, and 46 per cent in paper, printing and publishing was in firms headquartered within Greater Manchester. This is in very marked contrast to inner Merseyside where the leading industrial sectors are characterised by a very high level of external control.

Table 2.5: Location of Control of Manufacturing Employment, Inner Manchester, 1966 and 1975

	% employment controlled locally*	% employment controlled externally
1966	72.4	27.7
1975	61.9	38.1
% change 1966-75	– 49.4	– 30.1

* Employment in inner city plants (both single- and multi-plant) whose headquarters are located in Greater Manchester County.

Just as ownership structure and industry type are closely related, so too is plant size. Some industries are more closely associated with small and medium-sized plants than others and vice versa. Cutting across this relationship, however, is the general tendency for small plants to be associated with single-plant firms and for large plants to be associated with multi-plant firms. Thus in 1975 single-plant firms represented 75.2 per cent of all plants in inner Manchester but only 36.6 per cent of all employment. This relationship is shown in Figure 2.2. No single-plant firm in inner Manchester in 1975 employed more than 500 workers and only 11.4 per cent of all the single-plant employment is to be found in plants employing between 100 and 499 workers. The remainder of the workforce in the single-plant category is in small plants. In direct contrast, the multi-plant organisations favour the upper ranges of the plant-size spectrum. Only 9.4 per cent of all employment in multi-plant firms is to be found in factories with less than 50 workers. The bulk of the multi-plant workforce is concentrated in the 100-999 plant-size range which contains 62.8 per cent of the total.

In fact, there is a major break in the pattern at plants employing fewer than 100 workers. In the four plant-size categories covering the range 1-99 single-plant firms are more important than multi-plant firms though the proportions are more or less equal in the 50-99 group. But in plants employing more than 100 workers the single-plant/multi-plant relationship is completely reversed. To a certain extent, therefore, plant size offers a clue to corporate status. In broad terms, when we talk about the large plant we generally also imply multi-plant organisational status; when we allude to the small plant we are more likely to be dealing with a single-plant firm. Of course, the correspondence is by no means perfect. There are some relatively large single-plant firms (though as we have noted, none was larger than 500 employees in inner Manchester in 1975); equally many multi-plant firms operate small plants as well as some in the medium and large-size category.

There is also a clear relationship between size of plant and degree of external control. At the lower end of the plant size range most plants belong to locally-headquartered firms (not surprisingly given the point we have made regarding the prevalence of single-plant firms at this scale). Further up the plant-size scale the balance changes though the relationship is by no means as clear-cut as in the case of inner Merseyside. In that area, for example, all plants employing more than 1,000 workers are externally controlled; in inner Manchester the local/external split is more even though, of course, this size category is a good deal less important in inner Manchester than it is in inner Merseyside.

In summary, the industry type, plant size and ownership structure of inner Manchester had changed between 1966 and 1975 but not to any spectacular degree. Declining employment was spread rather evenly across industrial sectors, small plants tended to become rather more important and there was a tendency for control to shift to firms headquartered outside Greater Manchester. But locally-controlled firms remained a major part of the industrial scene. In terms of overall industrial concentration there was an increase between 1966 and 1975. In 1966 the five leading employers in inner Manchester employed 11 per cent of all manual workers in manufacturing, while the ten leading firms employed 18.1 per cent. By 1975 these concentration ratios had increased to 14.7 and 23.3 per cent. Again referring to inner Merseyside, these are relatively low levels of concentration: the five-firm concentration ratio in inner Merseyside for 1975 was 33.6

per cent and the ten-firm ratio was 44.5 per cent (Dicken and Lloyd, 1977).

However, despite the fact that much of inner Manchester's manufacturing industry was locally controlled in 1975 most of the leading employers have their headquarters outside Greater Manchester. Only two of the ten largest firms are headquartered locally; the remaining eight have their head offices elsewhere, primarily in London or abroad. So even though local control is still strong in inner Manchester, a considerable proportion of the decisions affecting inner area employment is made elsewhere and this is especially true of the larger firms.

The Corporate Element in the Components of Industrial Change

Each of the individual elements in the components of change equation for inner Manchester shown earlier has been subjected to a preliminary analysis in terms of its corporate characteristics. The sheer size of the operation – tracing the ownership of every manufacturing establishment in 1966 and 1975 and also searching for evidence of ownership change in the intervening period – led us to ignore plants employing fewer than ten workers. In fact, this is unlikely to distort the results in any major fashion. Although there is a large number of such plants, they account for a very small proportion of total manufacturing employment.

As we pointed out earlier, aggregate industrial change in inner Manchester between 1966 and 1975 was dominated by the closure of manufacturing plants. Decline of employment through *in situ* shrinkage was relatively unimportant and was, in any case, more than offset by employment generated by plants entering the system. Within this general context let us now examine each of the individual components to identify the contributions made to change by different types of firm.

Closures

The term closures or deletions in the present context refers to all those plants which were recorded as having been removed from the Factory Inspectorate registers between 1966 and 1975. In fact, the term masks a variety of possible situations including a change of name, though these have been accounted for wherever possible. Some of the closures coincide with the total cessation of business, others reflect the closure of operations at a particular site and their transfer to another site. Such transfers may be either to other locations within the inner city or to locations beyond its boundaries. Work is currently in progress which analyses transfers (Mason, 1979, forthcoming); for the moment we are concerned with closures as a whole, regardless of their subsequent behaviour.

The components of change equation shows that almost 46,000 manual jobs in manufacturing were lost to inner Manchester through the closure of plants. Approximately 93 per cent of this loss occurred in plants employing ten or more workers. Figure 2.3 shows that most of the closures were of small plants. In view of the relationship between small-plant size and single-plant firms, therefore, we would not be surprised to find that most of the small plants which closed between 1966 and 1975 were small single-plant organisations. The larger plant closures were those in multi-plant firms.

Table 2.6 demonstrates the general corporate composition of these closures. It shows that almost 42 per cent of the employment loss in this category was in single-plant firms. If we compare this percentage with the single-plant category's share of 1966 employment it is clear that the losses were not especially excessive in relative terms though, of course, they represented a very large absolute job loss. By comparison more than 58 per cent of employment loss in closures was in multi-plant firms, this loss being fairly evenly distributed between locally-headquartered and externally-headquartered firms. In both cases the job loss was more or less proportional to each category's share of 1966 employment. Again, comparison with inner Merseyside is instructive. There, a much higher proportion of job loss through closures was in externally-headquartered firms and, in addition, job losses in single-plant closures were relatively greater than in inner Manchester. In inner Manchester, closures were spread across all ownership categories.

Table 2.6: Plant Closures in Inner Manchester Classified by Ownership Category (Plants Employing ten or more Workers)

	Single-plant	Multi-plant	Locally HQd multi-plant	Externally-HQd multi-plant (domestic)	Externally-HQd multi-plant (foreign)
Percentage share of closure employment	41.8	58.2	31.4	26.2	0.6
Percentage share of *all* 1966 employment	37.0	63.0	35.5	23.8	3.7

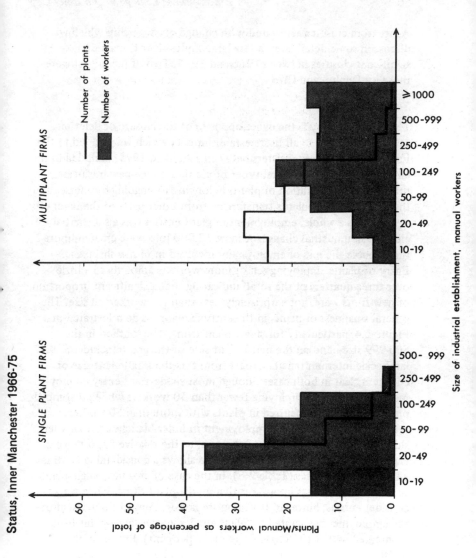

Status, Inner Manchester 1966-75

Apart from closures associated with change of ownership which we discuss in some detail later, a few large multi-plant firms did make significant closures between 1966 and 1975. Two of the largest were those by Dunlop and CWS.

Entries

The entry category is the exact opposite of the closure or deletion category. It refers to all those establishments which were added to the Factory Inspectorate registers between 1966 and 1975. Included in the entry class, then, are several types of plant: genuine new businesses (births), the in-migration of plants belonging to ongoing businesses and the destinations of plants transferring from other parts of the inner city.

Taken as a whole, employment in plant entries was a substantial element in industrial change. Almost 12,000 jobs were created, more than double the loss of employment involved in *in situ* shrinkage. Entry of plants employing ten or more workers amounts to a little over three-quarters of the total, indicating that a significant proportion of new firms were, not surprisingly, less than ten workers in size. The general smallness of plants in the entry category is demonstrated in Figure 2.4, particularly for single-plant firms. The 'outlier' in the 500-999 size-band on the multi-plant side of the graph includes a large-scale internal transfer. Apart from this the small-plant size of entries is clear in both cases; though most single-plant entry employment was in plants employing fewer than 50 workers while most multi-plant employment occurred in plants with more than 50 workers.

Table 2.7 relates entry employment in inner Manchester to ownership type and, as in the case of closures, to the relative importance of each ownership type in 1966. The table shows a considerable contrast with that for closures (Table 2.6). In the case of closures, single-plant firms were rather less important than multi-plant firms. When we consider entries, however, the opposite is true. Almost 60 per cent of the employment generated by plant entries was in single-plant firms (compared with a 1966 base share of 37 per cent). Entries in the multi-plant category were very evenly spread between locally and externally headquartered firms. Overall, some 79 per cent of all entry employment in plants employing more than ten workers was in locally headquartered firms (single-and multi-plant), presumably reflecting the well-documented tendency for most new businesses to start their lives in the locality with which their owners are already associated.

But although there clearly was considerable new firm development in inner Manchester between 1966 and 1975 it fell very far short of

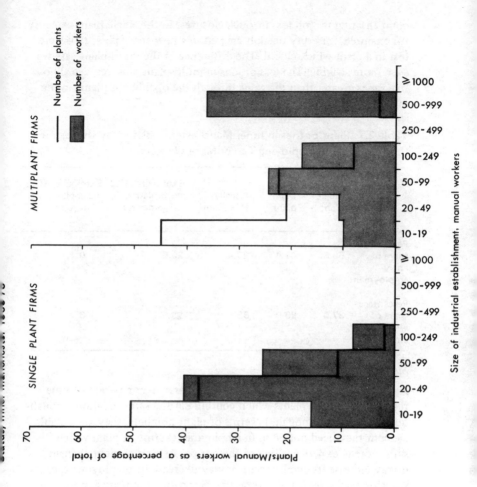

SINGLE PLANT FIRMS — MULTIPLANT FIRMS

— Number of plants

Number of workers

Plants/Manual workers as a percentage of total

Size of industrial establishment, manual workers

compensating for job loss through closures. In the single plant category, for example, for every one job created in a new entry plant two were lost in a plant which closed. The difference in the multi-plant case was even more striking. The loss of jobs in multi-plant closures was almost five times greater than the gains through the opening of plants in the multi-plant category.

Table 2.7: Plant Entries in Inner Manchester Classified by Ownership Category (Plants Employing Ten or More Workers)

	Single-plant	Multi-plant	Locally-HQd multi-plant	Externally-HQd multi-plant (domestic)	Externally-HQd multi-plant (foreign)
Percentage share of entry employment	58.6	41.4	20.4	20.6	0.4
Percentage share of *all* 1966 employment	37.0	63.0	35.5	23.8	3.7

Survivors

Amongst all the comings and goings in an area over a period of time there remain those plants which continue at the same location throughout the period. Although, in terms of plant numbers, they are a stable element they need not be so in employment terms. A plant which survives may experience one of three types of employment change: it may increase its employment, it may decrease its employment, or its workforce may remain the same size. Survivors, then, are a more complex category to analyse even without two additional complications associated with the present investigation.

The first of these is purely technical and occurs because of our use of an employment threshold of ten or more workers. A plant employing more than this number in 1966 may or may not do so in 1975. Conversely, a plant employing fewer than ten workers in 1966 may have grown to more than ten by 1975. Applying an employment threshold, then, may well mean that the population of surviving plants may be rather different in the two years being considered. Because of this, the present analysis of survivors refers to plant which employed ten or more workers in *both* 1966 and 1975.

The second complication is more substantive and is inherent in all work where plant ownership is concerned. A plant may well survive at the same location between 1966 and 1975 with more, fewer, or the same number of workers. But its *organisational status* may well change too. For example, a single-plant firm in 1966 may have become part of a multi-part organisation by 1975. Most likely this will have occurred through acquisition or merger, a process we discuss later. But it could also occur through internal expansion whereby a single-plant firm grows and in doing so opens up an additional plant. Conversely, a multi-plant firm may suffer contraction and close down plants, becoming a single-plant firm. These comments should be borne in mind when considering change among survivors over the 1966 to 1975 period.

Net shrinkage of employment in plants which were operating in inner Manchester in both 1966 and 1975 was the least important component of change contributing a balance of –5,580 jobs, about one ninth of the job loss through plant closure. This is in marked contrast to inner Merseyside where *in situ* shrinkage, especially in very large plants headquartered outside Merseyside County, was the dominant element in employment change. In inner Manchester there was a net loss of 5,226 jobs in survivors employing more than ten workers in both 1966 and 1975. Sixty per cent of this job loss was in multi-plant firms and 40 per cent in single-plant firms. A good deal of this shrinkage was associated with change of ownership, a topic to which we now turn our attention.

The Impact of Ownership Change

Some of the reduced employment in the survivor category undoubtedly reflects rationalisation following acquisitions and mergers taking place prior to 1966. But what of such activity during the 1966 to 1975 period? We noted earlier that the process of acquisition and merger has played a very important part in the evolution of business organisations at the national level. We would, therefore, expect to find some evidence of the same process operating at the level of the inner city and contributing towards industrial change.

Detailed information on acquisitions and mergers is difficult to obtain at a national level; at the scale of this study even more so. Yet because of the importance of the acquisition process some attempt has to be made to assess its importance locally. To do this, every 'closure' and every surviving plant in the study area was examined for evidence of ownership change. In the case of survivors this was simply a matter of comparing the parent company of a plant in 1966 and 1975 (no attempt was made to identify 'intermediate' changes). For plants which closed between 1966 and 1975 the procedure was slightly different. The aim was to discover whether a plant had experienced a change of ownership prior to closure. This is a massive operation requiring the search of ownership directories in consecutive years between 1966 and the date of closure. To make the task a little easier we again considered only those plants employing ten or more workers. The results of this analysis are tentative but, despite inevitable inaccuracies, we believe they throw some light on the issue.

Ownership Change and Plant Closure

Some 92 plant closures employing more than ten workers were identified as having experienced a change of ownership between 1966 and the date of closure. This represented roughly 14 per cent of all plants of this size involved in closure. In employment terms, however, the contribution of ownership change was very much greater. Approximately 9,700 job losses could be associated with this process, representing some 25 per cent of closure losses. Table 2.8 shows how this change was distributed between the different categories.

Table 2.8: Plant Closures Associated with Change of Ownership, Inner Manchester, 1966-75

		Employment Loss Status of acquired plant			
		Single-plant	Multi-plant local	Multi-plant external (domestic)	Multi-plant external (foreign)	Row Total
	Multi-plant local	167	889	—	—	1,056
Status of acquiring firm	Multi-plant external (domestic)	1,179	2,820	4,224	—	8,223
	Multi-plant (foreign)	160	275	25	—	460
Column total		1,506	3,984	4,249	—	9,739

In terms of the status of the *acquired* plant in 1966, the table shows that acquisition of single-plant firms was a much less important element of employment change than that of multi-plant firms. 1,506 jobs — 15.5 per cent of the total — were lost in single-plant firms acquired by others. By comparison 84.5 per cent of the employment loss in acquired firms was in multi-plant firms. Shifting attention to the *acquiring* firm reveals that the vast bulk of the acquisition activity was generated by multi-plant firms headquartered elsewhere in the United Kingdom. In all 8,223 lost jobs — 85.3 per cent of the total — were in plants acquired by such firms. Roughly half of these (4,224) were in plants already belonging to externally-headquartered firms.

Hence a good deal of the employment loss was the by-product of acquisitions taking place at the national scale which, because of the particular corporate mix in inner Manchester, also had repercussions locally. But the process itself is part of a much larger economic restructuring. Indeed the effects of some very large acquisitions and mergers were experienced locally. The most widely publicised were, of course, those resulting from the government-encouraged merger between GEC, AEI and English Electric in 1967. Almost 1,000 jobs in inner Manchester were lost in the aftermath of this major corporate up-heaval in plant closures alone, quite apart from employment reduction in acquired plants which survived. Large job losses were also associated with the Johnson and Firth Brown merger, with the takeover of English Steel by the British Steel Corporation, with Allied Polymer's acquisition of Greengate and Irwell, and by other major ownership changes.

Thus job loss in closures in inner Manchester was not just a function of the demise of single-plant firms, important though this was. An important element was the closure of plants belonging to firms acquired by others as part of the broader process of corporate rationalisation. Of course, we cannot conclude unequivocally that closure was *caused by* a change of ownership. Quite apart from problems of identifying ownership change especially among small firms, some of the plants may have had to close anyway — for example, because of compulsory purchase orders. All we can do at this stage is point to an observed association between closure and a prior change of ownership.

Ownership Change and Surviving Plants

We observed earlier in discussing surviving plants that one of the ways in which they might change over a period of time would be to alter their organisational status. By far the most common cause of such status

change is that associated with a change in ownership. A preliminary
estimate suggests that 84 plants employing more than ten workers in
both 1966 and 1975 changed ownership during the period. In 1966 these
plants employed a total of 12,312 workers. By 1975 their total
labour force had fallen to 10,594, a relative decline of almost 14 per
cent. Of course not every one of the 84 plants reduced its workforce.
In fact, 22 plants increased their employment and 27 plants held the
same level in both 1966 and 1975. But the 35 plants which did reduce
their labour force more than offset these. Their net employment loss
accounted for 33 per cent of all job losses in surviving plants employing
more than ten workers.

Table 2.9 allows us to see the detail of the ownership change among
surviving plants more clearly. Again, as with closures, it is evident that
externally-headquartered firms were responsible for most of the
ownership change. In fact, 60 of the 84 plants were acquired by such
firms and several of these were also involved in closures. In terms of
net change, however, employment was greatest in those plants acquired
by locally-headquartered multi-plant firms; employment in this group
fell by 22.5 per cent. The changes involving foreign-owned firms were
numerically very small so that the percentage change figure does not
have much significance.

An obvious question arising from the fact that some plants changed
ownership whilst others did not relates to their comparative employment
performance. Among survivors, did acquired plants change their
employment to a greater or lesser extent than non-acquired plants? This
is a difficult question to answer given the substantial differences in the
number of plants in each category. All that can be concluded at this
stage is that the 84 acquired plants lost 13.9 per cent of their 1966
employment. In comparison, the 392 non-acquired plants lost 11.0 per
cent of their 1966 employment. These would hardly seem to be significant performance differences. As we noted earlier, of course, it does
not necessarily follow that post-acquisition employment change occurs
immediately after the event. It may be some years before changes take
effect. Thus some of the employment change in the plants not
acquired between 1966 and 1975 may in fact be the result of acquisitions occurring prior to 1966.

The Overall Impact of Ownership Change

If we add those acquired plants which closed to those acquired plants
surviving between 1966 and 1975 we get some idea of the overall
contribution of ownership change to total employment change. A total

(A) EMPLOYMENT 1966/75

		Status of acquired plant			
		Single-plant	Multi-plant local	Multi-plant external (domestic)	Multi-plant external (foreign)	Row total
Status of acquiring firm	Multi-plant local	917/652	1,861/1,502	—	—	2,778/2,154
	Multi-plant external (domest-c)	549/494	5,392/4,542	3,265/2,774	—	9,206/7,810
	Multi-plant external (foreign)	—	160/470	140/140	28/20	328/630
Column total		1,466/1,146	7,413/6,514	3,405/2,914	28/20	12,312/10,594

(B) PERCENTAGE CHANGE 1966/75

		Single-plant	Multi-plant local	Multi-plant external (domestic)	Multi-plant external (foreign)	Row total
Status of acquiring firm	Multi-plant local	-28.9%	-19.3%	—	—	-22.5%
	Multi-plant external (domestic)	-10.0%	-15.8%	-15.0%	—	-15.2%
	Multi-plant externa (foreign)	—	+193.7%	NC	-28.6%	+92.1%
Column tota		-21.8%	-12.1%	-14.4%	-28.6%	-13.9%

of 176 inner city plants are believed to have changed ownership, 52.2 per cent of which, employing more than 9,500 workers, subsequently closed down. The 84 plants which, though changing ownership, still survived suffered a much smaller net loss of 1,718 workers. Taken together almost 11,500 job losses in inner Manchester could be associated with ownership change. This was equivalent to 30 per cent of total employment loss in plants employing more than ten workers and 28.8 per cent of employment loss in plants of all sizes. Quite clearly a significant proportion of *local* change is a reflection of corporate reorganisation at the *national* or even *international* level.

Conclusion and Policy Implications

It is perhaps appropriate to ask what the 'organisational' viewpoint adopted in this chapter contributes to the analysis of industrial change in inner Manchester and to policy prescriptions for the future. As we have shown, there is a general tendency within the nation as a whole, and within the western capitalist economies generally, for there to be an increasing concentration of industrial production and capital assets in the hands of fewer, larger companies. In the economico-political climate of ten years ago this was seen to be an inevitable, and even desirable, stage in the development of corporate capitalism. The larger corporate entities were regarded as being best able to promote and benefit from the new technologies and their associated scale economies. The Wilson government through its Industrial Reorganisation Corporation sought actively to promote such concentration by sponsoring and encouraging industrial merger and acquisition.

At that stage what later came to be called the 'small is beautiful' lobby following the exhortations of Schumacher (1973) found few converts. Merger, acquisition, rationalisation and restructuring were, together with comprehensive urban redevelopment, the dominant forces then influencing the population of industrial enterprises operating within an urban environment. For some areas with particularly 'receptive' industrial structures the process of effective industrial concentration was more active than in others. An earlier paper (Dicken and Lloyd, 1977) dealt with a particularly extreme case, that of inner Merseyside.

Other relevant corporate trends of the period from 1966 to 1975 in Britain were: falling average profit margins, increasing technical obsolescence, shrinking industrial investment and low productivity (for a full analysis of these problems see Singh, 1977). Indeed, recession — followed after 1973 by severe depression — has been the broader

backdrop against which industrial events in inner Manchester have
been taking place. Clearly, the nature of national, even global, economic
trends during the past ten years, however remote they appear to be in
both time and place, are vital to a causal analysis of those events which
have cost inner Manchester over 40 per cent of its 1966 manual job
stock.

In the corporate environment local events have reflected global
trends. We have shown, for example, the tendency towards the demise
of small indigenous manufacturing firms, with a relative rise in the
share of employment controlled by larger multi-plant firms whose headquarters are outside Manchester. We have shown how, for inner
Manchester, plant closure has been a more frequently applied option
against a background of recession than the alternative of shedding
labour and maintaining a number of plants running below effective
capacity. We have, albeit in a preliminary and incomplete analysis,
illustrated the regressive impact of ownership change on employment
in the case of inner Manchester. The study area has thus mirrored
within its own recent history events in the economy at large. The
interesting question to be asked, however, and one to which we shall
address ourselves in later research is to what extent, if any, those events
have been distorted by the inner city as a *particular* industrial
environment. It is only upon answering this question that the effective
design of more than palliative urban-industrial policy can be based.

In the absence of an overall context against which the problems of
industry in the inner city can be set, we can only proceed with a somewhat generalised review of the way the corporate viewpoint contributes to the analysis of inner urban industrial events. To begin with,
let us consider the question of differential response. Division of an
area's stock of factories into the single-plant or multi-plant categories
can tell us rather more than simply how industry is structured in enterprise terms. It can also tell us something of the repertoire of responses
available to an area's firm population when faced with changing
circumstances. Clearly for the single-plant firm responses to geographically localised problems are more limited than for the multi-plant firm.
Take, for example, a change in the working environment of a given
factory by the imposition of parking or access restrictions, the removal
of a valued local labour source by slum clearance or perhaps the impact
of a prolonged local strike.

For the single-plant firm, particularly in the smaller-size range, such
events might well be a threat to the very roots of its existence. For an
organisation supporting more than one factory, a threat to a single

plant is not, in the first place, a direct threat to the firm as a whole. Second, there is a possible response to the problem through a functional reorganisation of activities among the company's plants. Third, where, as we have shown is often the case, the multi-plant organisation tends to be part of a generally larger concern, it may be possible to 'ride out' the difficulties by some form of cross-subsidisation from other units within the company. For the single-plant firm it is possibly the bank manager's view of the overdraft rather than perhaps the longer-run, more tolerant view of the company accountant which might make it more vulnerable.

External control may also bring both benefits and disadvantages of the same order as those outlined for multi-plant firms in general. Sometimes it may, of course, be easier for a firm headquartered far from the site of one of its constituent plants to close it down while having little regard for the local impact of this action. Conversely, however, a factory under some short-term threat to its viability may well survive primarily by virtue of its association with a large company whose assets are large enough to support the temporary loss and whose constituent plants operate in regions or sectors unlikely to be afflicted simultaneously by adverse conditions. From time to time views of the 'branch-plant economy' appear to have reflected value judgements rather than hard fact.

A further critically important feature of the organisational character of the firms which make up an area's job stock is their *differential impact* on the nature of available job opportunities. For the single-plant firm, for example, all the functions exist at the same site — managerial, clerical, manual. For the multi-plant firm, however, this is not necessarily always so. The centralisation of management functions has been one of the key scale economies available to the large integrated multi-plant firm. As a result, many of the branch operations of such firms present only a truncated spectrum of the firm's employment opportunities. Frequently, for example, there may be provision of semi-skilled processing, fabrication or assembly tasks at branch factories while 'higher order' tasks in management, R & D and sales are retained at the corporate 'centre'. In regional or intra-urban terms, therefore, *which particular parts* of the multi-plant firms' employment spectra are provided may have a critical impact on job opportunities, promotion prospects and pay levels.

In the specific case of inner Manchester we have suggested that it is fortunate to still retain a substantial core of locally-controlled small business. Policy should indeed be devised and applied which will nurture this particular segment of the city's economic base. Here, more than in the case of inner Merseyside, *locally* applied measures for industrial promotion will find a substantial residual audience of *local* entrepreneurs able to benefit. There is, however, in the current climate of opinion a danger that the prescription of small business as the saviour of the inner areas will be received uncritically. We have already shown that despite the numbers of small firms operating in inner Manchester over the past ten years the key employment events have been generated by the arrival and departure of a handful of major firms. A dialogue with small business has been established and a climate towards positive discrimination fostered. In all this it should not be forgotten that even in Manchester the elements of the larger multi-plant firms which it possesses and new branches whose establishment it might encourage, will still hold a major key to the scale of job opportunities provided, as well as provide a doorway for its residents to the prized jobs in the mainstream labour market.

In the final analysis, however, the prospects for an industrial revival of the inner areas cannot be regarded as other than bleak. As analysis by firm shows unequivocally, the forces which generate observed 'on the ground' events in the inner areas are those operating in the economy at large. Solutions to the inner city problem at any level, and more especially in the case of manufacturing, are unlikely to be found in 'tinkering' with the existing order of things. The stagnation of British industry generally finds its way, in the extremist of forms, to the nature of industrial events in the inner city. Similarly, the ongoing processes of merger, rationalisation and re-equipment which seek to promote the necessary rises in national productivity and profitability may well have quite dramatic negative impacts on the availability of blue-collar jobs in the inner urban areas. One clear fallacy in evaluating and prescribing policy for manufacturing in the inner areas is to ignore the fact that the significant 'levers' of change lie outside them and that events within derive from decisions taken at the highest reaches of society at large.

Notes

1. The terms 'large' and 'small' are vague. As the Bolton Committee (1971) pointed out it is extremely difficult to find a single, unambiguous and empirically satisfactory definition of a small firm. In the case of manufacturing, the Committee opted for an upper limit of 200 employees. Manufacturing firms employing fewer than 200 workers were defined as 'small'.

2. The establishment data are derived from the records of the Factory Inspectorate and, as such, they refer to manual workers in manufacturing only.

3. In each of Tables 2.3, 2.4 and 2.5 the row labelled '% change 1966/75' refers to the change in absolute employment in each category.

References

Bannock, G. (1976) *The Smaller Business in Britain and Germany*, London: Wilton House

Cameron, C.G. (1973) 'Intra-Urban Location and the New Plant', *Papers of the Regional Science Association*, vol. 31, pp. 125-44.

Committee of Enquiry on Small Firms (Bolton Committee) (1971), *Small Firms*, London: HMSO

Dennis, R. (1978) 'The Decline of Manufacturing Employment in Greater London: 1966-74', *Urban Studies*, vol. 15, pp. 63-73

Dicken, P. (1976) 'The Multi-Plant Business Enterprise and Geographical Space: Some Issues in the Study of External Control and Regional Development', *Regional Studies*, vol. 10, pp. 401-12

—— and Lloyd, P.E. (1977) 'Inner Merseyside: Components of Industrial Change in the Corporate Context', North West Industry Research Unit, Working Paper No. 4, University of Manchester School of Geography

—— and Lloyd, P.E. (1978) 'Inner Metropolitan Industrial Change, Enterprise Structures and Policy Issues: Case Studies of Manchester and Merseyside', *Regional Studies*, vol. 12, pp. 181-97

Fagg, J.J. (1973) 'Spatial Changes in Manufacturing Employment in Greater Leicester: 1947-1970', *East Midlands Geographer*, vol. 5, pp. 400-16

Firn, J.R. (1975) 'External Control and Regional Development: the Case of Scotland', *Environment and Planning A*, vol. 7, pp. 393-414.

Gripaios, P. (1977a) 'Industrial Decline in London: An Examination of the Causes', *Urban Studies*, vol. 14, pp. 181-9

Gripaios, P. (1977b) 'The Closure of Firms in the Inner City: the South East London Case', *Regional Studies*, vol. 11, pp. 1-6

Hannah, L. (1976) *The Rise of the Corporate Economy*, London: Methuen

—— and Kay, J.A. (1977) *Concentration in Modern Industry*, London: Macmillan

Lloyd, P.E. (1977) 'Manufacturing Industry in the Inner City: A Case Study of Merseyside', North West Industry Research Unit, Working Paper No. 2, University of Manchester School of Geography

—— (1979) (forthcoming) 'The Components of Industrial Change for Merseyside Inner Area: 1966-1975', *Urban Studies*, vol. 16

—— and Mason, C.M. (1977) 'Manufacturing Industry in the Inner City: A Case Study of Greater Manchester', North West Industry Research Unit, Working Paper No. 1, University of Manchester School of Geography

—— and Mason, C.M. (1978) 'Manufacturing Industry in the Inner City: A Case Study of Greater Manchester', *Transactions, Institute of British Geographers*, New Series, vol. 3, pp. 66-90

Mason, C.M. (1979) (forthcoming) 'Structural and Locational Change in Metropolitan Manufacturing Industry: A Case Study of Greater Manchester', unpublished PhD, University of Manchester School of Geography

National Enterprise Board (1977) *Investment Potential in the North East and North West of England*, London: National Enterprise Board

Prais, S.J. (1976) *The Evolution of Giant Firms in Britain*, Cambridge: Cambridge University Press

Schumacher, E.F. (1973) *Small is Beautiful: A Study of Economics as if People Mattered*, London: Blond and Briggs

Singh, A. (1977) 'U.K. Industry and World Economy — A Case of De-industrialisation', *Cambridge Journal of Economics*, vol. 1, pp. 113-36

Westaway, J. (1974) 'The Spatial Hierarchy of Business Organisations and its Implications for the British Urban System', *Regional Studies*, vol. 8, pp. 145-55

3 THE INNER CITY LABOUR MARKET

Glen Bramley

This chapter is concerned with what may be happening in the inner city labour market, and in particular with explanations of the level and pattern of unemployment. The emphasis is on problems arising in Britain, and most of the empirical material discussed relates to London, although some comparisons are made with Liverpool and with other cities generally. This work grows out of the author's involvement with the Lambeth Inner Area Study (IAS), a multi-disciplinary, area-based research and action project commissioned by the Department of the Environment in 1972 and completed in 1976 (Great Britain, 1977a).

Some attempt is made to go beyond the practical questions asked by policymakers and consider some of the ideas being developed by academics working on theories of the labour market. Thus, in the following section, consideration is given to whether the inner city labour market has any distinctive structural characteristics and whether these can be related to various alternative models of labour market behaviour. In the third section some hypotheses are put forward to explain unemployment and related problems — underemployment, employment instability, low income — in the inner areas. Evidence on some of these hypotheses is discussed, including selected findings from a variety of studies, some detailed evidence analysed by the author in the course of the Lambeth IAS, and a special analysis of unemployment rates and changes across London boroughs.

The existence of a problem of high unemployment rates among inner city residents is well established; there is clear evidence that male unemployment rates are systematically higher in most inner areas than in their surrounding regions. This is shown for London by the Lambeth IAS (Great Britain, 1977a, chapter 4), the Greater London Council (1975, Table 6) and the Strategy for the South East Review (Great Britain 1976, Table 4.9). Similarly Corkindale (1976, Table 21 and Annex Tables 14 and 15) and the Department of the Environment (Great Britain, 1975a) summarise the pattern across all the conurbations, and studies of particular areas, e.g. Liverpool Inner Area Study (Great Britain, 1977b), have highlighted inner area unemployment concentrations. There is rather less strong evidence that residents of inner areas experience lower average earnings or household incomes;

the London situation being better documented than elsewhere in, for example Simon (1977) and the Lambeth IAS (Great Britain, 1975b, part 7).

It is far from clear, however, that the relative position of the inner areas has worsened in the last decade or so as unemployment nationally has grown. Neither can it be said to have improved, and absolute rates of unemployment are currently very high in some inner areas. The main debate which this chapter addresses, is how the inner areas' persistent disadvantage in unemployment (particularly) is to be explained or interpreted and what implications this has for policy.

Distinctive Characteristics of Inner City Labour Markets

Are there differences in the way that labour market processes operate in inner city areas as compared with local labour markets in other types of area? It is argued in this section that such differences do exist and help to explain some of the apparent disadvantages of inner area workers. These characteristics should be taken into account when interpreting evidence on employment conditions in the inner city. They follow from the geographical, industrial and social structure of inner areas, some of the main features of which are as follows:

(1) Geographical characteristics:
    (a) The market, in terms of total jobs or workers, is large;
    (b) The market is geographically concentrated;
    (c) The market is open (e.g. to commuting) rather than self-contained;
    (d) Internal accessibility by public transport within the market area is relatively good.
(2) Industrial structure tends to be:
    (a) relatively diversified;
    (b) biased towards service industries;
    (c) less dominated by major, individual employers (other than the public sector);
    (d) characterised by smaller firms.
(3) Demographic and social characteristics:
    (a) in-migrants are largely young and single;
    (b) most out-migrants are somewhat older and married;
    (c) large ethnic minorities are present;
    (d) the workforce is relatively low in skill, or socio-economic status.

These are put forward as generalisations which may be truer of one conurbation than another but remain a fair description of inner cities in general. In this regard by inner city we are referring to the inner London boroughs and more generally to the nineteenth-century cores of our conurbations. We now consider the implications of these characteristics for the operation of the labour market.

Competitiveness

One plausible implication is that the inner city labour market is more competitive, that is more subject to market forces and less institutionally structured, than other local labour markets. It can be argued that this follows from its larger scale, concentration, openness and internal accessibility which together with the service industry and small firms bias create a market with many potential buyers and sellers of any particular type of labour. If this competitive market model held we would expect local conditions of supply and demand to have more impact on local wages than appears to be the case more generally (MacKay *et al.*, 1971). We might also expect a more 'efficient' allocation of labour (as discussed by Stigler, 1962, p. 104), a corollary of which would be that the least skilled or productive workers were even less likely to find steady employment than elsewhere.

Job Mobility

Associated with this competitive market is perhaps the expectation that job mobility and turnover would be higher in inner cities, because the opportunities for horizontal movement are plentiful. Such mobility would, however, depend on the state of demand (see Great Britain, 1977c, pp. 40-1). High turnover means a high flow of job vacancies, which renders access to the job market relatively easy for newcomers. Hence labour turnover and mobility interact with migration patterns and the demographic, social and ethnic characteristics of the workforce. Turnover indeed probably reinforces the housing and cultural factors which lead to the in-migration of young single people and ethnic minorities. Young, single people are themselves more prone to job-changing, and thus migration and labour supply may exacerbate an instability inherent in the geographical and industrial structure. Again, firms for which high labour turnover was costly might tend to (re)locate elsewhere.

On the evidence available it is difficult to establish whether labour turnover is higher in the inner city areas, partly because it is difficult to control for the effects of industrial and occupational composition and the pressure of demand for labour. We would expect to find relatively more short-term, frictional unemployment in these areas, particularly at times of high demand, and the evidence for London supports this (Greater London Council, 1975, Table 14). The apparent concentration of inner city unemployment among younger workers (Great Britain, 1977a, 1977b; Greater London Council, 1975) is also consistent with this view of the labour market. Taking larger cities in general, Vipond (1974) found a positive relationship between city size and male unemployment rates, tentatively explained in terms of information diseconomies and in terms of a lesser tendency of employers in large cities to hoard labour, causing greater frictional unemployment.

Cycle Sensitivity

Would we expect unemployment to be more sensitive to national fluctuations in demand in the inner city than elsewhere? There is no clear answer to this question because, while characteristics on the demand side imply less sensitivity, some of the supply side factors would imply the opposite. An industrial structure which is more diversified and biased towards services would tend to generate less employment instability than one characterised by greater manufacturing specialisation, particularly in capital goods. This would suggest that the sharp employment declines experienced by London and other cities since the mid-1960s represent a long-term structural (or locational) problem rather than a cyclical downturn, and shift-share evidence supports this (see Greater London Council, 1975, Table 10).

However, when we consider the characteristics of the labour supply resident in the inner areas a different picture emerges. The workforce is likely to be disproportionately composed of those groups who tend to be most vulnerable to downturns in the demand for labour, whether through greater likelihood of redundancy or (perhaps more important) through lesser ability to compete for a greatly reduced flow of job vacancies. These groups are the young, in-migrants, ethnic minorities and the unskilled. Thus, although the number of jobs in the inner city may not fall disproportionately as a result of a cyclical downturn, the effects of any fall in demand are likely to be most marked in that sub-sector of the labour supply which lives in the inner areas, bearing in mind that the labour market under consideration is not self-contained.

Thus, we cannot predict whether we would expect relative unemployment rates in inner areas to worsen during recessions. Labour supply characteristics suggest they would, but labour demand characteristics and also the frictional unemployment phenomenon (if positively related to demand) suggest they would not. If inner area unemployment rates do increase in relative terms this may reinforce the case that what is observed is actually a longer-term trend. The evidence for London during the two recessions 1971-2 and 1974-5 (Greater London Council, 1975, Table 6) was that the inner sectors' male unemployment increased either equally or less in terms of ratios but more in terms of absolute differences when compared with the outer sectors, the Outer Metropolitan Area or the rest of the South-East Region. This could be explained in terms of a broadly similar cycle sensitivity superimposed on a higher base level of unemployment in the inner sectors, reflecting frictional and structural components. The same pattern of relative change (less in terms of ratios, more in terms of differences) is apparent when comparing Liverpool with the North-West Region or Great Britain between June 1974 and September 1975 (Great Britain, 1977d, Figure 4).

Women in the Labour Market

The participation of married women in the labour force responds to a range of factors on both the demand and the supply side. Factors on both sides tend to increase the observed activity rates in inner areas. A predominance of service and other industries (e.g. textiles in Greater Manchester) which employ high proportions of women increases the demand for female labour in the central and inner areas. The supply is increased by the concentration and internal accessibility of the inner urban labour market, and also arguably by the operation of the housing market and the selective migration patterns which result. As Evans (1973, chapter 9) argues, households where both husband and wife work in the central area will in equilibrium locate closer to the centre than households where the wife does not work. Wabe (1969) found among other things an inverse relationship between activity rates for married women and distance from the centre within the London region. Thus the housing market may work with demand and accessibility to produce high activity rates, although it would be dangerous to place too much emphasis on choice and market forces in the British housing system, because of the extent of public intervention.

The fact that activity rates are high in inner areas, sometimes very high (see Great Britain, 1975b, pp. 59-62) does not of itself indicate a favourable labour market for women, nor can it easily be related to measures of multiple deprivation (Holtermann and Silkin, 1976). Female unemployment rates, particularly registered (as opposed to

Census) rates, are also an unreliable indicator. However, taking a range
of evidence, including earnings and indices of labour demand, it was
concluded in the Lambeth context that the labour market for women
was much more favourable than that for men, problems being more to
do with low pay and day care for young children. Looking across the
155 largest British cities, Vipond (1974) found that female unemployment fell with city size after allowing for various other factors. For
these reasons, attention is focused in the rest of this chapter on male
employment and unemployment.

The Supply of Skills

Another implication of the structural characteristics of inner areas
may be that the supply of labour skills tends to be inadequate, except
where traditional skills have become redundant by technical change.
First, smaller firms (and service firms) may be less able or willing to
afford the overhead cost of training, whether formal or informal, on or
off the job. Second, the competitiveness/mobility thesis implies that,
wherever skills or experience are transferable, there will be greater
opportunities for poaching, a higher risk of wastage among trainees,
and hence a lower incentive for firms to invest in training. Third, the
differential out-migration of the more skilled occupational groups and
the more experienced age groups in the labour force (Dugmore, 1975;
Jones, chapter 8 in this volume) would progressively drain the pool on
which inner-area employers draw or increase the cost of retaining
workers who have to commute farther. Finally, it is widely believed
that levels of educational attainment among inner city school leavers
are markedly lower than elsewhere, and some relevant evidence is
presented by the Department of the Environment (Great Britain,
1975a, chapter 10).

The Dual Labour Market

A number of these suggested characteristics of inner city labour
markets may be put in a broader theoretical perspective by considering
an alternative to the orthodox, neoclassical economic approach which
has gained some currency in the last decade. The dual labour market
approach, which was developed in an American context, is usefully if
critically reviewed by Wachter (1974). The economy is seen as divided
into two distinct sectors, a primary (high-wage) sector characterised
by specific training and structured internal labour markets, and a
secondary (low-wage) sector without these features and hence characterised by job instability. Disadvantaged groups such as blacks, women,

the young and the poorly educated tend to be trapped in the secondary sector by the lack of 'good' (primary) jobs and barriers to the primary sector, including discrimination, feedback (bad work habits, inter-generational effects) and life-cycle effects. It is argued that secondary workers are underemployed relative to their potential, and that high unemployment in the secondary sector reflects not a lack of job openings but rather frequent spells of unemployment resulting from the lack of incentive to remain in 'bad' jobs. Thus, the dual hypothesis puts a different interpretation on both low pay and structural unemployment from orthodox neoclassical economic models, which stress demand, wage rigidities, information and 'human capital'.

Bosanquet and Doeringer (1973) examine the applicability of the dual model to the British labour market, and although they find much evidence that is consistent with it, they qualify their argument by pointing to important differences between British and American conditions. Higher long-term unemployment, the lower unemployment rates for women and the importance of apprenticeships giving general training in transferable skills are three examples. However, they argue that, in the long term, the British labour market may become more dualistic for various reasons.

Some propositions as to the characteristic features of the inner city labour market were put forward above, and there are significant parallels between these and the dualists' descriptions of the secondary sector. The emphasis on labour mobility and turnover and on the preponderance of disadvantaged groups in the labour force are common elements in both. Yet it would be a simplification to argue that the inner city employment problem is that of the secondary sector in a dual labour market. The characteristics of the resident workforce show some secondary bias, in terms of industry competition, demographic, ethnic, skill, sex and age composition, while the typical secondary problems of low pay and short-term unemployment are in evidence. However, this cannot be attributed to the characteristics of employment located in these areas, for example in terms of industry or earnings levels, but rather is a function of patterns of residential location which derive from the operation of the housing system. This line of argument is developed in the Lambeth IAS (Great Britain, 1975b). It may still be the case that the inner city environment encourages firms to adopt 'secondary' characteristics, to the extent that they have some choice as to their personnel policies, for example by accepting labour turnover and adapting production techniques, skills required, promotion and pay structures accordingly.

Factors Affecting Unemployment
We now focus on the problem of major concern, inner city unemployment. We consider in this section how factors which are possible causes
of unemployment relate to the characteristics of the inner city. In
particular we examine the roles of physical accessibility, information,
housing immobility, skill barriers and skill creation, the demand for
labour and personal attributes. Labour disadvantage, although not
considered explicitly here, could also be analysed in such terms.
Unfortunately a close look at some of these factors suggests constraints
as to the appropriate analysis of the problem, and these, too, are discussed in this section.

Accessibility

It is undoubtedly the case that people with low incomes are constrained
in their journey to work patterns than those on high incomes. Low
income restricts car ownership and hence restricts freedom to travel in
non-radial directions within the city, to inaccessible workplaces or at
unsocial hours. Lack of a car also increases the marginal cost of travelling further to work. Low income directly restricts journey to work
expenditure and hence distance. It also tends to oblige workers to use
slower, less reliable or less comfortable modes of transport like buses
or walking. Berthoud (1975) presents an interesting discussion of this
issue in the London context, concluding that professional, managerial
and other non-manual workers can travel much further and consequently
have a much wider choice of potential work places than semi- or unskilled
manual workers. Part of their advantage derives from the radial rail
network and the concentration of non-manual jobs in the central area.
    In the Lambeth IAS (Great Britain, 1975b), both potential and
actual work journeys from the study area were mapped. The evidence
suggested that the average male worker, earning rather below the
average and lacking the use of a car, would be effectively confined to a
zone comprising the southern sector of inner London plus the central
area. Household survey data revealed a clear positive relationship
between working outside these confines and income, while married
women and young males (aged 16-20) were more likely to work within
the borough itself. From this analysis it was concluded that Greater
London should not be regarded as a single travel to work area but
rather as a series of overlapping ones, and that as far as the more
vulnerable groups in the labour force were concerned this localisation
was particularly important. Some parts of inner (and outer) London
have poorer accessibility than Lambeth, notably Docklands. London

is a special case by virtue of its size, but similar arguments were developed in the Liverpool context (Great Britain, 1977d, pp. 14-15), namely that most inner city residents were effectively restricted to a choice of work places within the city, the growth areas of the sub-region being inaccessible.

Information

The evidence on sources of information on new jobs indicates the importance of informal channels, in other words direct approaches to employers and 'the grapevine' of friends and relatives. For example, the 1972 General Household Survey showed that 55 per cent of people who had been in their present job for less than a year first heard of it through such informal channels (Great Britain, 1972). Daniel (1974) found this proportion (among those previously unemployed) highest with the less skilled manual worker, and indeed Rees and Shultz's study of Chicago (1970) revealed a striking reliance on informal sources for manual hirings. Furthermore, these and other sources (Dunnell and Head, 1975, p. 56) suggest a preference for informal methods, and their greater efficiency, both from employees' and employers' viewpoints. Rees (1966, p. 566) summed up the reasons for this preference as 'richness and reliability of information'.

It can be argued that informal information channels are inherently more localised than agencies, employment exchanges or advertising. Reliance on personal contacts implies that the employer will tend to continue, over time, to draw on labour from the same locality, most probably (though not necessarily) adjacent to the workplace. Direct approaches by job applicants will tend to be localised because of knowledge about where to try and the costs of travel during job search set against the uncertainty of outcome. Thus, a case can be put that information channels and job search costs represent additional constraints on less skilled manual workers seeking or obtaining jobs outside their locality within the conurbation. This reinforces the constraints associated with the journey to work. Informal methods may, it seems, be used somewhat less in the major cities (see General Household Survey regional analysis, distinguishing London), but this could be a response to the size and complexity of the urban labour market which forces inferior and more costly (Rees, 1966, p. 563) channels to be used. Such tendencies perhaps reinforce the view that information is a problem in a large urban area.

Housing and Mobility

Housing in Britain has been subject to increasing public intervention
since the First World War, the side effects of which on the labour market
have rarely been considered. The housing system hinders geographical
mobility in general, and hence hampers individuals trying to adapt to
personal job changes, but in addition it tends systematically to house
certain groups in certain places, which may be the wrong places relative
to the pattern of job opportunities. The reasons for this can be seen if
we briefly examine the characteristics of the main tenure groups before
relating these to the inner city.

Entry into owner-occupation is restricted primarily by income, and
the need for large deposits reflects building society conservatism in
lending policies on the older properties in the inner areas (see Karn,
chapter 7 in this volume). Entry into the council sector is rationed
bureaucratically and although waiting times vary greatly between areas
entry is largely restricted to people who have lived for some time in
the local authority area. Mobility within the public sector is rarely
positively encouraged and little provision is made for inter-authority
moves, that is moves between labour market areas, except in the special
case of the new and expanding towns, which have tended to be selective
in terms of occupation. The private rented sector is divided into
protected tenancies and subletting by owner-occupiers. The latter sub-
sector facilitates mobility but is inevitably limited in scale and provides
little family accommodation. Protected tenancies are shrinking steadily
and when vacancies occur they are not necessarily relet. Such reletting
as does take place tends to involve the payment of premia, which again
excludes the poor, or requires local knowledge and contacts which
discourages geographical mobility.

Apart from the absolute constraints on access to housing, there
are also disincentives to residential mobility in many areas. There are
the direct costs of moving, but perhaps more important is the insidious
tendency for rents on new lettings (like initial mortgage repayments) to
be very high compared with rents in existing tenancies (Berthoud,
1975; p. 23). Loss of security of tenure or place in the council waiting
list, problems with longer work journeys for the carless or for wives,
loss of seniority or pension rights associated with job change, and
general uncertainty about an unfamiliar environment would all tend to
discourage movement, especially over a longer distance.

The constraints on mobility arising out of the institutional
structure of housing supply are more pressing in the inner city areas,
because their housing stock is largely in the public and private rented

sectors. London poses more serious problems than other cities because the price level, and hence the income threshold to owner occupation, is higher, reflecting demand pressures emanating from high-income jobs concentrated in the central area together with an inelastic supply. In the Lambeth IAS the phenomenon of 'the housing trap' was identified as a major issue affecting the less skilled, lower-income population of the area and, by analogy, much of inner London (Great Britain, 1977a, chapter 6). It was argued there that this constraint increased the vulnerability of that population to changes in the demand for labour in the accessible zone; in other words, the assumption of a fixed place of residence when defining the relevant labour market area was far from unrealistic. To the extent that mobility exists it is selective, giving rise to the demographic and social characteristics of the inner city labour supply identified earlier and the movement patterns discussed by Jones (chapter 8 in this volume).

Skill Barriers and Skill Creation

The three factors just considered are explicitly spatial elements in the explanation of inner city unemployment and related problems. However, it is impossible to avoid considering aspatial elements which are important in the functioning of labour markets, particularly the structuring of the market in terms of skill levels and occupational groups. In this chapter it is assumed that some form of occupational disaggregation is the best approach, reflecting a view that attachment to individual firms or particular industries is not such a pervasive constraint in Britain as are the limits on mobility associated with levels of human capital (education, training, experience) and the nature of skills, which are often specialised without being firm or industry specific. Various alternative hypotheses as to the causes of inner city unemployment could be considered in this context.

First, it could be argued that the aggregate demand for labour in the inner city, or indeed the whole of a conurbation, is deficient, due to the decline of a broad range of economic activity. The obvious prediction from that would be that unemployment would increase in all or most occupational groups, but there are reasons for expecting the greatest increase to be in the unskilled category. It is suggested that redundant skilled workers 'bump down' the hierarchy and either become unskilled unemployed or, more likely, displace the truly unskilled in competition for the limited number of available jobs. This assumes an employer preference for over-qualified recruits on grounds of quality or stability and a willingness of the formerly skilled workers to lower their sights in terms of status and earnings. Evidence for this model is to be found in Daniel (1972), Berthoud (1975, pp. 3-10), and the Liverpool IAS (Great Britain, 1977d, para 3.13). Young people entering such a low demand labour market would stand less chance of acquiring skills because of the lack of incentive for employers to take on apprentices or trainees. This would reinforce the concentration of unskilled unemployed and appears as a striking phenomenon in the Liverpool context (Great Britain, 1977d, pp. 33-6).

A second hypothesis, which is conceptually distinct but may be difficult to distinguish in practice, is that there is a mismatch in the occupational composition of supply and demand in the inner city with unsatisfied demand in some categories not accessible to the unemployed who have different (or no) skills. The Lambeth IAS (Great Britain, 1977a, chapter 4) argued that this model characterised inner London. To identify such a mismatch it would be necessary to measure labour demand as well as unemployment in a suitably disaggregated way and to see if there was an inverse correlation between demand and unemployment. Explanation of such a mismatch would require that barriers to occupational mobility be identified. It would also be helpful to distinguish the origins of the mismatch which lay on the demand side, such as unbalanced industrial decline or technological change affecting skill requirements, from supply-side factors like selective migration, associated with housing and the environment. Two distinctions between this model and the previous one would be that excess demand was evident in some job categories and that the barriers to skill creation were institutional rather than through lack of demand. One could incorporate under the 'institutional' label the problem of externalities in training transferable skills and the problem of low educational standards, as argued in the Lambeth context (Great Britain, 1977c).

A third hypothesis is the dual labour market argument, either that the inner city has a secondary sector bias inherent in its industrial structure, or that the environment is conducive to secondary patterns of behaviour predominating. This would predict underemployment (difficult to measure) and low pay plus abnormal job instability and short-term unemployment. It would also predict a concentration of these problems among women, blacks and the young. As was argued earlier, such a model has some plausibility but also some severe limits in the British inner city context. It is not entirely clear what it implies about skills, perhaps because conventional categories are inadequate.

We should recognise, though, that it can be tied in with both the previous models. The phenomenon of 'bumping down' the skill hierarchy can be related to the dualists' emphasis on internal labour markets where ports of entry are at the lower levels, while it shares with the mismatch thesis an emphasis on institutional barriers to training opportunities which lead to 'better' jobs. If distinctions can be drawn, it is again in terms of the demand for labour, for the dual model predicts unsatisfied demand at the bottom end of the market, unlike either of the two previous models. While other aspects might be stressed, it is striking that discussion of these alternative models implies that discrimination between them involves some explicit and disaggregated measurement of the demand for labour. This may be related back to the preceding comments on journey to work patterns and information, and are arguments in favour of analysing labour markets at a local scale within conurbations, for it is perhaps at this spatial scale that such tests should be applied.

The Demand for Labour

An economic perspective naturally leads to an attempt to explain unemployment and other labour market phenomena in terms of supply and demand. Other perspectives, including institutional and sociological approaches, have been brought to bear on unemployment, but it is argued in this chapter that while these offer additional insights they suggest factors which modify rather than override the pressures of supply and demand. Indeed, the arguments of the preceding and the following sections all suggest an interaction between social or institutional factors and the demand for labour, rather than wholly separate and competing causal explanations.

No attempt is made in this chapter to look behind the pattern of labour demand in inner city areas and to identify causes, important though this may be for policy analysis. (See Dicken and Lloyd, chapter 2 in this volume.) In the Lambeth IAS (Great Britain, 1977a) and a number of other studies these causes have been examined explicitly. The main concern has been with the decline in manufacturing employment, and four general categories of reason for decline have been identified:

(1) Structural change in the economy, reflecting technological change, demand elasticities and international competition;
(2) locational disadvantages of inner areas, including land values, physical congestion and obsolete premises and environments;
(3) planning and regional policies, including redevelopment, control

of non-conforming uses, development plan land allocations,
industrial and office Development controls;
(4) labour market rigidities, including wage controls and wage
bargaining, trade union pressures and restrictions, recruitment and
training practices.

The last category may not be so directly related to employment
decline, but it is often a factor in specific imbalances between supply
and demand and their persistence over time, and emphasises the point
that supply and demand are not independent of price.

We are here concerned with the impact of demand on unemployment. It is somewhat surprising that much previous work on unemployment in British cities (for example, Metcalf and Richardson, 1976;
Evans and Russell, 1976; Vipond, 1974; Corkindale, 1976) has paid
relatively little attention to the demand for labour, suitably disaggregated at the local scale. In some cases this may have reflected an
implicit identification of unemployment with deficient demand, but
where studies have sought to stress other determinants of unemployment (e.g. personal attributes) the neglect of demand could have led
to biased results. It is clear, though, that data on demand at the
local level and in disaggregated form have been difficult to obtain and
problematic to use.

The concept of demand in this context is ambiguous because there
are several distinct dimensions to demand which may all have some
impact on local unemployment. We have already discussed the
occupational dimension, but for any occupational group there are
three further dimensions to consider. First, there is the *pressure* of
demand at a point in time, represented for example by unfilled job
vacancies, and perhaps deducting redundant or hoarded labour which
has not yet been released for institutional or other reasons. Apart from
being very difficult to measure accurately, the pressure of demand is
very sensitive to the economic cycle. The second dimension is the
temporal change in the demand for labour, which comprises seasonal,
cyclical and trend components, of which the latter is of greatest
interest in the inner city context. However, since we can only measure
trends by taking employment changes over a number of years, there
are problems of interpreting such changes and their impact on unemployment. The level of unemployment at a point in time (e.g. the end
of the period) will reflect the speed of supply-side adjustment as well
as the extent of job decline. Also, actual employment may at times be
constrained by supply rather than demand.

The third dimension is the *spatial* one: physically nearer job opportunities represent a more effective demand than more distant jobs, as argued above. This dimension can be measured by taking ratios of jobs by workplace to resident workers in a defined sub-area of the conurbation in a particular occupational group. However, such measures are very sensitive to where boundaries are drawn in relation to employment concentrations, and it is also very difficult to assess the extent of competition for jobs in one area with workers commuting in from other areas. Temporal and spatial dimensions can be combined by measures of the change of jobs (workplaces) relative to workers (residents). Measures on all these dimensions are used in the empirical work that follows.

Personal Attributes

The final set of factors to be considered is a range of personal attributes which, it is suggested, influence an individual's propensity to be unemployed (see McGregor, chapter 4 in this volume). It may be that workers with such characteristics are concentrated in the inner city areas and that this helps to explain high unemployment rates in these areas. Younger and older workers are generally seen as vulnerable groups, but as Metcalf and Richardson (1976) point out the nature of their disadvantage differs. Younger workers are more mobile and hence it is their greater frequency of becoming unemployed rather than difficulty in finding a new job, reflected in unemployment duration, which is in general their problem. However, the dual labour market thesis predicts higher unemployment rates among the young because of barriers to the primary sector, while the tendency of employers to reduce labour requirements through natural wastage would increase young people's unemployment disproportionately during cyclical downturns. Furthermore, evidence from London (Greater London Council, 1975, Table 14) suggests spatial variations in unemployment rates and durations within the 16-24 age group. Older workers' disadvantage lies in their greater difficulty securing new jobs reflected in much greater unemployment duration.

The family situation of men is thought to have a significant impact on their unemployment propensities. Metcalf and Richardson (1976) argue that married men are less likely to become unemployed voluntarily or to remain unemployed for long, owing to their greater preference for income over leisure and perhaps also to employer discrimination. However, men with large numbers of dependent children will be eligible for much higher supplementary benefit and consequently the cost of unemployment for them is more likely to be small or negative. The Lambeth household survey (Great Britain, 1975b, pp. 50-1) revealed some tendency for less skilled manual men with wife not working and several dependent children to be more likely to have experienced unemployment in the preceding twelve months. It is only some parts of inner London, for example the Lambeth study area, which have above average proportions of children and large families.

Ethnic minorities, particularly coloured groups, are expected to experience more unemployment as a result of discrimination, whether or not this is set in the context of a dual labour market model. Some fairly direct evidence of discrimination in Britain is presented by Smith (1974), while it is of course a characteristic of many inner areas to house fairly substantial numbers of ethnic minorities. The Lambeth survey (Great Britain, 1975b, pp. 47-9, 70-1) suggested that significantly greater unemployment propensities and low pay were characteristic of skilled manual coloured men, but not of other occupational groups, compared with white men in the same area. This implies discrimination in some of the skilled manual trades, which could be reconciled with the dual labour market view of barriers to good jobs. The experience of different ethnic groups seems to vary, only some experiencing abnormal unemployment, while particular age and ethnic groups experience very high unemployment, notably West Indian youths (Great Britain, 1975b, p. 25).

Physical or mental disabilities, or simply a greater liability to sickness would be expected to be associated with unemployment experience at the individual level. The Lambeth study of multiple deprivation (Great Britain, 1977a, chapter 3) showed just such a close association. What this implies at the area level is less clear depending as it does on the spatial distribution of sickness and disability. Adjusted mortality rates are higher in the conurbations and large urban areas (Great Britain, 1975a, Table 45). There was no evidence of more disability in the Lambeth study area though, than nationally. Disability and sickness may cause some unemployment directly through interruption of jobs, but whether it creates a more general disadvantage depends in part on the local state of labour demand, as argued by Hill *et al.* (1973, pp. 7 and 8).

Empirical Evidence

In this section a systematic attempt is made to establish the relative importance of some of these factors in explaining the pattern of inner city unemployment, with a particular emphasis on London. First, regression analysis is used to analyse the level and changes in male unemployment across the 32 London boroughs. Second, indices of unemployment and the demand for labour disaggregated by occupation are analysed for parts of the city accessible to the inhabitants of the Lambeth study area. Using these indices comparisons are then made with the pattern of demand in Liverpool.

Unemployment Variations between Boroughs

This analysis builds on the earlier work of Metcalf and Richardson (1975). They regressed 1971 census male unemployment rates for the 32 boroughs against a number of variables, concluding that male unemployment in London is primarily determined by certain individual characteristics, especially skill and marital status. However, there are certain shortcomings in their approach which need to be recognised and can, to some degree, be remedied.

First, little explicit attention was paid to the underlying spatial trends in the data, reflecting the spatial structure of the city. These could easily give rise to apparent correlations, explicable in terms of location directly or in terms of third factors associated with location. Second, their emphasis on hypotheses about individuals would be more appropriately tested by survey data analysed at the level of the individual, or perhaps by census data analysed at the small-area level, rather than analysis at the very aggregated borough level. There is no guarantee that a lack of correlation between, say, immigrants and unemployment does not hide higher unemployment rates among immigrants within boroughs.

Third, the most important variable in their model, the proportion of unskilled workers, is suspect on the grounds discussed earlier, namely that it may be partially endogenous, affected by labour demand and unemployment. In other words, boroughs with poor job opportunities and high unemployment may have more unskilled residents because of inadequate skill creation among the young and the 'bumping down' of older, skilled workers. The coefficient on unskilled in their model is too high to be consistent with merely the effect of greater numbers of unskilled suffering the average unemployment rate for unskilled workers. And indeed the unemployment rate within the unskilled group (and other groups) tends to be higher in areas of high unemployment (Great Britain, 1977a, Tables 9 and 10; Greater London Council, 1975, Table 12).

Fourth, no adequate attempt is made to incorporate measures of

labour demand for different locations within London, apart from the
rather limited redundancies variable. Manufacturing workers are
included, but not certain other industry/occupation groups, which,
a priori, one would expect to show higher unemployment of a
frictional kind, for example, construction and personal services. Finally,
while observing the relative stability of the pattern between 1966 and
1971, no attempt is made to explain what relative changes in the
pattern did occur in that period.

What follows is a selection of findings from a broadly similar
approach to the same data which takes the above points into consideration. Additional variables measuring location, occupation groups, and
occupationally and spatially disaggregated indices of demand, are
incorporated. A major problem with this data is the high degree of
multi-collinearity reflecting the first point made above, the underlying
spatial structure of the city. This makes it desirable to select certain
combinations of variables and to avoid other combinations, and in some
cases it reduces the size and significance of coefficients. It therefore
means that we cannot reach firm conclusions about which are the true
relationships and which are fortuitous; there are several competing
models, which achieve similar goodness of fit and are equally plausible.
Holtermann (1978) argues that a regression approach is inappropriate
in these circumstances, but if the above qualifications are recognised
it is argued here to be at least suggestive of possible causal effects. The
results are summarised in Table 3.1.

Model (1) describes the spatial pattern of male unemployment in
London in 1971 in a way which is fairly crude but fits the data quite
closely, namely a quadratic function of average distance from the
centre and dummies to represent the eastern and southern sectors.
Precise definitions of all the variables are found in Table 3.2. Unemployment falls at a decreasing rate from about 6 per cent near the centre to
about 2 per cent at the periphery, while boroughs to the east have
unemployment rates two-thirds of a percentage point higher on
average. This simply confirms the picture that unemployment is an
inner city phenomenon and that the East End is worst off. It is
interesting to contrast the pattern when the ratio of 1971 to 1966
male unemployment (including temporarily sick) is the dependent
variable, although in this case the model is not quite statistically
significant. This represents a shallow inverted U ranging from 1.65 at
the centre and periphery to just over 2.0 in the middle ring; again, the
eastern sector deteriorated.

It is difficult and perhaps dangerous to interpret these patterns in any causal sense. Distance may be a proxy for demand, given the decentralisation of jobs, and there are also significant positive correlations between distance and the ratio of 1971 workplaces to 1966 workplaces in the cases of transport, distribution and unskilled occupations.

Table 3.1: Selected Regression Results for London Boroughs

Dependent variable: 1971 male census unemployment rate (per cent)

Independent variables	Model number		
	(1)	(2)	(3)
Location variables:	-0.38		-0.34
DIS	(4.44)		(3.71)
DISSQ	0.0072		0.0065
	(2.24)		(2.00)
DDEW	0.64		
	(3.09)		
DDSN	0.082		
	(0.37)		
Demographic variables:			
PMM			
PCH			
PEAU 24			
PEA 604			
Occupational variables:			
PUS			
PSS			
PPS			
PR715			
PR723			
PR7GC			
Sectoral demand indices:			
SVAC		-2.63	-1.75
		(3.00)	(3.29)
SRED		0.19	
		(0.39)	
Borough demand indices:			
DIGJ		0.71	-0.17
		(2.03)	(0.74)
D2GJ		-8.67	-2.46
		(3.63)	(1.60)
D2GD			
D2GE			
D2GH			
CONSTANT	6.75	12.05	9.43
R^2	.82	.58	.89

Numbers in brackets are the t statistic of the respective coefficient.
The male unemployment rate excludes temporary sick.

Table 3.1 continued

Dependent variable: Male unemployment rate (per cent)							
				Model number			
Independent variables	(4)	(5)	(6)	(7)	(8)	(9)	(10)
Location variables:							
DIS							
DISSQ							
DDEW							
DDSN							
Demographic variables:							
PMM	-0.155 (5.52)		-0.053 (1.25)	-0.227 (9.80)		-0.103 (8.73)	-0.113 (5.72)
PCH	0.032 (2.08)		0.037 (1.97)	0.090 (5.38)			
PEAU 24	0.045 (0.68)	0.284 (3.70)	0.306 (3.92)		0.41 (5.17)		0.295 (4.04)
PEA 604	-0.12 (1.11)	0.106 (0.79)					
Occupational variables:							
PUS	0.18 (6.24)	0.276 (5.80)				0.194	
PSS		-0.116 (1.96)					
PPS		0.310 (4.15)			0.393 (8.90)		
PR715			0.377 (1.93)				
PR723			0.292 (4.81)				
PR7GC			-0.0007 (0.03)				
Sectoral demand indices:							
SVAC				-1.70 (4.06)		1.204 (3.47)	
SRED				0.11 (0.42)	-0.063 (0.18)		
Borough demand indices:							
D1GJ				0.049 (2.26)	-0.035 (0.10)		
D2GJ				-4.04 (3.35)		-1.44 (1.63)	
D2GD							-0.007 (0.00)
D2GE					-3.28 (3.21)		
D2GH						-5.22 (2.19)	
CONSTANT	11.03	-3.71	-4.38	17.14	-1.15	11.14	10.87
R^2	0.93	0.91	0.92	0.92	0.80	0.94	0.83

Table 3.2: Definitions and Sources

DIS and DISSQ: Simple average of straight line distances from Trafalgar Square to nearest and furthest points in each borough, in kilometres.

DDEW = 1 if borough lies predominantly to east of N-S line through central area.
DDSN = 1 if borough lies predominantly to south of E-W line through central area.
PMM: Married males 16-64 as percentage of all economically active males 1971 (Great Britain, 1971a).
PCH: Children aged 0-14 as percentage of all EA males 1971 (ibid.).
PEAU 24: Economically active males aged 16-24 as percentage of all EA males 1971 (Great Britain, 1971a).
PEA 604: Economically active males aged 60-64 as percentage of all EA males, 1971 (Great Britain, 1971a).
PUS Resident EA males in SEG groups 11, 10 and 7 respectively as
PSS : percentage of all resident EA males, 1971, 10 per cent sample data
PPS (Great Britain, 1971b).
PR715 . Resident EA males in occupation orders XV, XXIII respectively as
PR723 ˙ percentage of all resident EA males, 1971, 10 per cent sample data (Great Britain, 1971b).
PR7GC: Resident EA males in occupation orders I-XIV + XVII as percentage of all resident EA males, 1971, 10 per cent sample data (Great Britain, 1971b).
SVAC: All notified unfilled vacancies as a percentage of all male jobs by workplace, sectors, 1971 (Greater London Council, 1975).
SRED: Sector's share of 1971-2 male redundancies divided by sector's share of 1971 male employment (Greater London Council, 1975).
D1GJ: Male employment in manual occupations by workplace divided by resident EA males in manual occupations, boroughs, 1971, 10 per cent sample data (Great Britain, 1971b).
D2GJ Male employment by workplace in 1971 divided by male employ-
D2GD . ment by workplace in 1966, and by occupational groups, 10 per
D2GE ˙ cent sample data (Great Britain, 1966, 1971b).
D2GH
        (GJ = all manual; GD = less skilled manual; GE = transport and service manual; GH = all manual other than skilled.)

Equally, though, distance may be a proxy for a number of demographic and social characteristics. Interpreting the pattern of 1966-71 change is even more difficult, though it does perhaps confirm the observations of other commentators (Evans and Russell, 1976; Lomas, 1974) that parts of the middle ring have deteriorated. Whether this represents the outward spread of the 'inner city' residential areas (see Great Britain, 1977a, pp. 33-4), employment decline in the inner and middle rings, or whatever is unclear.

Before proceeding to consider the impact of the demand for labour we need to establish some measures of this demand. Four types of

index of labour demand were used in the analysis. Two relate to the
nine sectors (one central, three inner, five outer) used by the Greater
London Council (1975), and give the male vacancy rate and the relative
share of 1971 redundancies, aggregating all occupations for males. The
other two types of index used are measures of the 1971 male job/
worker ratios within boroughs (D1GJ) and the change in male employment by workplace 1966-71 (ratios of 1971 to 1966) (D2GD, etc.),
both disaggregated by occupations. The rationale for using measures
of local and sectoral demand rests on the arguments developed in
the previous section about accessibility and information.

It should be recognised that these measures are far from being ideal
and better explanations might be obtained from more subtle measures.
In addition the first two types of index suffer from major deficiencies.
The Department of Employment's notified unfilled vacancy data are
somewhat suspect and certainly understate the true level of vacancies,
by nearly two-thirds on average (Great Britain, 1978). There are almost
certainly variations between industries and occupations in the extent of
notification. Redundancies are regarded as a poor measure of demand
because they only measure one component of demand, and probably
not the most important one for unemployment. Many employers, as
noted earlier, run down their labour forces by natural wastage and
avoid formal redundancies so far as possible.

In the analysis, these measures of labour demand are combined
selectively with the demographic, occupational and locational variables.
Model (2) shows how 58 per cent of the variance in 1971 male unemployment can be explained by demand factors alone. Vacancy rates
and the decline in manual jobs appear to be significant. Combining
demand indices and the distance function in model (3) achieves a good
fit (R^2 = .89) and, as was pointed out, distance could be regarded as in
part a proxy for demand. At the borough level, it is generally the
employment change indices rather than the job/worker ratio indices
which relate in the predicted (negative) way with unemployment.

Model (4) uses approximately the same formulation as Metcalf and
Richardson (1975), concentrating on unskilled, marital status,
dependants and age groups (immigrants are excluded from this particular
analysis). Although this model achieves a good fit, it is to be regarded as
suspect for the reasons already outlined. Comparing models (5) and (6)
with (4) shows that a significant positive coefficient on the 16-24 age
group variable emerges when other variables in the model are changed,
reflecting multi-collinearity problems. The 60-64 age group is not
significant, however. Marital status is usually significant when included

Table 3.3: Selected Indicators of the Demand for Labour and Unemployment (Males): Inner South London (ISL), Greater London (GL) and Great Britain

Indicator		Socio-Economic Groups					
		Professional, managerial, intermediate (1,2,3,4,5)	Junior non-manual (6)	Personal service (7)	Skilled manual (8,9)	Semi-skilled (10)	Un-skilled (11)
1973 Vacancies as % of 1971 jobs	ISL	.10	1.07	1.43	1.47	1.11	1.04
	GB	.61	1.52	4.31	1.71	1.34	2.11
1971 Job/ worker ratio, x 100	ISL	125	86	53	96	88	63
	GL	119	130	116	113	120	102
1971 Jobs (workplace)/ 1966 jobs, x 100	ISL	109	84	101	85	78	70
	GL	114	83	102	88	84	84
1971 Job/ worker ratio ÷ 1966 Job/ worker ratio, x 100	ISL	99	89	100	102	97	88
	GL	106	101	105	101	101	99
1973 registered % unemployed	ISL	1.04	1.95	2.46	1.88	2.40	11.2
Index, all SEG's = 100	ISL	38	70	89	68	87	404
1971 census unemployed%	ISL	3.14	2.82	3.84	4.76	5.26	7.08
Index, all SEG's = 100	ISL	66	60	81	100	111	150

Source: Great Britain (1977a, Table 20).
Numbers in brackets are the appropriate Census grouping.

but its coefficient is quite unstable for the same reason of multi-collinearity.

Demand variables are combined with personal variables in model (7) and it can be seen that vacancies and manual job decline have the predicted sign and are statistically significant. Models (5), (6) and (8) illustrate the point that the occupation/industry characteristics of the resident work force may also be used to explain variations in unemployment. Not only the unskilled but also service workers and construction workers are positively related to unemployment, probably reflecting the high frictional unemployment in these sectors, tying in perhaps with the concept of a secondary labour market. The changing pattern of borough unemployment rates is more difficult to explain, but tests show an association with location, declining manufacturing jobs, vacancies and the manual job/worker ratio.

Clearly, caution must be exercised when interpreting regression results subject to considerable multi-collinearity. However, the results suggest that to the factors stressed by Metcalf and Richardson must be added a number of other factors which probably also affected male unemployment in 1971. These factors are location, age (the 16-24 age group), construction and service occupations, the sectoral pressure of demand (vacancies) and the rate of decline in employment in certain manual occupations at borough level. Thus, there is some support in the case of London for a number of the hypotheses put forward in the previous section, and specifically for the relevance of locational factors and the demand for labour as well as personal attributes and skills.

Labour Demand and Unemployment in Lambeth and Liverpool

The approach just described is still quite aggregated in the measurement of demand and unemployment. In the context of a local case study it is possible to undertake a more thorough analysis, as was attempted for example in Lambeth and Liverpool. It is not proposed to discuss these cases in detail, for they are described elsewhere (Great Britain, 1975b, 1977c, 1977d). However, they do allow one to identify the relevant labour market area for a particular population in a particular location, and to identify the relationship between demand and unemployment across occupations.

Table 3.3 compares inner south London (ISL), the labour market immediately relevant to the Lambeth study area, with Greater London or Great Britain on four different indices of demand, and gives two separate measures of unemployment across six broad occupational groups for males. It shows that the demand for labour was generally low or declining in ISL compared with the wider areas in most occupational groups. However, more significant is the way that the relative demand varies between occupations being not particularly unfavourable in the professional, etc. and skilled manual groups, less favourable in the junior non-manual and semi-skilled groups, and highly unfavourable in the unskilled manual category. While this pattern is consistent with the mismatch hypothesis discussed earlier, the low vacancy rate for unskilled men is inconsistent with the dual labour market prediction, and some of the indices for professional, etc. and skilled manual men are also inconsistent with a hypothesis of deficient aggregate demand at the local scale. Incidentally, notified vacancies are an unreliable index for the professional, etc., group.

The two measures of unemployment rates within occupations are the author's own estimates. They are not directly comparable because of the different stage in the economic cycle they represent and because of the different definitions of unemployment and occupation used by the Census and the Department of Employment. The latter tend to allocate formerly semi-skilled or even skilled men to the general labourer and factory-hand categories for administrative reasons, which accounts for the apparently very high unskilled unemployment rate. There may be an opposite bias in the Census figure, which excludes the unclassified.

However, it can be seen that some elements of the pattern of demand are replicated in the relative unemployment rates, particularly the position of the professional, etc. group and the relative ranking of the manual groups. But the relative position of, for example, junior non-manual and skilled manual workers is less clear. The difficulty may lie in the differing propensities to frictional unemployment in the different groups, or alternatively in a tendency for the effects of demand to be displaced into other occupations. While this evidence is consistent with the mismatch thesis, the high unskilled unemployment figure might also owe something to the 'bumping down' or lack of skill creation arguments developed earlier. A much more disaggregated approach, distinguishing types as well as levels of skill, was attempted in the Lambeth IAS (Great Britain, 1977c, Section 2 and Appendix I) but this evidence is not easy to interpret.

Finally, Table 3.4 presents a comparison between inner south London and Liverpool County Borough in terms of three census-based indices of labour demand disaggregated by socio-economic group. While the overall unemployment position in Liverpool was much worse than in inner London, it is interesting to see the similarities in the labour demand trends between 1966 and 1971. The job/worker ratios are not really comparable because Liverpool includes the central area. The trend indices perhaps suggest that ISL displayed more differences between occupations than Liverpool, particularly in the manual sector, which might support the view that inner London is characterised more by a problem of mismatch, whereas Liverpool suffers from an overall shortage of job opportunities.

Table 3.4: Three Measures of Employment Demand for Males by Socio-economic Group in Inner South London and Liverpool

Socio-economic group	A — % change in jobs (by workplace) 1966-71		B — Ratio of jobs to resident workers, 1971		C — Ratio of change in jobs to change in resident workers, 1966-71	
	IS London	Liverpool CB	IS London	Liverpool CB	IS London	Liverpool CB
Professional, managerial (1,2,3,4)*	+9	– 1	1.25	1.85	.99	.97
Intermediate non-manual (5)		+12		1.27		1.13
Junior non-manual (6)	–16	–21	.86	1.62	.89	.95
Personal service (7)	(+1)	(–41)	.53	1.08	(1.00)	(.69)
Skilled manual (8,9)	–15	–20	.96	1.03	1.02	.97
Semi-skilled manual (10)	–22	–24	.88	.99	.97	.94
Unskilled manual (11)	–30	–25	.68	.71	.88	.92

Sources: 1971 Census 10 per cent Economic Activity Tables by workplace and residence, converted from occupations to SEGs (Great Britain, 1971b).

* Numbers in brackets are the appropriate Census grouping.

Conclusion

This chapter has examined a number of factors which influence labour market behaviour in general and unemployment in particular, in the inner city context. Four themes emerge and these should perhaps be emphasised in conclusion. The first is that the inner city labour market differs to some extent from other local labour markets; and that such differences as greater competitiveness and labour mobility, greater female participation and problems of skill creation can be explained in terms of the geographical, industrial and demographic characteristics of the inner city. It is possible to link these features to the dual labour market hypothesis, but it can also be argued that the more traditional economic concepts of supply and demand can still explain a great deal when suitably disaggregated in terms of location and occupation.

Third, it is important to recognise that labour markets are localised within the conurbations, and that workers are immobile, particularly the less-skilled, lower-paid groups in the labour force. Finally, the evidence suggests that, in a high-demand region like London, local declines in job opportunities or local mismatches between demand and supply do help to explain the pattern of unemployment. This lends some support to current policy attempts to regenerate employment in these inner areas, though perhaps such policies should look more broadly than just at manufacturing jobs, to encompass other industries and also such issues as training, education and housing mobility.

The argument has been couched in general terms, although most of the evidence has referred to London with some limited references to Liverpool. There are limits to the validity of any generalisations about inner city labour markets from the experience of London. The geographical scale of London makes it somewhat unique and certainly increases the plausibility of conceiving localised labour markets within the conurbation, although scale is somewhat offset by better public transport. Two other distinct features of London are the magnetic effect of central London as an international and a capital city, reflected in the demand for both labour and housing, and the peculiarly restricted housing market. The major provincial conurbations are more likely to be sharing the experience of Liverpool, which as we have seen is dominated by the problem of deficient aggregate demand for labour, while none of them shows the same degree of dynamism as either London or the newer growth areas.

References

Berthoud, R. (1975) *Employment in a Changing Labour Market*, London: Centre for Environmental Studies, Seminar Paper

Bosanquet, N. and Doeringer, P.B. (1973) 'Is There a Dual Labour Market in Great Britain?', *Economic Journal*, vol. 83, pp. 421-35

Corkindale, J.T. (1976) *Employment in the Conurbations*, CES Inner City Employment Conference, York

Daniel W.W. (1972) *Whatever Happened to the Workers in Woolwich?* London: Political and Economic Planning

—— (1974) *A National Survey of the Unemployed*, London: Political and Economic Planning

Dugmore, K. (1975) Migration and Social Change in *GLC Research Memorandum 443*, London: Greater London Council

Dunnell, K. and Head, E. (1975) *Employers and Employment Services*, London: Office of Population Censuses and Surveys Social Survey Division. SS 1012

Evans, A. (1973) *The Economics of Residential Location*, London: Macmillan.

—— and Russell, L. (1976) *A Portrait of the London Labour Market – Some Preliminary Sketches*, CES Inner City Employment Conference, York

Foster, C. and Richardson, R. (1973) 'Employment Trends in London in the 1960s and Their Relevance to the Future', in Donnison, D. and Eversley, D. (eds.), *London: Urban Patterns, Problems and Policies*, London: Heinemann

Great Britain (1966) *Census, Economic Activity County Reports*, London: HMSO

—— (1971a) *Census, County Report for Greater London*, London: HMSO

—— (1971b) *Census, Economic Activity County Reports*, London: HMSO

—— (1972) *General Household Survey, 1972*, London: HMSO

—— (1974) Department of Employment, 'Vacancy Study', in *Dept of Employment Gazette*, vol. 81, no. 5, p. 223, London: HMSO

—— (1975a) Department of the Environment, *Study of the Inner Areas of Conurbations Volume 2 Detailed Studies*, London: HMSO

—— (1975b) Department of the Environment, *Labour Market Study, IAS/LA/4*, London: HMSO

—— (1976) Department of the Environment, Strategy for the South East 1976 Review, *Report of the Economy Group*, London: HMSO

—— (1977a) Department of the Environment, *Inner London: Policies for Dispersal and Balance: Final Report of the Lambeth Inner Area Study*, London: HMSO

—— (1977b) Department of the Environment, *Change or Decay: Report of the Liverpool Inner Area Study*, London: HMSO

—— (1977c) Department of the Environment, Lambeth Inner Area Study, *Local Employers' Study IAS/LA/16*, London: HMSO

—— (1977d) Department of the Environment, *Economic Development of the Inner Area IAS/LI/21*, London: HMSO

—— (1978) Survey of Engagements, *Department of Employment Gazette*, vol. 85, no. 6, London: HMSO

Greater London Council (1975) *Employment in Greater London and the Rest of the South East Region*, Submission to Strategy for the South East Review

Hill, M., Harrison, R. Sargeant, A. and Talbot, V. (1973) *Men Out of Work: A Study of Unemployment in Three English Towns*, London: Cambridge University Press

Holtermann, S. (1978) 'Unemployment in Urban Areas', *Urban Studies*, vol. 15, pp. 231-2.

—— and Silkin, F. (1976) 'Low Economic Activity as an Indicator of Deprivations', *Urban Studies*, vol. 13, pp. 343-7.

Lomas, G. (1974) *The Inner City*, London: London Council of Social Services

Mackay, D., Boddy, D., Brack, J., Diack, J. and Jones, N. (1971) *Labour Markets under Different Employment Conditions*, London: George Allen and Unwin

Metcalf, D. and Richardson, R. (1976) 'Unemployment in London', in Worswick, G.D.N. (ed.), *The Concept and Measurement of Involuntary Unemployment*, London: George Allen and Unwin

Rees, A. (1966) 'Information Networks in Labour Markets', *American Economic Review*, vol. 45, pp. 559-66

Rees, A.R. and Shultz, G.P. (1970) *Workers and Wages in an Urban Labour Market*, Chicago: University of Chicago Press

Simon, N.W.H. (1977) 'The Relative Level and Changes in Earnings in London and Great Britain', *Regional Studies*, vol. 11, pp. 87-98

Smith, D.J. (1974) *Racial Disadvantage in Employment*, London: Political and Economic Planning

Stigler, G.J. (1962) 'Information in the Labour Market', *Journal of Political Economy*, vol. 70, supplement, pp. 94-105

Vipond, J. (1974) 'City Size and Unemployment', *Urban Studies*, vol. 11, pp. 39-46

Wabe, J.S. (1969) 'Labour Force Participation Rates in the London Metropolitan Region', *Journal of the Royal Statistical Society*, series A, vol. 132, part 2

Wachter, M.L. (1974) 'Primary and Secondary Labour Markets: A critique of the Dual Approach', *Brookings Papers in Economic Activity*, vol. 3, pp. 637-80

4 AREA EXTERNALITIES AND URBAN UNEMPLOYMENT

Alan McGregor

Within the last decade Britain's policy makers discovered a new area of concern, the problem of urban deprivation (see Norris, chapter 1 in this volume). There was a rapidly growing awareness of the marked diversity in social and economic wellbeing between different neighbourhoods in given towns and cities. Systematic documentation of these area inequalities was provided by statistical analyses of the 1971 Census (Great Britain, 1975). The authorities have moved increasingly in the direction of area-based approaches to the problem of urban deprivation. The most recent initiatives along these lines have been the inner city partnership agreements and the Glasgow Eastern Area Renewal project (Great Britain, 1977).

The relevance of area-based policies has been disputed by a number of writers (see, for example, Townsend, 1976). Although such policies can be justified on a number of criteria (Holtermann, 1978) the strongest case can be made where area externalities are present. An area externality exists where an individual's welfare is lower as a *consequence* of residence in a deprived area. Within the labour market an example of an area externality would be a situation where residence in a deprived area increased the likelihood and/or duration of unemployment of an individual relative to others possessing identical employment characteristics, but resident in non-deprived areas of the same town or city. In such circumstances there is a clear justification for channelling extra resources towards deprived areas.

In this chapter we examine the evidence for the existence of area externalities by considering the problem of unemployment in a severely deprived housing estate in the West of Scotland. In the next section we consider in general terms the factors generating differences in unemployment rates within urban areas. Next, we discuss the existing empirical evidence on the relative importance of individual and area factors. This section is followed by a statistical analysis of unemployed individuals from the deprived Ferguslie Park estate and a control group drawn from the adjoining urban area. Finally, we discuss the implications of our findings for labour market policies towards deprived areas.

Individuals, Areas and Unemployment

Unemployment is not distributed randomly across the population.
Particular sets of individuals are more likely to experience unemployment than others. Likewise the probability of being out of work varies
across areas. In this section we restrict the discussion to a single labour
market area and consider a situation where location *per se* does not
influence the individual's experience of unemployment. That is, we
abstract from the possibility that spatial variations in the demand for
labour or in physical access to employment influence the unemployment rates in one neighbourhood relative to another. This is not to deny
the general importance of such factors. It is well established that
spatial variation in the excess demand for labour plays a major role in
explaining inter-regional variations in the extent of unemployment. It
is argued elsewhere in this volume (Bramley, chapter 3) that similar
influences are important in explaining unemployment variations
within London.

Within a given labour market area we anticipate that the extent and
nature of unemployment will vary in a systematic fashion between
individuals with differing personal characteristics. The relevant
characteristics are those which proxy either 'quality' differences
between workers or variations in labour-supply behaviour. For example,
unemployment rates tend to be relatively high amongst the young and
the old, the unskilled, men with large families, etc. The simplest explanation of area variation in unemployment rates within a single labour
market is that it is a reflection of variations in social composition
between areas. The most deprived areas contain concentrations of
workers who have a high likelihood of being unemployed irrespective
of their location within the labour market. This proposition has been
tested with some success in studies analysing variations in unemployment rates within London (Metcalf and Richardson, 1976) and within
each of the four Scottish cities (Mair and Wood, 1977).

However, in certain instances the concentration of poor people in
particular locations does not simply create deprived areas; rather, it
produces a situation where certain areas become notorious and residence in such areas carries with it a social stigma. Damer (1974) has
described the historical development of the stigmatisation of the
'Wine Alley' estate in Glasgow. Many towns and cities have similar
housing areas, generally located in the public sector housing stock.
It does not automatically follow that this form of residential stigmatisation will carry over into labour market behaviour. However, it is not
difficult to see how residential stigmatisation can be incorporated into

conventional theories of discrimination in the labour market to yield the hypothesis that residence in such an area raises the probability of being unemployed, other things being equal.

First, an analogy can be drawn with the standard economic model of discrimination which takes as its starting point the aversion felt by members of one group towards members of another (see, for example, Arrow, 1973). In general, this model begs the question of the origin and wider social rationale of such aversions. Nevertheless, it is clear that the residents of Ferguslie Park (and other stigmatised areas) are held in low regard by the adjoining communities. Perhaps one behavioural indication of the aversion many people feel towards stigmatised areas is the short waiting period required to gain access to housing in such estates.

Second, given the notoriety and mythology surrounding the residents of stigmatised areas it may be appropriate to apply one of the statistical models of discrimination (Phelps, 1972). Local employers may use residence in a stigmatised estate as an index of unsuitability. Detailed scrutiny of job applicants is a costly process and employers tend to adopt simple screening devices to economise on hiring costs. Both sets of theories predict group differentials in earnings in situations where labour markets clear leaving no unemployment. Where wage flexibility operates within restricted margins the effects of discrimination will spill over into differential unemployment rates.

To summarise, it is known that specific neighbourhoods within given labour market areas are characterised by exceptionally high unemployment rates relative to the area average. This may simply reflect the clustering of people with similar characteristics. In certain circumstances, that is where some areas are heavily stigmatised, it may partly reflect area externalities. In the next section we review the fairly scant empirical evidence on this question and discuss some of the problems of testing for the existence of area externalities.

Evidence on Intra-Urban Unemployment Variations

In principle, the most straightforward test for the existence of area externalities within an urban labour market is to set up the null hypothesis that such externalities do not exist. That is, the hypothesis to be tested is that variations in area unemployment rates are purely a reflection of variations in the characteristics of the labour forces of different residential areas. In practice, it is often difficult to measure precisely, or even proxy, the relevant individual characteristics.

The most important single study is an analysis of variations in unemployment rates across London boroughs using data collected in the

1971 Census (Metcalf and Richardson, 1976). Although employing an extremely limited set of explanatory variables to capture labour market disequilibrium effects and differences in labour force composition between the boroughs, the analysts were able to explain well over 90 per cent of the variations in unemployment rates. This work has been replicated with minor adjustments in the four Scottish cities (Mair and Wood, 1977). Again, extremely good levels of explanation were attained. However, an analysis of the residuals for Glasgow suggested that the personal-characteristics model consistently underpredicted the unemployment rate in areas with the highest unemployment rates.

The London study is comprehensively re-examined elsewhere in this volume (Bramley, chapter 3). In the context of the present chapter, a number of points can be made. First, although collinearity and aggregation may give an artificially high estimate of the influence of personal characteristics it has to be pointed out that very few personal characteristics were included in the set of explanatory variables as a result of the limited nature of the Census data. The model based on personal characteristics could be filled out considerably, thus producing better levels of statistical explanation.

Second, this chapter is not concerned with an overall explanation of the differences in unemployment rates between the various neighbourhoods that make up an urban area. Rather, we are concerned with the most deprived areas and, in particular, with those areas that carry a social stigma. This issue is difficult to analyse at a high level of aggregation as such areas contain a relatively small proportion of the population of any town or city.

Third, Mair and Wood's analysis of the residuals in the Glasgow study is consistent with the existence of externalities operating in the worst areas of the city. Thus, for example, the simple model underpredicts the unemployment rate for Blackhill, an area of council housing which has gained a notorious reputation in the city of Glasgow. However, we must reiterate the point that the set of explanatory variables utilised in the studies based on Census data is extremely limited.

Empirical Problems

Before considering our own statistical evidence it may prove useful to examine the problems which beset any attempts to establish empirically the existence of area externalities in an urban labour market. Many studies have demonstrated the systematic relationship between certain individual characteristics and the probability of unemployment.

In particular, a large volume of work on the duration of unemployment has identified the key role of factors such as age, skill, marital status, benefit income, etc. In some instances the influences can be viewed as pure supply-side effects; for example, the low unemployment durations of married versus single man. In other cases the influences stem primarily from employer behaviour; for example, the disadvantage experienced by older workers confronted with restrictive, age-related hiring standards. Nevertheless, there will always be a degree to which all dimensions of supply behaviour or worker quality cannot be fully captured in an empirical analysis. There is simply less heterogeneity than in the case where these measured variations are not captured.

These problems are inherent in empirical work in labour economics but often they can be set to one side on the assumption that the omitted variables do not correlate closely with measurable personal characteristics. However, this assumption is less tenable in the analysis of the employment problems of deprived areas. Allocation to such areas is a social rather than a random process. Where deprived areas are located in the private housing stock people are forced into them (or are unable to leave) because their incomes can sustain the consumption of only poor quality housing. Traditional housing allocation policies and differential waiting periods have enforced a quasi-market system of allocation within the public sector stock (Damer and Madigan, 1974; English, 1976). Hence unmeasured indicators of worker quality and worker 'motivation' are likely to be correlated with residence in deprived versus non-deprived areas.

Bearing this caveat in mind we now move to consider the findings of a statistical analysis of unemployment in a severely deprived area in the West of Scotland.

Unemployment in Ferguslie Park

In this section we analyse the problem of unemployment in Ferguslie Park, a council estate located in the town of Paisley which lies just outside Glasgow. This estate scores badly on most observed indicators of deprivation and on this basis is one of the most deprived areas in the west of Scotland (for a fuller description, see English, chapter 5 in this volume). The extent of deprivation can be illustrated by the indicator of unemployment. According to the 1971 Census, Ferguslie Park had a male unemployment rate (Census definition) of 22 per cent compared to 8 per cent in Paisley as a whole (that is, including Ferguslie Park) and 4 per cent in Britain. It should be noted that Paisley is traditionally a relatively buoyant labour market area with unemployment rates consistently below the average for Scotland and well below the average for Clydeside. Within Paisley, Ferguslie Park is reasonably well located relative to existing employment, and the estate is adjacent to one of the town's major employers, the Chrysler car plant.

In an attempt to analyse the estate's unemployment problem we extracted data from a cross-section of the male unemployment register in Paisley in January 1975. (For details of the sampling procedure, see McGregor, 1977.) By sampling from the Paisley area as a whole we are able to analyse the experiences of Ferguslie Park men within their wider labour market context. We have already outlined in broad terms the factors which might generate high unemployment rates in deprived areas relative to the norm for their locality. In the statistical analysis we attempt to establish the extent to which men from Ferguslie Park experience less favourable unemployment experiences relative to men with similar characteristics living in other parts of Paisley.

The analysis is conducted in two stages in recognition of the two processes which can generate unemployment-rate differences between separate labour force groups.

(1) Do Ferguslie Park workers have a higher incidence of unemployment spells, *ceteris paribus*?
(2) Do Ferguslie Park workers experience longer spells of unemployment, *ceteris paribus*?

The distinction between the number of unemployment spells and the duration of these spells has proved a fruitful analytical device in explaining variations in unemployment rates between different groups of workers. For example, unemployment rates tend to be relatively high for younger and older workers. This apparent similarity disguises a qualitative difference in unemployment experiences. Younger workers tend to have a high incidence of unemployment spells whereas older workers experience lengthy durations of unemployment.

Unemployment as a social problem has traditionally been defined in terms of lengthy spells out of work. Prewar studies (for example, Pilgrim Trust, 1938; Eisenberg and Lazarsfeld, 1938) documented the debilitating effects of long-term unemployment. Postwar research on unemployment has concentrated on the analysis of unemployment duration. More recently, increasing attention has been paid to the high incidence of unemployment experienced by particular groups (for example, Hall, 1970; Marston, 1976). In considering the costs unemployment imposes on individuals recurrent spells of unemployment may be equivalent to one lengthy spell.

Incidence of Unemployment Spells

We analyse variations in the incidence of unemployment between Ferguslie Park and the rest of Paisley by considering a restricted sub-sample of the Paisley unemployment register. Many of the Paisley unemployed had been out of work for considerable periods of time. This made them unsuitable subjects for a study of unemployment incidence. Their problem was clearly one of long-term unemployment. Therefore, we analysed the unemployment experiences of short-term registrants only (men who had been out of work for less than three months), and looked at the number of spells of unemployment they had experienced over a period of approximately four years.

Within this sample of men Ferguslie Park registrants had experienced an average of 2.56 separate spells of unemployment over the four years relative to a figure of 2.05 spells for the sample of men from other areas of Paisley. It seems clear that a relatively high incidence of unemployment contributes to the difference in unemployment rates between the two parts of Paisley. We now attempt to ascertain whether this differential incidence of unemployment is simply a reflection of compositional differences in the samples of men drawn from Ferguslie Park and from the rest of Paisley.

There are two basic influences on the incidence of unemployment spells. First, men who exhibit a high rate of job changing over a given period are likely to experience more unemployment spells than men with stable employment patterns, simply because they are more often at risk. Second, for a given amount of job changing some men will experience more spells of unemployment than others. Many people change jobs without experiencing intervening spells of unemployment; the others may be unemployed for relatively long periods. We expect that factors similar to those influencing the duration of unemployment will also exert an influence on the probability of becoming unemployed on changing jobs.

With the use of multiple regression analysis it is possible to test whether the Ferguslie Park job seekers experienced a higher incidence of unemployment after controlling for variations in employment stability and personal characteristics. The procedure followed is to estimate an equation of the general form:

$$S = f(J, X, R, e) \tag{1}$$

where S is the number of spells of unemployment, J is the number of jobs, X is a vector of personal characteristics, R is a dummy variable coded 1 for Ferguslie Park registrants, and e is an error term.[1]

Data and variable definition problems restrict the X-vector to three variables — age, skill and marital status. The time taken to find work rises on moving from young, through prime-age to old workers. The good performance of young workers may reflect an expectation of short tenure in a job, once found. Therefore, they have little incentive to engage in lengthy job search. Older workers are faced with restrictive hiring standards which limit the jobs available to them. Skilled workers tend to find jobs more rapidly than the unskilled, principally as a result of the more favourable labour market conditions they face. Finally, married men are generally out of work for less time than single men. The simplest explanation is that single men are under less pressure to return to work quickly.

The results from estimating equation (1) are shown in Table 4.1.

Table 4.1: Regression on Incidence of Unemployment Spells

Residence	(Ferguslie Park)	0.54 (0.16)**
	(Rest of Paisley)	—
Age	(up to 19)	- 0.86 (0.29)**
	(20 to 49)	—
	(50 and over)	0.25 (0.34)
Skill	(skilled)	- 0.41 (0.20)*
	(semi-skilled)	- 0.16 (0.23)
	(unskilled)	—
Marital status	(married)	0.27 (0.16)
	(others)	—
No. of jobs		0.78 (0.03)**
Constant		- 0.40
R^2(F)		0.738 (81.09)**
No. of observations		210

Note: Standard errors of coefficients are in parentheses and significance at the .05 (.01) level is indicated by *(**).

The coefficients on the jobs, age and skill variables, support our expectations. However, the coefficient on the marital status variable has the wrong sign. Turning to the residence variable we can see that the

Ferguslie Park registrants experience significantly more spells of unemployment, other things being equal. In fact, controlling for employment stability, age, skill and marital status has very little effect on the difference in unemployment incidence between the two areas. The net difference of 0.54 spells is virtually the same as the gross difference (0.51 spells) noted above. We postpone further discussion of these findings until we conduct our preliminary analysis of variations in the duration of unemployment.

Duration of Unemployment Spells

Our data set allows us to examine the question of variations in the duration of unemployment in two different ways. First, we analyse variations in the length of the spell of unemployment experienced by those individuals who found work during the period of our study. The procedure adopted is similar to that used in the analysis of the incidence of unemployment spells. Using multiple regression we estimate an equation of the following general form:

$$\ln D = f(Y, R, e) \tag{2}$$

Here the left-hand side of the equation is the logarithm of the length of an individual's completed unemployment spell,[2] Y stands for a set of personal characteristics influencing unemployment duration, R is the residence dummy variable and e is an error term. The personal characteristics include age, skill and marital status which are common to the analysis of unemployment incidence. Additionally, we introduce variables based on the industrial affiliation of each man, and a proxy for health problems based on a distinction between men registered for light capacity work and all others.

Second, we look at the probability of individuals moving from unemployment into employment within a given period of time. This is simply another way of considering the question of unemployment duration. Individuals who have a relatively low probability of finding work within a given number of weeks will also tend to experience relatively long durations of unemployment. The statistical analysis again involves the use of multiple regression. The estimated equation is:

$$\Pr(N) = f(Z, R, e) \tag{3}$$

Here Pr(N) takes the value of 1 if a man found work within eight weeks of the date the sample was drawn and 0 if he remained on the unemployment register for the full eight weeks. It should be noted that this formulation of the dependent variable creates statistical difficulties (Goldfeld and Quandt, 1972). Z is a set of factors likely to influence the probability of re-employment. We include all the personal characteristics used in the analysis of unemployment duration. In addition, we allow for the considerable variation in the lengths of time men had been out of work at the time our sample was conducted. It is well known that increasing time out of work is associated with declining probabilities of leaving the unemployment register within a given period (Fowler, 1968).

In terms of simple averages the men from Ferguslie Park take markedly longer to get back into work. On the measure of the duration of unemployment the average length of spell is around 50 per cent greater for the Ferguslie Park sample relative to the sample from the rest of Paisley. Similarly, whereas 34 per cent of men from the rest of Paisley left the register for employment within eight weeks the corresponding Ferguslie Park figure was only 17 per cent. By estimating equations (2) and (3) we can find out the extent to which these differences reflect differences in the characteristics of the people living in the two areas. The results of these estimations are shown in Table 4.2.

Table 4.2 demonstrates the importance of certain personal characteristics. Most of the variables have the expected impact on unemployment and re-employment probability, although marital status in equation (2) works in the direction opposite to that predicted. However, holding constant these various characteristics men from Ferguslie Park still have significantly lower probabilities of finding work, and those finding work take significantly longer to do so, although the differences are reduced by controlling for age, skill, etc. As these results stand they are consistent with the existence of area externalities which disadvantage job seekers from the Ferguslie Park estate.

To summarise so far, we have established that, other things being equal, in our analysis the Ferguslie Park job seekers experience a higher incidence of unemployment spells, have lower probabilities of re-employment within a given time period and, if they find work, take significantly longer to do so. These findings are consistent with a situation where workers from Ferguslie Park operate under an area disadvantage in the labour market. However, this finding cannot be considered conclusive for the reasons noted earlier. Principally, we have been able to control for only a limited number of individual factors. In an attempt to shed further light on the situation we conduct two further sets of tests.

Table 4.2: Regressions on Speed and Likelihood of Finding Work

		Equation (2)	Equation (3)
Residence	(Ferguslie Park)	0.35 (0.12)**	−0.09 (0.03)**
	(Rest of Paisley)	——	——
Age	(up to 24)	−0.53 (0.13)**	0.04 (0.04)
	(25 to 49)	——	——
	(50 and over)	0.40 (0.20)*	−0.08 (0.04)*
Skill	(skilled)	−0.65 (0.14)**	0.19 (0.04)**
	(semi-skilled)	−0.24 (0.17)	0.10 (0.05)*
	(unskilled)	——	——
Marital Status	(married)	0.14 (0.12)	0.05 (0.03)
	(others)	——	——
Health	(light capacity work)	0.47 (0.32)	−0.05 (0.04)
	(other)	——	——
Industry	(construction)	−0.49 (0.18)**	0.13 (0.05)**
	(engineering)	——	——
	(services)	−0.37 (0.18)*	0.03 (0.05)
	(other)	−0.35 (0.19)	−0.00 (0.05)
Time out of work	(less than 3 months)		0.14 (0.04)**
	(3 to 6 months)		——
	(6 to 12 months)		−0.04 (0.05)
	(1 to 2 years)		−0.12 (0.05)*
	(2 years and over)		−0.17 (0.05)**
Constant		3.30	0.21
R^2 (F)		0.199 (7.01)**	0.209 (14.58)**
No. of observations		294	786

Note: Standard errors of coefficients are in parentheses and significance at the .05 (.01) level is indicated by *(**).

The Influence of Family Size

If a missing characteristic is to play a significant role in influencing the differences observed between the Ferguslie Park and Paisley samples two conditions must be fulfilled. First, it must be a characteristic which is significantly related to our measures of unemployment. Second, it must be a characteristic which is significantly more or less common in Ferguslie Park relative to the rest of Paisley. One characteristic which meets both these conditions is family size.

We know from the Census of Population that there is a crude

association between male unemployment and the family size. Males with large numbers of dependent children tend to have relatively high unemployment rates. This is not to say that large families cause high unemployment rates in any direct sense. However, benefit income tends to rise with increases in the number of dependants, and it is known from a number of studies (for example, Mackay and Reid, 1972) that benefit income and unemployment duration are positively related, other things being equal. Nickell (1977) finds that the probability of leaving unemployment within a given period falls as the number of dependent children increases, holding benefit income constant. We also know that family sizes are large in Ferguslie Park relative to Paisley as a whole (English, 1978).

Two other pieces of relevant evidence are worth noting. First, an analysis of a household survey conducted in Ferguslie Park (McGregor, 1978) found that male heads of households were more likely to be unemployed the larger the number of dependent children. This result held after controlling for the influence of age, skill and industry on unemployment. Second, in the statistical work in this paper we found that married men had a higher incidence of unemployment spells and longer durations of unemployment. This is contrary to expectations and is consistent with a situation where the true relationship between marital status and unemployment is being obscured by the effect of the higher benefit incomes generally available to married versus single men.

Lacking a direct source of data on family size and benefit incomes we must resort to more indirect methods of testing the influence of these factors. One such test involves considering married and single men separately. As family sizes are relatively large within Ferguslie Park we anticipate that area differences in unemployment experiences will be more significant for married men relative to single men, other things being equal. If the experiences of married and single men do indeed differ in the manner hypothesised this could not be easily explained by demand-side factors. It is difficult to see why employers should discriminate against married men from Ferguslie Park and not against single men from the estate.

More generally, it is difficult to conceive of any type of area externality which would generate such differentiation of behaviour by marital status. There is one possible source of differentiation which does not rely on benefit income, family size effects or area externalities. The sample of single men from Ferguslie Park will largely consist of men who were raised in the estate, or who moved there on the basis of parental choices and circumstances. On the other hand, it is likely that the sample of married men contains a higher proportion of men allocated into the estate on the basis of their own circumstances. Amongst this group it is probable that some will have been forced to accept housing in the estate as a result of an employment problem which our crude indicators do not pick up.

The test was carried out by estimating equations (1), (2) and (3) separately for married and single men. The results are summarised in the first three rows of Table 4.3 where we show the coefficients on the residence dummy variables derived from the separate, marital-status regressions. These results were hostile to the case for area externalities. In every case where we consider married men there is a significant difference between the unemployment experiences of Ferguslie Park and Paisley residents. However, although the area coefficient consistently shows a disadvantage associated with Ferguslie Park residence in the sample of single men, the difference between the two areas is not statistically significant in two of the three cases, and is only on the margin of significance in the third case.

Table 4.3: Coefficients on Residence Variable from Separate Marital Status regressions

Dependent variables	Single men	Married men
1. Spells of Unemployment	0.10 (0.28)	0.78 (0.19)**
2. Logarithm of Unemployment Duration	0.14 (0.19)	0.50 (0.15)**
3. Re-employment Probability	– 0.10 (0.05)*	– 0.09 (0.04)*
4. " " (short-term registrants)	– 0.17 (0.10)	– 0.29 (0.08)**
5. " " (long-term registrants)	– 0.02 (0.05)	– 0.03 (0.04)

Notes:
Standard errors of coefficients are in parentheses. Differences significant at the .05 (.01) level are shown by *(**).
Short-term registrants are all those out of work for under three months when the sample was drawn.
Comparisons of the absolute values of coefficients should not be made as the units of measurement differ between the regressions.

We carried the test further by examining the experiences of men who had been out of work for different lengths of time at the date of drawing the sample. Nickell (1977) has shown that the influence of benefit income on the likelihood of leaving unemployment declines as the period without work increases. To the extent that the benefit-income effect is relevant in the present study we would expect a more pronounced area disadvantage for short-term married registrants relative to long-term. This was tested by dividing the sample into two groups, taking three months as the criterion for differentiating short- and long-term registrants. Regressions on the probability of re-employment were then re-estimated and the coefficients on the residence variables appear in the last two rows of Table 4.3.

Within the group of short-term registrants married men from Ferguslie Park have significantly lower re-employment probabilities than their counterparts in other areas of Paisley. However, there is no evidence of significant area differentiation when we consider the case of married men who had been out of work for more than three months. This lends further support to the hypothesis that failure to correct for family-size differences exaggerates the poor unemployment experiences of the Ferguslie Park job seekers.

This conclusion must be qualified to some degree. Although the difference between areas (as measured by the coefficients on the residence dummy variables) is not significant for either short- or long-term single registrants the significance level is clearly higher for the short-term registrants. This mirrors the result for married men and suggests that the phenomenon observed for married males is not simply the result of a family size/benefit income effect but is partly the reflection of a more general process.

Residential Differentiation within Ferguslie Park

Up to this point we have treated the Ferguslie Park estate as a homogeneous residential area. This is an oversimplification of the situation. The estate contains housing which is varied in terms of age, type and quality. Similarly, Census data at enumeration district level show that some parts of the estate have relatively good scores on observed indicators of deprivation (see English, 1978). Can we divide up Ferguslie Park in such a way as to indicate the relative importance of individual and area factors in the problem of unemployment?

If we subdivide Ferguslie Park according to some systematic or arbitrary grouping criterion and find that, other things being equal:

(1) there are significant differences in unemployment experience between some areas of Ferguslie Park and the rest of Paisley, and
(2) there are no significant differences between other areas of Ferguslie Park and the rest of Paisley,

what interpretation can we place upon the results? We can conclude that to the extent that area externalities are important, they do not affect all parts of the estate. It is not obvious that we can completely reject the notion of area externalities. This depends on the nature of the hypothesised externality. For example, if we relax our assumption of a unified labour market we might argue that high unemployment rates in a particular deprived area are a reflection of relatively poor physical access to employment. Findings (1) and (2) above would not be consistent with such a hypothesis under certain reasonable assumptions (for example, assuming that access variations *within* the deprived area can be disregarded).

We progress the statistical analysis by considering a number of different residential groupings within the Ferguslie Park estate. The following breakdowns were adopted:

(1) 'Good' versus all other streets. Using census indicators a distinction was drawn between unambiguously good streets in the estate and all other streets.

(2) Streets with 'Ferguslie Park' in the name versus the rest. A number of street names incorporate the title Ferguslie Park.

(3) Arbitrary split. We listed the 42 street names alphabetically and drew a simple distinction between streets 1 to 20, and 21 to 42.

Equations (2) and (3) were re-estimated substituting each of these residential groupings for the simple Ferguslie Park-rest of Paisley split. The resulting area coefficients are presented in Table 4.4.

We can briefly summarise the results in the following way. Whichever subdivision of Ferguslie Park is employed residents of the estate have consistently longer unemployment durations and lower re-employment probabilities than their counterparts from other parts of Paisley. Nevertheless, it appears that Ferguslie Park should not be considered a homogeneous area from the perspective of unemployment experiences. Residents of the good streets in the estate, the 'Ferguslie Park' streets and the high-numbered streets do not have unemployment experiences which are significantly different from those of men from the rest of Paisley.

We have already suggested that this type of evidence is not necessarily inconsistent with the existence of area externalities operating to the disadvantage of some residents of Ferguslie Park. This type of test cannot provide definitive answers. The distinction in unemployment experiences between 'good' and 'bad' streets within Ferguslie Park could reflect individual factors or discrimination by local employers. The problem is identical to that of interpreting differences between

Ferguslie Park and the rest of Paisley. To the extent that a problem of employer discrimination does exist we would expect this to be reflected in the relatively poor performance of individuals who are clearly identified as residents of the estate; that is, people from streets where Ferguslie Park appears in the street name. In fact, these workers do not perform significantly more poorly than their counterparts in the rest of Paisley. Finally,the arbitrary division of the estate yields the most clear-cut evidence of differential experiences within Ferguslie Park. This demonstrates the heterogeneity of Ferguslie Park with respect to experiences of unemployment.

Table 4.4: Coefficients on Residence Variables Representing Different Areas of Ferguslie Park

	Dependent variables	
	Logarithm of unemployment duration	Re-employment probability
1. Good areas of Ferguslie Park	0.35 (0.25)	−0.02 (0.06)
All other areas of Ferguslie Park	0.34 (0.13)**	−0.10 (0.03)**
2. Streetnames with 'Ferguslie Park' prefix	0.36 (0.19)	−0.07 (0.05)
All other streets	0.34 (0.13)**	−0.10 (0.03)**
3. Low-numbered streets	0.45 (0.14)**	−0.11 (0.03)**
High-numbered streets	0.16 (0.17)	−0.05 (0.04)

Notes:
Standard errors of coefficients are in parentheses and significance at the .05 (.01) level is indicated by *(**).
In each case the coefficients are to be interpreted as differences between the specific area and the rest of Paisley.
The proportions of men resident in the good streets and in streets with Ferguslie Park in the name were relatively small. As this led to very small absolute numbers in these categories in the regression on the number of spells of unemployment we restricted the analysis to variations in the speed and likelihood of unemployment.
I am grateful to John English for providing me with the breakdown of Ferguslie Park into 'good' streets. The possible utility of differentiating areas within Ferguslie Park was suggested by Alan Evans and Ray Richardson.

Although residential differentiation *within* Ferguslie Park need not
be inconsistent with the discrimination hypothesis, it certainly places
it under strain. First, it assumes a detailed knowledge of the estate on
the part of employers or their hiring agents. Second, as we would now
be hypothesising discrimination against a smaller group of workers the
applicability of standard theories of discrimination must be questioned.
For example, the use of residence as a cheap screening device is of
little help to employers when it screens out only a small proportion of
job applicants.

Third, by narrowing the problem down to smaller and smaller numbers of workers we intensify the difficulty of differentiating area and
individual factors. The further we move into the tail of the distribution
of the working population by unemployment experience the more we
must expect to find individuals with special employment problems;
that is, the greater becomes the problem of unmeasured characteristics.
Finally, it is difficult to conceive of other kinds of area externalities
which would generate the patterns of residential differentiation observed
within Ferguslie Park.

We can summarise the statistical analysis in the following way. The
starting point of the analysis was the observation that Ferguslie Park
has much higher unemployment rates than prevail in the town within
which the estate is situated. Our analysis showed that Ferguslie Park
workers tended to experience more spells of unemployment and
longer durations of spells than workers from other parts of Paisley
possessing similar employment characteristics. This finding was consistent with the existence of area externalities operating to the disadvantage of Ferguslie Park workers. Alternatively, it may have been
simply a reflection of the influence of employment-related characteristics which our study was unable to capture.

Further statistical testing suggested that the latter was the more
likely explanation of the relatively high incidence of unemployment
spells and lengthy durations of unemployment experienced by the
Ferguslie Park job seekers. The differential experiences of married
versus single men strongly supported this kind of explanation, and
could not be reconciled easily with the existence of area externalities.
Similarly, the evidence of residential differentiation within Ferguslie
Park militates against explanations based on employer discrimination
or other area externalities, although it does not rule them out altogether. On the other hand, we should not lose sight of the fact that
however Ferguslie Park was subdivided (single versus married, one area
versus another) the men from Ferguslie Park were consistently in an

unfavourable position relative to men with similar characteristics resident in other parts of Paisley.

Conclusions and Policy Implications

In this chapter we have focused on the problem of unemployment in the
Ferguslie Park estate, a highly deprived area in the west of Scotland.
From a number of perspectives Ferguslie Park constitutes a useful area
of study. First, it is not an isolated pocket of population. The estate
contains around 10,000 people, roughly one-tenth of the population
of the town within which it is located. Second, it is not situated in an
'inner-city' area. Labour market conditions in Paisley as a whole have
been relatively good and unemployment rates have traditionally been
low relative to adjoining areas. Yet Ferguslie Park had an unemployment
rate of 22 per cent in 1971, a rate of unemployment exceeding that
prevailing in many of the older inner city areas of the adjacent city of
Glasgow. The existence of Ferguslie Park (and similar areas) is a useful
corrective to the notion that urban deprivation is synonymous with
inner city deprivation.

The most important reason for studying Ferguslie Park is that this
estate has acquired and retained a notorious reputation. To the extent
that area-specific factors play a causal role in the generation of deprivation we would expect to see them highlighted in a heavily stigmatised
area like Ferguslie Park. In our statistical analysis we tried to establish
whether there was any reason for believing that area externalities
played some role in generating the extremely high unemployment rates
typical of the estate. We hypothesised that a major externality might
be the operation of discriminatory hiring practices by employers in the
Paisley area. Although this statistical analysis cannot be considered
conclusive the balance of the evidence points to the predominance of
individual factors in the explanation of the relatively high unemployment rates to be found in Ferguslie Park.

Many qualifications can be placed against this conclusion. Perhaps
the major problem is that some of the factors which we have considered
to be individual factors may partly reflect area influences. For example,
do school leavers from Ferguslie Park have the same opportunity of
learning a skill compared to their educational counterparts from other
parts of Paisley? On the other hand, we utilised only a limited number
of individual characteristics. It could be argued that the introduction
of further measures of worker quality and motivation would provide
a more complete explanation of the differences in unemployment
experiences between the Ferguslie Park and Paisley men.

We would also urge caution when generalising from this finding. The case study methodology is naturally limited. At best the findings of this study might be generalised to similar situations in other towns or cities. Thus, we have thrown no light on the question of physical access to employment which is claimed to be an important factor in generating high unemployment rates in the inner cities. We have abstracted from this question by considering a relatively small urban area. More generally, no attempt has been made to explain the overall variation in residential unemployment rates within an urban area. Rather, we have compared the unemployment experiences of the population of the most deprived area of a town with the experiences of the population of the remaining areas of that town.

In considering the policy implications of our findings several preliminary points can be usefully made. First, the emphasis on the importance of individual factors in explaining area variation in unemployment rates should not be taken to mean that a problem does not exist. Indeed residential concentrations of the unemployed highlight the general problem of unemployment and, in particular, underline the fact that unemployment is unevenly distributed within the working population. Second, we have examined the evidence for the existence of area externalities in only one sphere of activity. Although individual factors appear to be the major influence in the employment sphere we cannot go on to conclude that area externalities are unimportant in all other activities influencing the welfare of individuals in deprived areas like Ferguslie Park.

Our broad policy conclusion would be that area-based employment initiatives are difficult to justify. The statistical analysis suggests that unemployment varies systematically with certain individual characteristics but is probably not causally related to residence in a deprived area. This being the case it is difficult to see how one would formulate a specifically area-based employment or manpower policy instrument. There is nothing for such a policy to attack. An alternative to implementing new area-specific manpower policies would involve the allocation to deprived areas of a disproportionate share of the resources available under the existing national manpower programmes. For example, this could involve allowing easier access to training programmes for residents of deprived areas. Such a development raises problems of equity. To the extent that unemployment is less an area problem and more a problem for certain types of individuals (for example, the unskilled irrespective of where they live) it would seem fair to allocate resources for tackling the problem on the basis of individual and not residential criteria.

The analysis also has implications for the utility of policies on the housing front aimed at breaking up or preventing the emergence of deprived areas. Our analysis suggests that the concentration of the deprived in specific areas does not necessarily lead to additional labour market disadvantages for the individuals concerned. That is, if the population of Paisley (including Ferguslie Park) was distributed at random within the town the same individuals and groups would still suffer relatively high unemployment rates. Problem areas like Ferguslie Park would disappear but the problems of the individuals affected by unemployment would remain. However, this is not to deny that there may be many other good reasons for avoiding situations where concentrations of deprived people are created.

In the last analysis we would argue that the unemployment problems of the people living in deprived areas like Ferguslie Park are not susceptible to easy solution. In crude terms, the deprived area is the spatial manifestation of the labour market inequalities which have traditionally characterised the economy. These inequalities are translated into concentrations of deprived people by the 'rules' governing the private and public housing sectors. Only in the process of reducing these inequalities can the employment problems of the residents of deprived areas be ameliorated.

Notes

1. Dummy variables are used in much of the analysis in this chapter. The coefficient on the residence dummy variable shows the difference in the number of spells of unemployment between Ferguslie Park and the rest of Paisley after controlling for the influence of the other relevant variables.
2. The distribution of the duration of unemployment is badly skewed by the presence in the sample of a small number of individuals with very lengthy periods out of work. In these circumstances it was advisable to take the logarithm of unemployment duration as the dependent variable.

References

Arrow, K.J. (1973) 'The Theory of Discrimination', in Ashenfelter, O. and Rees, A. (eds.), *Discrimination in Labour Markets*, Princeton: Princeton University Press
Damer, S. (1974) 'Wine Alley: The Sociology of a Dreadful Enclosure', *Sociological Review*, vol. 22, no. 2, May, pp. 221-48
—— and Madigan, R. (1974) 'The Housing Investigator', *New Society*, vol. 29, no. 616, pp. 226-7
Eisenberg, P. and Lazarsfeld, P.F. (1938) 'The Psychological Effects of Unemployment', *Psychological Bulletin*, vol. 35, June, pp. 358-90
English, J. (1976) 'Housing Allocation and a Deprived Scottish Estate', *Urban Studies*, vol. 13, no. 3, October, pp. 319-23
—— (1978) *A Profile of Ferguslie Park*, Glasgow: Strathclyde Regional Council

Fowler, R.F. (1968) *Duration of Unemployment on the Register of Wholly unemployed*, Studies in Official Statistics, Research Paper No. 1, London: HMSO

Goldfeld, S.M. and Quandt, R.E. (1972) *Nonlinear Methods in Econometrics*, Amsterdam, North Holland

Great Britain (1975) Department of Environment, *Census Indicators of Urban Deprivation*, Working Note No. 6, London: HMSO

—— *Policy for the Inner Cities*, Cmnd. 6845, London: HMSO

Hall, R.E. (1970) 'Why is the Unemployment Rate so High at Full Employment?', *Brookings Papers on Economic Activity*, 3, pp. 369-410

Holtermann, S. (1978) 'The Welfare Economics of Priority Area Policies', *Journal of Social Policy*, vol. 7, no. 1, January, pp. 23-40

McGregor, A. (1977) 'Intra-Urban Variations in Unemployment Duration: A Case Study', *Urban Studies*, vol. 14, no. 3, October, pp. 303-13

—— (1978) 'Family Size and Unemployment in a Multiply Deprived Urban Area', *Regional Studies*, vol. 12, no. 3, pp. 323-30

Mackay, D.I. and Reid, G.L. (1972) 'Redundancy, Unemployment and Manpower Policy', *Economic Journal*, vol. 85, no. 4, December, pp. 1256-72

Mair, G. and Wood, C.L. (1977) Paper on Unemployment in Scottish Cities, SSRC Urban and Regional Economics Study Group, University of Glasgow, May

Marston, S.T. (1976) 'Employment Instability and High Unemployment Rates', *Brookings Papers on Economic Activity*, 1, pp. 169-210

Metcalf, D. and Richardson, R. (1976) 'Unemployment in London', in Worswick, G.D.N. (ed.), *The Concept and Measurement of Involuntary Unemployment*, London: George Allen and Unwin

Nickell, S. (1977) 'Estimating the Probability of Leaving Unemployment', *Centre for the Economics of Education Discussion Paper No. 7*, London School of Economics

Phelps, E.S. (1972) 'The Statistical Theory of Racism and Sexism', *American Economic Review*, vol. 62, pp. 659-61

Pilgrim Trust (1938) *Men Without Work*, Cambridge: Cambridge University Press

Townsend, P. (1976) 'Area Deprivation Policies', *New Statesman*, 6 August, pp. 168-71

5 ACCESS AND DEPRIVATION IN LOCAL AUTHORITY HOUSING

John English

Local authority housing was first built on a significant scale in Britain in the 1920s and its growth, broadly coinciding with that of owner-occupation, has transformed the tenure structure and largely replaced privately rented accommodation. The public sector, which also includes new towns and housing associations, accounted for 31 per cent of dwellings in 1975 (54 per cent in Scotland) (Great Britain, 1977). Council housing set new standards for the working class: before the First World War it was exceptional for them to have dwellings equipped with hot water, baths and inside WCs. The lack of these basic amenities has conventionally been used as an indicator of unsatisfactory housing and on this basis practically all purpose-built council housing is satisfactory. Housing problems have been mainly located in that part of the stock built before 1919 and policies have been directed at its replacement or improvement. The public sector has been seen as a solution to housing problems, by making available good quality accommodation to those in housing need who often had little chance of obtaining it in the market and, most specifically, by rehousing people from demolished slums.

While council housing as a whole should be counted as a major success, it is far from homogeneous and includes, as well as much accommodation of high quality, some that is extremely unsatisfactory. Failures have arisen from a variety of causes and, usually, good intentions: standards were pared down in the 1930s to minimise rents for rehoused slum dwellers; remote green field sites were used in the 1950s to facilitate large-scale building programmes; and system-built blocks of flats seemed to offer advantages of speed and land saving in the 1960s. Many factors affect what makes for more and less attractive housing and these cannot be discussed at length here; but in any area there is almost bound to be a hierarchy of acceptability or popularity. Indeed, the relative attractiveness of housing is in many ways more significant than its quality in an absolute sense. A great deal depends upon the alternatives available. Some council housing is unsatisfactory by any standards but a great deal more would be considered reasonable in one area and poor in another. The importance of this distinction is borne out when one moves from physical to social conditions: almost invariably unpopularity is associated with the existence of a deprived population. The processes whereby deprived people are concentrated in parts of the public sector are the central concern of this chapter.

It should come as no surprise that deprived populations exist in the public sector; good housing solves only one problem of poverty and a move to a council estate may, indeed, itself cause difficulties with, for example, higher travel and heating costs and fewer opportunities for part-time female employment. With the rapid decline of the private rented sector the poorest sections of the community have increasingly been moving to council housing in recent years. But a key issue is the concentration of deprived people in unpopular estates. After all, council housing is not bought and sold in the market but is allocated, ostensibly according to need, and it is not immediately obvious why the least well-off applicants should so often get the worst accommodation.

One broad explanation is that poorer applicants are channelled into the lowest quality accommodation by explicit policies of local housing departments. The clearest instance of this occurred in the 1930s when council housing was reoriented from meeting general needs to rehousing people from the first large-scale slum clearance programme in Britain. Practically all new housing was used to accommodate people who, almost by definition, included disproportionate numbers of the economically insecure. Ever since, estates built at that time have suffered from the twin disadvantages of lower physical standards (often with flats rather than houses) and stigmatisation as 'rough' areas. The tendency to build higher than normal proportions of large units to accommodate bigger families has also often resulted in concentrations of children in such estates. As will be seen, for all these reasons the problems of slum clearance rehousing estates have been self-perpetuating (Great Britain, 1970; Damer, 1974).

More generally, however, a great deal of attention has been given to the practice of grading prospective tenants. At least until recently most housing authorities have, with more or less formality, classified applicants according to their supposed suitability for different quality accommodation. (In practice this has usually meant the popularity of housing: for example, even new maisonettes, which are notoriously unpopular, may be allocated to applicants with low gradings.) Grading is generally undertaken by housing visitors or inspectors with a heavy workload and minimal training: a cursory evaluation is made on the basis of apparent housekeeping standards (Great Britain, 1969; Damer and Madigan, 1974). Grading undoubtedly does restrict the housing opportunities of some applicants and contributes to the creation and perpetuation of deprived council estates. But the role of grading should

not be over-emphasised for two reasons: first, local authorities are
increasingly abandoning the practice and, second, deprived people
appear actually to choose to live in less popular housing. This second
factor is at least as important as grading and arguably much more
important. An implication is that the abolition of grading is unlikely
to have any great effect on the pattern of allocations.

One line of argument which has some currency, amongst housing
department staff as well as the general public, is that poorer people
actually prefer run-down estates. They are alleged to feel more at home
with the less demanding life style to be found there. They are said to
prefer the lower rent levels of older housing though this consideration
cannot have much force since the introduction of the generous national
rent rebate scheme in 1972. But even if there is a modicum of truth in
this interpretation of the situation an infinitely more potent factor is at
work: the very large differences in waiting time required for different
council housing within the same area. Although waiting lists are still
almost universal, some council housing is available in most areas
virtually immediately or after only a short delay. This is true even of
central London where the GLC has had to evolve novel methods to find
tenants for 'difficult to let' housing, generally unimproved walk-up flats.

The chief price of a popular council house is a relatively long period
on the waiting list. The existence of points schemes does not fundamen-
tally alter the situation if, as is usually the case, additional points are
given for waiting time. Applicants differ widely in their ability and
willingness to wait; the most obvious factor is existing housing circumstances. People who are already reasonably well housed may be ready
to wait literally years until accommodation of the type and in the
location they prefer becomes available. But someone who is living in
appalling conditions or is threatened with homelessness is constrained
to accept whatever council house is available without delay. One cannot be certain of the other circumstances of such a person or family
but there is a high probability that they will be deprived in other ways
apart from their housing conditions: they may have a low income
because of unemployment, chronic sickness or unskilled work; or an
unsupported mother may have been left without a home following a
domestic crisis.

Wide differences in waiting times seem to be the chief means whereby
deprived estates are perpetuated. But before research findings which
illustrate the process are examined it is useful to look at the allocation
of council housing in general terms. All social services have allocation
systems of one sort or another, though in none are potential users in the
least acute need able systematically to obtain the highest quality

of provision as they are in the field of council housing.

The Allocation Process

Ordinarily the allocation of commodities is determined in the market through the operation of the price system but a characteristic of social services is that they are provided at zero or subsidised cost to the consumer. Consequently demand usually exceeds supply and a rationing mechanism is required. This is generally the case even when a service purports to meet all demand: rationing then appears as a restriction on or dilution of the quality of provision. Rationing may be implicit rather than explicit: deterrence or secrecy are used to deflect demand (Parker, 1967). Council housing has a relatively explicit rationing mechanism: first, through eligibility rules and, second, through waiting lists. But the rationing process for council housing has certain features which differentiate it from superficially similar procedures, for example hospital waiting lists. These relate primarily to the manifest lack of homogeneity of housing as a consumption good and to the relative lack of legitimacy extended to claims for professional expertise in the allocation of housing as against consumer preferences.

Although there are variations in the quality, for example, care in different hospitals and education in different schools, variations in the quality of council housing are probably relatively greater and are certainly more obvious to the ordinary man or woman. The acceptability of housing depends on a whole range of factors. Some of these are personal or idiosyncratic in the sense that they vary randomly between individuals: for example, nearness to relatives or work or the possession of an exceptionally large garden. But overall demand tends to approximate to a single hierarchy; in other words, some housing is generally popular and some generally unpopular. Each individual trades off a large number of considerations which relate to the type and condition of the dwelling itself, to the estate and to the nearness of amenities for shopping and entertainment. Recent research has suggested that perceptions of the estate are of more salience than type of dwelling (Great Britain, 1976) but, other things being equal, houses are likely to be more popular than flats, central than peripheral areas, modern than old-fashioned dwellings and 'respectable' than 'rough' neighbourhoods. Two factors which are of relatively little significance in the public sector are price and size of dwelling: rent structures are usually relatively flat with only modest variations·according to quality while housing departments are generally only willing to allocate accommodation of the 'correct' size.

A second difference between council housing and most social services is that consumers have few qualms about judging for themselves the quality of the available accommodation. There is little parallel to the veil of professional obfuscation which is drawn over the standard and type of medical care or of education. Housing managers do not attempt to decide what is appropriate for particular applicants beyond a few very basic considerations such as adequate size to prevent overcrowding and ease of access for the elderly and disabled. Most people regard themselves as the best judges of their housing needs; these are transmitted to housing departments which on the whole do their best to meet them.

The difficulty is that demand for some housing far exceeds supply and criteria necessarily have to be evolved to determine to whom it shall be allocated. There are, as will be seen, criteria of need but these relate essentially to the need for housing as such rather than for particular houses; in the allocation of the latter desert is crucial. The basis on which particular houses are allocated and the priority given to different applicants are a matter of policy for each local authority.

Housing allocation has in fact two separate though interrelated functions: first, to determine who shall become council tenants and, second, to determine which applicants shall have particular houses. Until fairly recently the first function was of paramount importance and the housing management literature concentrates upon it. This reflected the fact that there was a healthy demand for any council house and that the majority of vacancies were in new units rather than relets. Neither of these factors applies today in most areas. Sometimes there is no excess of demand over supply in the public sector as a whole so that overall the need to ration does not exist. More often there is a shortfall of demand for some council housing which co-exists with lengthy waiting lists in the same authority.

The second function of housing allocation, deciding who shall have which house, has become the more important. Housing departments usually attempt to meet individual needs and desires in terms of nearness to employment or relatives, for example, but this does little to counteract general preferences. A few areas have draconian policies of severely restricting choice by automatically offering the first suitable vacancy (from an official point of view) to the applicant at the top of the waiting list with substantial penalties for refusal. This procedure would not generally be regarded as good housing management practice and it does not appear to be widespread. In the past desert, through the process of grading, very often determined who should be allocated the best housing; but this practice seems to be diminishing in importance.

In towns and cities with large slum clearance programmes it has been usual to give priority to people who require to be rehoused. In some areas much of the most popular housing is allocated to existing council tenants who wish to transfer.

Though most authorities attempt to give priority to applicants who have the least adequate accommodation in relation to their needs, this policy rarely seems to be successful in relation to the allocation of houses of differing popularity. Even where a points scheme exists priority achieved by waiting may be of crucial importance in getting access to the best housing. The result is that very frequently waiting time is, either directly or indirectly, of crucial importance in determining the quality of housing allocated to an applicant. Thus applicants with the least acute need tend to obtain preferred housing in preferred locations while the economically and socially deprived get the least attractive.

This process has been identified in outline in a number of areas. For example, a study of housing allocation in the Greater Manchester area (Mylan and Jennings, 1975) showed that there were large differences in the length of wait required to obtain a less desirable property and a house in a popular estate in many pre-reorganisation authorities. A study of housing in the Dundee sub-region made by the Scottish Development Department concluded that '. . . allocation data showing relative waiting periods for different districts and housing types . . . can be interpreted as a type of cost in the absence of a conventional pricing system' (Great Britain, 1976, p. 44). In Dundee itself the least popular estates, which constituted 28 per cent of the public sector stock, were the most socially and economically deprived and in 1973 had an average waiting time of 9 months compared with 26 months for the city as a whole. The author was, however, able to undertake rather more extensive research into this aspect of housing allocation in Paisley with particular reference to a very deprived and unpopular estate, Ferguslie Park. Conditions in Ferguslie Park will be outlined before the allocation system is discussed.

Ferguslie Park: A Deprived Estate

Most areas have deprived council estates but the problem is particularly severe in the central Clydeside conurbation. There are a number of reasons why this should be the case: first, the public sector is relatively large; second, differences in quality between the best and worst council housing are extreme; and, third, the conurbation as a whole suffers from severe deprivation (Silkin, 1975). A recent report on urban deprivation in the Strathclyde Region (Strathclyde Regional Council, 1976) identified 114 Areas for Priority Treatment. Out of 27 APTs in the most severely deprived category 14 were council estates; eight of these were located in Glasgow but the largest and most deprived outside the city was the Ferguslie Park area in Renfrew District. The significance of Ferguslie Park, however, does not lie in uniqueness but in the fact that it is representative, albeit in an extreme form, of the situation in most local authorities throughout Britain. Until 1975 the estate was situated in the former Paisley Large Burgh but, although the research overlapped local government reorganisation, the change did not significantly affect housing allocation during the relevant period. Ferguslie Park is therefore discussed in the context of Paisley rather than the larger Renfrew District.

Conditions in Ferguslie Park have been described elsewhere (English, 1978) and it is here only necessary to outline their most salient features. Paisley is situated a few miles west of Glasgow and the estate is surrounded by industry (the Chrysler factory at Linwood is nearby), railway lines and open country. Though Ferguslie Park is no more than a mile or so from the town centre, bus services are indifferent and local shops small and expensive, factors which add to the unpopularity of the area.

The estate was built over a period of about 40 years from the 1920s to the 1960s; there were a number of distinct phases of building the differences between which are of great importance. The earliest houses, which were built for general needs, are mainly cottage flats and form a pleasant enclave in Ferguslie Park. The bulk of the estate was built in the 1930s for rehousing families from slum clearance schemes and consists mainly of blocks of tenement flats. When for a number of years around 1970 the Housing Department was unable to let all the houses which became vacant in Ferguslie Park these bore the brunt of the problem. Substantial numbers became derelict and have since been demolished. Thus the inherent shortcomings of tenement buildings have been exacerbated by a great deal of dereliction. The postwar housing is much more variable in condition; some of it is in a relatively good state while some shares the problems of the prewar tenements.

The loss of population from Ferguslie Park had largely ceased by the mid-1970s, which probably reflects a tightening up of the local housing market. About 2,600 occupied houses remain after a loss of nearly 1,000, with a population of between 9,000 and 10,000 people. The estate accounts for about 13 per cent of the 20,000 council houses in Paisley which make up some two-thirds of the total stock.

Deprivation in Ferguslie Park has many aspects which are closely interrelated. Though all the houses are equipped with basic amentities, housing conditions over much of the estate are poor. The tenement buildings are unattractive and the houses are old-fashioned by modern standards. But not only is modernisation needed; the state of repair of many of the houses is far from satisfactory. Environmental conditions are also often poor, especially where buildings have become vacant or have been demolished.

The most salient aspect of economic deprivation in Ferguslie Park is the serious and persistent problem of unemployment. The 1971 Census indicated a male unemployment rate of 22 per cent in the estate compared with 9 per cent in the Clydeside conurbation (see McGregor, chapter 4 in this volume). Almost 30 per cent of economically active and retired men from Ferguslie Park were or had been unskilled manual workers, two and a half times the proportion in the Clydeside conurbation. Nine out of ten households did not have a car compared with about two-thirds in Clydeside. And at least two-fifths of households in Ferguslie Park were dependent on social security benefits which means that they had incomes at or below the Supplementary Benefit poverty line.

The Ferguslie Park population contains a disproportionate number of children and young persons, larger families and incomplete families. This is not to say that large families or one-parent families are a problem in themselves but, given the relatively low levels of family income support and the shortcomings of the social security system in Britain, they tend to be economically deprived and other difficulties flow from this. Furthermore, the presence of a large number of children in housing which is not designed to cope with them results in overcrowding and a great deal of pressure on the environment.

In 1971 no less than 38 per cent of the Ferguslie Park population was aged under 15 years, compared with 27 per cent in Paisley as a whole, and almost half was aged under 20 years. Household size is related to the large proportion of children in the population. About one-fifth of households contained six or more persons compared with 8 per cent in Paisley, but less than two-fifths were small households with one or two persons compared with almost half. There is a considerable concentration of one-parent households in Ferguslie Park. Nearly one-fifth of households with children in the estate were headed by single parents (10 per cent of all households), double the proportion for Paisley as a whole.

Ferguslie Park, like many deprived estates, has a disproportionately large number of bigger houses. But, paradoxically, overcrowding is severe. Nearly one-fifth of households were overcrowded on the Census definition of living at a density of more than one and a half persons per room. One-third had insufficient bedrooms on the standard used by the Government Social Survey, including four-fifths of households with six or more members.

Housing Allocation in Paisley

The allocation system in Paisley for waiting list applicants (that is excluding transfers and exchanges) was operated basically according to waiting time. In theory simple queueing was mediated by a system of quotas whereby proportions of available lets were supposed to be allocated to various categories of applicants such as the overcrowded, the badly housed and the homeless. This last category, which is of considerable importance in the research findings, referred to applicants without a home of their own such as those sharing accommodation. In fact the quotas appeared to have little or no significance in the day-to-day operation of the allocation system. The categories are nevertheless of interest as an indication of the circumstances of applicants. The chief categories of allocations in 1974, 1975 and 1976 were the homeless, taking 40, 41 and 46 per cent of allocations to waiting list applicants, and the badly housed, with 33, 25 and 33 per cent respectively. Altogether waiting list allocations amounted to about two-thirds of the total of around 1,200 lets in these years, the remainder going to transfers and exchanges.

A set of housing rules laid down matters such as who was eligible to apply for a house and the number of offers that would be made. With the exception of servicemen, applicants normally had either to live or work in Paisley. The refusal of two offers of accommodation was supposed to result in an application being suspended for two years. But in practice neither of these rules was applied to Ferguslie Park and persons who did not fulfil the normal residential qualifications in fact provided a substantial proportion of applications for the estate. This reflected the fact that for some years at least the task had been not to ration the supply of houses in Ferguslie Park but to seek out sufficient demand to ensure that vacancies were filled. Officials were clearly reluctant to exclude any potential tenant from consideration. Until 1975 applicants were graded and the choice of a few was probably limited to the estate though the abolition of grading had no apparent effect on the pattern of allocations.

It was characteristic of how the problem was approached that Ferguslie Park allocations were dealt with separately from those elsewhere in Paisley. One officer in the Housing Department had particular responsibility for allocations in the estate and he maintained a file of applicants who were believed to be willing to accept a house there (or were ineligible on grounds of residence for anywhere else). Without ignoring the considerable variations between other estates in Paisley, the distinction between Ferguslie Park and elsewhere can be said to overshadow them. This was demonstrated by the preferences expressed on application forms which were not infrequently in terms of Ferguslie Park and any other estate. Officials believed that the chief attraction of Ferguslie Park was the relatively short wait required to obtain a house in the estate and the large difference in waiting times between it and other areas was confirmed by the research findings.

The objectives of the research were to discover, first, whether deprived people were continuing to move to Ferguslie Park, and second, if they were doing so, how this was happening. The availability of records varies between authorities and those in Paisley were not very extensive. Two principal sources of data were available: applications for houses in the estate and a routine analysis of allocations throughout Paisley made by the Housing Department. The latter is the more salient inasmuch as it relates to actual allocations but the former contained some information about household structure which is indicative of that of those who actually moved to the estate.

The file of applications for houses in Ferguslie Park was analysed in March 1975: there was a total of 229 applications (182 waiting list and 47 transfer applicants). The waiting list applications were for the most part very recent: 19 per cent had been made during the previous three months, 60 per cent during the previous fifteen months and practically all during the previous two years. Transfer applications were older with 40 per cent outstanding for over two years. The place of residence of applicants is of considerable significance. Two-fifths of waiting list applicants lived outside Paisley (most of whom would have been ineligible for any other estate) though very few such persons actually moved to Ferguslie Park. But particularly striking was the large proportion of applicants who already lived in the estate: 42 per cent of waiting list applicants and 83 per cent of transfer applicants. The first figure is an indication of the extent of sharing in Ferguslie Park and the second of the absence of any substantial demand from council tenants elsewhere in Paisley to move there. Thus only a small minority of applicants who were eligible to apply for a house in another estate did not already live in Ferguslie Park. Furthermore, as many as 82 per cent of waiting list applicants did not have a house to themselves: most were sharing accommodation with a few in hospitals and the services. Practically all of them would fall into the homeless allocation category.

The mean household size of waiting list applicants was substantially less than that of existing Ferguslie Park residents and, surprisingly, below that for all households in Paisley. There are perhaps two explanations of this finding: first, many of the households had probably been recently formed and were still growing and, second, those from outside Paisley (which rarely moved to the estate) may have been relatively small. Transfer applicants, however, had much larger households, over 40 per cent containing six or more members. This reflected the problem of overcrowding in Ferguslie Park and the shortage of four and five apartment houses. Over 20 per cent of applicants were lone parent households, virtually all headed by women. The concentration of lone parents in Ferguslie Park seemed likely to continue. While therefore the available data on the characteristics of applicant households were limited they are compatible with the continued recruitment of a deprived population. The evidence of existing housing circumstances strongly suggests that, except possibly for some of those already living in Ferguslie Park, nearly all applicants were constrained to consider the estate by the ready availability of houses there or, as non-residents of the burgh, were ineligible for anywhere else.

Data on allocations were compiled from monthly returns prepared by the Housing Department. The principal information available about each allocation was the category into which it fell (such as overcrowded, badly housed and homeless) and the date of application. A preliminary point which is worth touching on is the rate of turnover of tenancies, also derived from this source, which throws further light on conditions in Ferguslie Park. A high population turnover is generally felt to be indicative of dissatisfaction on the part of residents with an area. During 1974, 1975 and 1976 the turnover rate in Paisley as a whole was about 6 per cent whereas the rate in Ferguslie Park was more than twice as great at over 12 per cent. But there were substantial differences within the estate: while the turnover rate was over 20 per cent in some streets, in others (particularly those of houses built in the 1920s) it was below 3 per cent.

The pattern of allocations in Ferguslie Park has been very different from that in Paisley as a whole; Table 5.1 shows statistics by allocation category for 1974, 1975 and 1976. The most striking difference is the very large proportion of allocations in Ferguslie Park to homeless applicants (that is persons without separate houses) which amounted to

70, 61 and 60 per cent of all the allocations in the three years, at least twice the proportion in Paisley as a whole. Looking at the statistics in a different way, although Ferguslie Park contains only about 13 per cent of occupied council houses in Paisley, in the three years 56, 49 and 55 per cent of allocations to homeless applicants were in the estate. The importance of these statistics is that it can reasonably be assumed that applicants without separate accommodation of their own were under the greatest pressure to obtain a council house quickly and that they included some of the most vulnerable and disadvantaged members of the community.

The other major category of allocations in Ferguslie Park was transfers which amounted to 18, 26 and 32 per cent of the total in 1974, 1975 and 1976 respectively. These proportions are very similar to those for Paisley as a whole but in each of the three years about 90 per cent of the transfers were to applicants already living in Ferguslie Park. Furthermore, transfers together with allocations to homeless applicants amounted to about 90 per cent of all allocations in the estate during the three years leaving few in any of the other categories.

The tendency for houses in Ferguslie Park to be allocated to existing residents of the estate was not confined to transfers; in 1975, 1976 and 1977 the proportion of waiting list allocations to existing residents was 55, 57 and 59 per cent respectively. Taking transfers and waiting list allocations together, existing residents received 62, 67 and 69 per cent

Table 5.1: Categories of Allocations 1974, 1975 and 1976

	Ferguslie Park			Paisley		
	1974 %	1975 %	1976 %	1974 %	1975 %	1976 %
Waiting list						
Overcrowded	—	2	1	6	8	5
Badly housed, slum clearance	5	3	5	24	16	22
Homeless	70	61	60	28	27	30
Medical cases	2	1	1	8	7	3
Other	2	6	2	8	8	5
Transfers	18	26	32	18	26	25
Exchanges	3	2	2	9	8	10
Total (100%)	281	261	322	1,274	1,213	1,183

of all allocations in the estate. To a very considerable extent, therefore, allocations in Ferguslie Park represented a movement of existing tenants to different houses within the estate and households which had been sharing accommodation there getting homes of their own. The relatively small numbers of outsiders moving into Ferguslie Park reflected the pattern of applications except that few of the non-Paisley applicants actually took houses there.

An important issue in housing allocation is the availability of transfers; the significance of an initial allocation to an applicant may depend in part on the possibility of subsequently moving to a different house or area. It is difficult to judge the adequacy of the availability of transfers from Ferguslie Park; there certainly appears to be a considerable demand to move from the estate, much greater than in the case of other areas in Paisley. Data for transfers are available for 1974, 1975 and 1976; during these years Ferguslie Park residents leaving the estate obtained more than a proportionate share of all transfers in Paisley (including those within estates). It cannot be said therefore that it was difficult to transfer out of Ferguslie Park in absolute terms though this may have been so relative to demand. There were, however, only a handful of exchanges with people from outside the estate.

The households which left Ferguslie Park for council houses elsewhere in Paisley (through transfers and exchanges) represented only about one-fifth of tenancies which were given up during the three years. The remainder amounted to some 200 households each year. It is not suggested that all these represent a problem: some will have ceased to exist through death or for other reasons and some will have moved to satisfactory accommodation in other tenures or outside Paisley. But there can be little doubt that a substantial number was evicted or absconded, usually in the face of rent arrears, without satisfactory alternative accommodation. There is evidence that some remained in Ferguslie Park sharing with other households and thus increasing overcrowding.

Data were collected about the length of time that had elapsed since applications were made for waiting list allocations in 1974 and 1975; the statistics are set out in Table 5.2. In both years about 80 per cent of applicants allocated houses in Ferguslie Park had applied during the previous two years (two-fifths within a year) and practically all within five years. Waiting times in Paisley as a whole were, however, substantially longer; only one-third of applicants had waited for less than two years and more than one-fifth had waited for more than five years. The mean waiting time in both years before allocations in Ferguslie Park was about 10 months, but for all houses in Paisley it rose from 35 months in 1974 to 45 months in 1975. The differential in waiting times appeared to be increasing: while, on the one hand, this indicated a further decrease in the relative demand for houses in Ferguslie Park, on the other hand the trend may have been to the advantage of the estate inasmuch as it became easier to let houses there.

These statistics about actual waiting times confirm the earlier conclusions drawn from analysis of applications for Ferguslie Park: the ready availability of houses there was a powerful factor in inducing applicants, who were constrained to obtain accommodation quickly, to move to the estate.

Table 5.2: Waiting Time of Waiting List Allocations 1974 and 1975

	Ferguslie Park		Paisley	
	1974 %	1975 %	1974 %	1975 %
1 yr ⟨ 1 yr	44	39	15	13
1 yr ⟨ 2 yrs	38	39	20	18
2 yrs ⟨ 3 yrs	9	9	14	18
3 yrs ⟨ 4 yrs	3	2	6	10
4 yrs ⟨ 5 yrs	2	1	7	7
5 yrs ⟨ 10 yrs	—	3	14	17
10 years and over	—	—	7	7
Not stated	4	8	17	11
Total (100%)	219	190	905	809

Policy Options

Council housing has a number of characteristics which are of crucial importance to how it is distributed or allocated: these include very wide differences in its attractiveness (related to factors such as building type, location and, perhaps above all, social standing); normally a relatively flat rent structure which means that pricing is ineffective; and only a weak professional role in determining need for different accommodation. In most areas length of wait is of crucial importance in determining who has access to popular housing; and differential demand is manifested in the time required (other things, such as household size, being equal) to obtain accommodation in different estates and of different types. But ability or willingness to wait depends primarily upon existing housing circumstances which in turn are related to the level of the economic and social well being or deprivation of applicants. Therefore, even in the absence of grading of applicants, deprived households tend to move to less popular estates. These areas, which are usually of at least relatively low amenity, have increasingly deprived populations.

These processes have been illustrated by research on one housing authority and one estate. Ferguslie Park is heavily stigmatised, as far as can be judged primarily because of its position as the location of practically all the prewar slum clearance rehousing in Paisley. In recent years its unpopularity has been exacerbated by physical dereliction resulting from empty housing and problems, such as vandalism, stemming from a very high child density. Many social indicators demonstrate the plight of people living there: the very high rate of male unemployment may be recurred to as simply the most striking. In an attempt to find enough tenants to fill houses becoming vacant most of the normal restrictions on eligibility had been waived. Deprived people were still moving to Ferguslie Park.

The allocation of council housing is almost entirely a matter for the discretion of individual local authorities; the statutory requirements laid upon them are so vague and generalised that they can have little salience at the operational level. Over the years local authorities have been bombarded with advice, for example from the former Central Housing Advisory Committee and its continuing Scottish counterpart, on topics such as the desirability of reducing residential qualifications. Whether or not these exhortations have had much independent effect, the advice has been little concerned with access to different parts of the public sector. In short, attention has in the past been largely confined to considerations of who shall have access to council housing as a whole. The way in which the differential popularity of housing and the concentration of deprived people are approached is, therefore, very much a matter for local decision.

While the condition of estates such as Ferguslie Park and the circumstances of residents are undoubtedly seen as serious problems by most local authorities, it would be wrong to assume that policies to end the concentration of deprived people would necessarily find favour. Indeed, it is not frivolous to suggest that a situation where the disadvantaged, who are often seen as both undeserving and as uncongenial neighbours, are effectively segregated in less sought-after housing fits in with what is thought right and proper by the general public and their elected representatives. Though this is not to suggest that segregation reflects a deliberate policy (except perhaps where grading is used), attempts to alter the situation may well be resisted. Whether or not the existing situation is seen as a problem requiring new policies is a question which revolves around different notions of equity or social justice. On the one hand is the view that the concept of need should be the chief criterion in housing allocation. Consequently action should be taken to ensure that those in greatest need have at least the same opportunity as any other applicant of gaining access to good housing. On the other hand is the view which concentrates on deserts: those who have lengthy local residence and registration on the waiting list and, perhaps, high grading should continue to obtain the best accommodation. Public responsibility for meeting need is satisfied if accommodation of a decent minimum standard is provided: the gratification of personal tastes is something to be enjoyed by the deserving. But even this view implies that action should be taken to improve conditions in those parts of the public sector which can scarcely be accepted as providing even decent minimum standards. Local autonomy and the absence of a strong professionalism in housing allocation mean that policy decisions in this field are particularly dependent on the need for political legitimacy. Political considerations would undoubtedly be a greater barrier to any attempt to alter the existing situation than practical difficulties though the latter would not be insubstantial.

Physical Improvement

Before some possible approaches to improving the access of the deprived to public sector housing are discussed it is worth making two preliminary points. First, as was pointed out above, whatever view is taken of the main issue there is an extremely strong case for substantial investment in estates such as Ferguslie Park to make good the disrepair of houses and environmental dereliction. Whether or not their present condition reflects under investment in the past is often a sore point with local authority officials: but the reality is that such areas require above average expenditure on maintenance to achieve average standards. To say that conditions are the fault of residents, even if true, is to bury municipal heads in the sand. Building types and large child populations are in any case amongst the chief causes. Furthermore, action to reduce existing high child densities by transferring a proportion of larger families to other estates and by restrictions on new allocations to these estates would be useful. But this could not be done unless adequately sized houses are available elsewhere.

Second, it would be a delusion to believe that even if deprived people could be successfully dispersed throughout the public sector their problems would be solved. There is no doubt that the social composition of certain estates exacerbates the familial and individual problems of people living in them and this is surely one of the strongest arguments for dispersal. But it should be recognised that most aspects of deprivation, for example low incomes, single parenthood or unemployment, are not chiefly caused by housing policies and would for the most part continue to exist in the absence of concentration. Dispersal might result in problems appearing to be solved but the change would be no more than a statistical artefact. It can at least be said that the existence of severely deprived areas has focused attention on the problems which they manifest.

The very close interrelationship between deprivation and unpopularity has been emphasised and if means could be found of making unpopular housing more acceptable the concentration effect could be reduced if not eliminated. But the difficulty is that unpopularity results from a whole range of factors, both social and physical, and it is difficult to conceive, even in principle, how some of these could be acted upon. First, reputation and stigma are major causes of unpopularity and these cannot easily be eradicated. Experience with improvement schemes suggests that success has tended to be associated with a more or less complete change of population. But such a radical course is rarely practicable, particularly in the case of larger estates. Second, as far as physical factors are concerned, building types can only be modified to a very limited extent and, other things being equal, flats and maisonettes, for example, tend to be relatively unpopular. Action can, however, be taken to improve physical conditions and possibly to reduce child densities. The effectiveness of these improvements in altering the pattern of consumer preferences cannot be guaranteed but two points can be made in their favour: they are desirable in any case to ensure decent minimum standards in the public sector and, unlike some of the other options outlined below, they increase the supply of good housing rather than seeking to redistribute an existing supply. In other words it is not a zero sum game.

Changes in Rent Structures

A different approach to altering consumer preferences is to modify rent structures. At present variations in the rents of council housing are relatively modest in most areas. There are two arguments for greater

differentiation of rents: one relates to equity, that residents in housing
of low amenity should enjoy cheaper costs. The other is that rents
could be used to equalise the relative supply of and demand for
different housing. The direct effect of such a change would be principally on better-off tenants inasmuch as poorer ones would be largely
insulated from increases through rent rebates and Supplementary Benefit rent allowances. But the latter would potentially benefit if some of
the demand for the more desirable housing from the better-off was
deflected.

There are, however, a number of difficulties. First, given the relatively low level of public sector rents in relation to the incomes of
even the moderately better-off, rent increases would probably have to
be very large to induce significant numbers of applicants to shift their
demand; such increases would be politically difficult to achieve. Second,
and perhaps more serious, even if a shift in demand is achieved there is
no reason to expect that this would be mainly into other parts of the
public sector. The main effect might well be a shift into owner-
occupation. This result, which might also arise from some of the changes
to allocation priorities which are discussed below, could have large
implications for local housing systems and the role of the public sector.

Changes to Allocation Criteria

One possible modification of allocation procedures which should be
touched upon, though it is perhaps unlikely to command widespread
support, is the elimination of choice of dwelling on the part of applicants.
A suitable offer would be made on whatever criteria seemed appropriate
with severe penalties in terms of lost priority if it were refused. This
would be a reversion to the practice of some housing authorities in the
past though few follow it today. It would generally be felt to be out of
tune with good housing management practice to treat applicants in
such a cavalier fashion and likely to be productive of much dissatisfaction. Restriction of choice would also be likely to result in many of
those who were able to do so moving into owner-occupation.

A potentially more fruitful approach to the modification of allocation procedures is a change in priorities so that greater weight is
placed upon various aspects of need, such as quality of existing
accommodation, overcrowding and medical problems. The role of
waiting time could be reduced or even practically eliminated. To be
effective these changes would have to apply to the allocation of particular houses. It is sometimes suggested that in areas where council
houses are available with little delay sophisticated allocation systems,

such as points schemes, are unnecessary and that allocation on the basis of queueing is satisfactory. But this view overlooks the fact that only some council housing is readily available so that segregation according to ability to wait results. The design of suitable points schemes, which above all must very severely limit any additional priority given for waiting time, should not present serious difficulties at a technical level; but such a change might well, rather like changes in rent structures and the restriction of choice, diminish the attractiveness of the public sector for some applicants.

At present the role of council housing is ambiguous and radically different views are held, particularly at the level of political debate. Perhaps the most striking way in which these are manifested is in the controversy over selling council houses. One view is of council housing as a public utility serving a wide section of the community. The other view is of a small public sector catering only for those with demon-strable special needs: the elderly, the disabled and the poor. The argu-ment in this chapter relates particularly to those local authorities, which include most major urban areas, which have large public sectors inasmuch as it is here that the non-deprived make the most substantial use of council housing. In such areas many members of what can be called, for want of a better term, the mainstream of the working class look to council housing to provide them with good quality accommo-dation which by and large is situated in the more popular estates. They do not often face acute housing crises and may be willing to wait for a considerable time to obtain what they desire. But if they cannot obtain it as new entrants to the tenure they may be willing to accept some-thing less satisfactory in the expectation of eventually moving through the transfer system. It must be recognised that changes to the terms of access to council housing, through altered allocation priorities, higher rents, restriction of choice or any other measures which resulted in more of a fixed quantity of good quality housing going to the deprived, would cut across the interests of a large section of the working class. Another factor which cannot be ignored is that the prospect of greater social mixing may diminish the attractiveness of council housing for some people.

If this interpretation is correct it has at least two implications. First, the political resistance to change is likely to be considerable and it is perhaps not very realistic to expect action along these lines. Second, if action were taken the effects on local housing systems could be con-siderable. Reduced demand for council housing might make it impossible to fill houses becoming vacant while prices in the owner-occupied sector

were inflated. In such circumstances the sale of council houses on a
large scale might seem appropriate though such a policy would be unlikely to overcome the concentration of the deprived. Nor, for that
matter, would sales necessarily be especially harmful given that at
present deprived people tend not to obtain the better quality housing
which would undoubtedly be sold: it is rather the potential for change
that would be destroyed. Differences between estates would increasingly
be mirrored by tenure differences instead of existing within the public
sector. For these reasons physical improvement and measures to reduce
child densities, together with two policies outlined below, seem potentially more fruitful.

A Wider Range of Council Tenants

In the past council housing has been little used by the single and the
young and, though the priority given to families and the elderly
reflected a perfectly reasonable view of what were the most urgent
needs, the lack of provision for certain groups in the community has
called forth increasing criticism. But in the last year or two there has
been growing interest in attempts to let council housing, usually the
least popular part of the stock, outside conventional allocation
systems. Probably the best known and most important scheme is that
pioneered by the Greater London Council under the label 'ready
access' which seems to have had a good deal of success in finding
tenants for difficult-to-let housing.

The new tenants will probably not stay very long but on balance
their presence is likely to have a good effect on the communities into
which they move: for one thing more non-family households reduce
child densities in deprived estates. Clearly the scope for this approach
varies on the demand side from area to area and is likely to be greater
in, say, centres of higher education with large student populations.
Nevertheless, the attraction of new types of council tenant, who have
different preferences and are likely, for example, to find flats more
acceptable than families with children, provides a useful though modest
approach to the problems of unpopular council housing.

Greater Use of Transfers

The second policy relates to the role of transfers. Council houses are
allocated not only to households entering the public sector for the first
time but also to existing tenants through transfers. The housing
management profession has a somewhat ambiguous attitude to transfers: on the one hand, they are seen as a way of ensuring the most

efficient use of the housing stock while, on the other hand, some are regarded as no more than an expensive satisfaction of whims. Tenants are naturally keen to obtain transfers into more popular estates and types of accommodation; in many areas a good deal of the best housing is pre-empted in this way and is thus never available to new entrants. At the same time housing departments are inevitably somewhat reluctant to transfer people out of unpopular estates because this will result in vacancies that are difficult to fill. Thus the extensive use of transfers may make it more rather than less difficult for the deprived to obtain sought-after housing.

One reaction to the problem outlined in this chapter is that transfers should not be allowed to pre-empt many of the vacancies in popular housing. This view has much to be said for it if the allocation of council housing were to be altered so that those in greatest need gained effective access to the public sector as a whole. But the obstacles to changing the terms of access to the public sector are very great and, realistically, it could be to the advantage of the deprived if transfers were used even more extensively than at present.

It has to be recognised that if applicants had a free choice there is some council housing that few people would choose to live in; but someone has to live there (except where there is a substantial surplus in an area and the least popular housing of all can be written off and demolished). An alternative approach, however, would be to accept queueing as the chief criterion for access to popular housing, for which people could wait either within or outside the public sector as they preferred. The quality of accommodation (in the sense of popularity and demand) which people moving to council housing were allocated would depend on their length of registration on the waiting list (though special provision would have to be made for those rehoused because of the demolition of their previous home). In essence applicants could be expected to trade off the attractions and disadvantages of their existing housing and the council housing for which they qualified at a particular time. Council tenants could also transfer to better housing on the basis of their length of residence.

The aim would be to ensure that an applicant could expect eventually to obtain similar council housing whether or not he decided initially to move to less preferred accommodation. Those in acute housing need would tend to move quickly but they would not, as now, be penalised in the long term for so doing. Furthermore, the non-deprived may be expected to be readier to move to less popular housing if they know that they will have a virtual guarantee of a transfer after a number of years. This approach is, frankly, a method of sharing out the misery of living in the less satisfactory parts of the public sector but, given that this has to be done on some basis, it is both reasonably fair and has perhaps some chance of being politically acceptable at the local level. Such an approach would at least be likely to prove less unacceptable than more radical policies aimed at increasing the housing opportunities of the deprived within the public sector.

Conclusion

The problems which are associated with the differentiation of council housing in Britain, in terms of the existence of deprived estates and of the unequal access of different groups in the community, are increasingly being recognised but it is probably fair to say that little progress has yet been made in elaborating solutions. The circumstances within which local authorities formulate their policies are continuously changing. Restrictions on public expenditure have slowed down the rate at which council housing can be modernised; but Housing Investment Programmes (Housing Plans in Scotland) have given local authorities greater freedom to determine their own priorities and some may switch resources from new building to the improvement of the existing stock. Then there is the Housing (Homeless Persons) Act, 1977 which may find a new use for unpopular estates though not one which on the whole is likely to be to their advantage. In the final analysis, however, the question which has to answered is how far council housing is to exist outside the market and be allocated according to need or how far the best is to be sold for a price, the length of time people are able to wait. If the political decisions are taken the practical means of change can be found.

References

Damer, S. (1974) 'Wine Alley: The Sociology of a Dreadful Enclosure', *Sociological Review*, vol. 22, no. 2, pp. 221-48.
—— and Madigan, R. (1974) 'The Housing Investigator', *New Society*, vol. 29, no. 616
English, J. (1978) *A Profile of Ferguslie Park*, Glasgow: Strathclyde Regional Council
Great Britain (1969) Ministry of Housing and Local Government and Welsh Office, *Council Housing Purposes, Procedures and Priorities*, London: HMSO
—— (1970) Scottish Development Department, *Council House Communities: A Policy for Progress*, Edinburgh: HMSO
—— (1976) Scottish Development Department, *Local Housing Needs and Strategies*, Edinburgh: HMSO
—— (1977) *Scottish Housing: A Consultative Document*, Cmnd. 6852, Edinburgh: HMSO

Mylan, D. and Jennings, C.A. (1975) *Housing Waiting Lists in Greater Manchester*, Manchester: SHELTER

Parker, R.A. (1967) 'Social Administration and Scarcity: The Problem of Rationing', *Social Work*, vol. 24, no. 2, pp. 9-14

Silkin, F. (1975) *Census Indicators of Urban Deprivation, Working Note No. 10, The Conurbations of Great Britain*, London: Department of the Environment,

Strathclyde Regional Council (1976) *Urban Deprivation*, Glasgow: Strathclyde Regional Council

6 POLITICS AND PLANNING OF URBAN RENEWAL IN THE PRIVATE HOUSING SECTOR

Tim Mason

Urban renewal policy is concerned with two major housing objectives, first to improve the housing stock of the nation by concentrating on some of the worse conditions to be found in it and second, to improve the housing situation of those who are obliged to live in the same. It is now recognised that the physical objective is not always compatible with the social one (Duncan, 1974) and a large part of the debate over urban renewal policy can be characterised as a juggling of these objectives for various political, economic and professional reasons.

It has also been the case that the worst housing conditions have been concentrated in older privately rented and owner-occupied property (Great Britain, 1977a, chapter 9). Therefore much of the debate over urban renewal and housing policy in general has also revolved around the extent to which the public sector should take over from those parts of the private sector which contain the worst housing conditions (Donnison, 1967, chapter 3). Thus urban renewal policy has often supplied a platform for municipal and parliamentary debates which have demonstrated a greater concern for the simplistic orthodoxies of state socialism and laissez-faire Toryism than for the economic and social realities of inner-city housing. The sophistication of the analysis has not usually been improved, however, by the contributions from those professions in housing who have argued that we should 'keep politics out of housing'.

Urban Renewal Since 1945

The conditions in Britain after the Second World War, however, necessitated action rather than sophisticated analysis. There had been no systematic slum clearance since 1939, 450,000 houses were rendered useless by enemy action, the building labour force was down to one-third of its prewar size and a major increase in demand was on the way with the return of the men and women from the armed forces and the resultant 'baby boom'. The most obvious approach was to emphasise the need for certain physical targets to be achieved and to give local authorities the powers needed to deal with the general housing needs of all their population as quickly as possible.

In the event the response was ambitious, but not radical; there was no major long-term reform in the provision or finance of housing in the way there was for the National Health Service for example. In particular the problem of rent control (Nevitt, 1966, chapter 8) and the declining and deteriorating privately rented sector, then covering over 50 per cent of households in England and Wales, was not tackled. In effect the immediate postwar policy of building for general needs was a repetition of the expansion of state intervention in housing which had taken place after the First World War. Marian Bowley (1947) described this as a 'limited emergency theory' in her classic study of interwar housing policies. Such a programme of building would have had to be continued for ten to twelve years at the rates which were envisaged by the government (Donnison, 1967, pp. 163-8).

A Limited Liability Programme

This did not happen, however, due to the balance of payments crisis of 1947, and the return of a Conservative government in 1951 made a return to such policies even less likely. Council house building was turned into a limited liability programme for dealing with the slums, new towns and special groups such as the pensioners. For most people, however, the Conservative government thought that owner-occupation should provide the answer (Cullingworth, 1966, pp. 40-1). Yet the problem remained, of how to deal with those who, for whatever reason, did not gain access to decent housing through the two main housing tenures of owner-occupation and council renting. The Conservatives' policies of the 1950s sought an answer in easing rent restriction and making improvement grants for older property more easily available. Faith and competitive returns on investment in the private rented sector were so low, however, that the easing of restrictions and the subsidy of private improvement actually encouraged some private landlords to sell their property to owner-occupiers (Donnison, 1967, p. 170). By 1960 the privately rented sector accounted for under one-third of all households in England and Wales.

As it became clear that the supply and the conditions of privately rented property were not likely to be increased by such measures the Conservatives turned to less direct forms of 'social housing' by setting up the Housing Corporation in 1964 in order to encourage housing associations, co-ownership schemes and cost-rent housing. Any rapid expansion of these forms of tenure was inhibited, however, by the small size of most of these housing organisations and their lack of a subsidy scheme which would enable them to cater for many of those least able to gain access to decent rented accommodation. Nevertheless these initiatives in housing policy did demonstrate a realisation by the political right that the decline in the privately rented sector had gone too far for an unmodified return to the 'sanitary policies' of the 1930s (Bowley, 1947) which had confined direct state intervention to the very worst housing conditions.

The Conservative approach to urban renewal which dominated the 1950s and the early 1960s did not attempt to break away from the 'limited liability' role for public housing, yet it did not find or create a suitable alternative in the private or voluntary sector that could take on the responsibility of providing for the areas of working-class demand left outside owner-occupation or the council sector. Those who could afford to buy new houses were reasonably well catered for, although they did have to accept falling standards in terms of housing density and internal space compared with prewar owner-occupiers, due in part to the successful planning policy of containing urban sprawl (Hall, 1973).

The policy was to some extent successful in doing away with the worst conditions in the inner city and transferring many people to the better conditions of a council house on the outskirts or overspill estates, but it did much less to tackle the problems of the 'grey' intermediate areas which are not slums. These areas were providing housing for those who were in the privately rented sector for long or short periods and those who could only afford to buy the older type of property which had often been recently transferred from the rented sector. The improvement of conditions in these areas could only be tackled by facing the problems of the rented sector and considering why it was that private investment was so difficult to attract. At the same time, it was necessary to instigate some wider policy of urban renewal, which could counter the increasing social and physical blight that was created by the uncertain future of all pre-1919 housing areas in those cities that had an active clearance policy and no strategic use of area improvement.

Area Improvement

The Conservative government made some small changes in its approach to the improvement of rented property in the 1964 Housing Act. This halted the previous trend of trying to achieve improvement by making the return to private landlords more attractive and it introduced an element of compulsion into the policy. Local authorities were empowered to declare 'improvement areas' of a few hundred houses and to encourage or, in some situations, to compel improvement. The legislation was cautious in its introduction of compulsory powers and instituted long waiting periods in which the owners could show their willingness to comply with the improvement notices; only after such periods could compulsory improvement be entered into.

This approach proved rather cumbersome and was not greatly used by local authorities. It also failed to look into the complex reasons for which landlords might refuse to improve their property. Accordingly the proportion of grants going into the privately rented sector remained at approximately one-fifth of all grants being approved although this sector did represent 61 per cent of unfit dwellings and 48 per cent of those lacking basic facilities in England and Wales in 1967 (Great Britain, 1968a). Like the compulsory improvement scheme, the improvement area concept was an attempt to divert the existing subsidy system into sectors of the housing stock that were not being covered by the existing distribution of subsidies in proportion to their perceived need. The improvement area powers were not widely used by local authorities, only 400 areas were declared between 1964 and 1968 and only 4,000 houses were actually improved in that time (Spencer, 1970).

One reason for this was that many of the big cities were committed to large-scale clearance programmes. The powers to achieve comprehensive redevelopment were readily available and understood by a dedicated Public Health Inspectorate. Ambitious plans stretching a decade ahead were laid out and provided obvious goals to be pursued. The aim became to rid the city of slums by a certain date and there seemed little inducement to divert manpower and money into the unknown difficulties of area improvement. It would not be too much to say that in some of our largest cities there was a professional objection among many officers, and a political objection among many of their councillors, to the idea of prolonging the life of older terraced properties by public subsidy (see Figure 6.1).

The new Labour government was in the process of considering its housing policies in the mid 1960s. The main points of their initial policy were described in the White Paper, 'The Housing Programme 1965 to 1970' (Great Britain, 1965), which voiced a need for more detailed information on a whole range of housing matters. In response to this need the government initiated the 1967 House Condition Survey which was to be so influential in opening our eyes to the scale and nature of the urban renewal problem (Great Britain, 1968a). Its results showed 1.8 million 'unfit' houses in England and Wales, with a further 4.7 million being in an unsatisfactory condition requiring repair and improvement. Altogether 11.5 per cent of the housing stock was

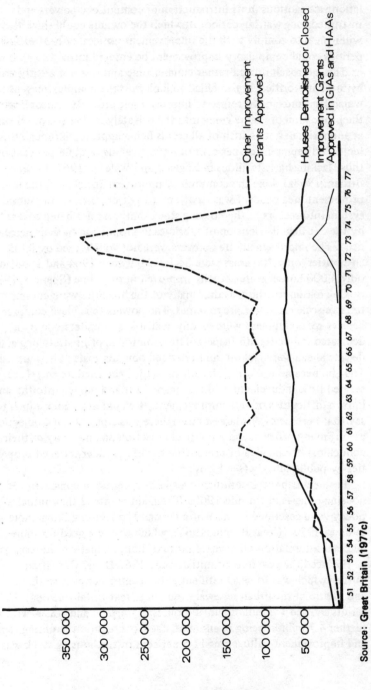

Figure 6.1: Urban Renewal Programmes in England Wales, 1950-1977

Other Improvement Grants Approved

Houses Demolished or Closed

Improvement Grants Approved in GIAs and HAAs

350 000

300 000

250 000

200 000

150 000

100 000

50 000

51 52 53 54 55 56 57 58 59 60 61 62 63 64 65 66 67 68 69 70 71 72 73 74 75 76 77

Source: **Great Britain** (1977c)

judged to be 'unfit' and a further 30 per cent unsatisfactory.

It was immediately obvious that even with Labour's much heralded, but never achieved, target of 500,000 new houses per year described in the 'Housing Programme 1965 to 1970', there could be no possibility of those in some of the poorest houses having new homes in the near future. The survey also revealed that half of the remaining unfit properties were not suitable for large-scale clearance schemes, because they were scattered and not so concentrated in the large towns as was previously thought. Thus the extent and physical distribution of bad housing was encouraging a re-consideration of the standard municipal-socialist solution of slum clearance.

At the same time, the economic crisis which precipitated the deval-uation of the pound in November 1967 made it more attractive to consider ways of improving existing older housing as that approach held out the possibility of quicker returns and lower immediate expense. A further politico-financial influence which favoured the development of an improvement-based urban renewal programme was the fact that slum clearance was moving into areas with large proportions of owner-occupied houses. The resistance to clearance was much greater in such areas because of the low compensation levels, and resistance to the idea of becoming tenants. At the same time the Labour party was beginning to look more favourably on owner-occupation and it became increasingly difficult for them to defend transference of large numbers of working-class owner-occupiers to the council housing sector.

The official explanation of the change in emphasis, as the Govern-ment announced in the White Paper of April 1968 (Great Britain, 1968b) was rather different, however:

> As a result of the very large increase in house building in the last few years it is possible to plan for a shift in the emphasis of the housing effort; the need for new house building programmes will remain for many years ahead but the balance of need between new house building and improvement is now changing so there must be a corresponding change in emphasis of the local programmes. The government intend that within a total of public investment at about the level it has now reached, a greater share should go to the improvement of old houses.

The 1969 Housing Act which followed the White Paper tried to achieve two main objectives. First, to increase the total amount of improvement work in line with the quotation above. This was to be achieved by removing restrictions on the resale of property after a grant had been given, introducing a repair element into the grant and various other modifications and liberalisations of the grant system. The second main objective was to encourage the local authorities in England and Wales to direct more effort to certain areas of their towns by declaring General Improvement Areas (GIAs). The GIAs were envisaged as quite small areas of 300-400 homes that would be given a 30-year life after improvement.

At the same time the lack of investment in privately rented property was not really tackled. No encouragement was given to compulsory improvement or purchase, but on the other hand orthodox left-wing Labour MPs would not accept any substantial increase in private rents. The resulting compromise of a slow decontrol of rents and the introduction of special controls on the standard of improvements and the level of rent increases for poorer tenants did nothing to resolve the problem.

The effect of the new legislation was in fact to achieve a dramatic rise in improvement grants from approximately 120,000 in 1969 to 450,000 in 1973 (see Figure 6.1) with a steady increase in the intervening years. To this extent the policy was successful, but the rapid rise in grants caused the government, both central and local, to look more closely at their distribution. It was still the case, for example, that the use of improvement grants within improvement areas was still a very small proportion of the total (see Figure 6.1). In addition there was the continuing low take-up among private landlords (22 per cent of all grants in England and Wales 1969-72) although they contained about one in four of the dwellings lacking an amenity in 1971 (Great Britain, 1973a, Tables 1 and 4). There was also growing evidence of the high profits that were being made from the transference of rented property into owner-occupation with the assistance of improvement grants and that this was encouraging harassment, eviction and speculation at the expense of the most poorly housed households (Counter Information Services, 1973, pp. 40-4).

By the early 1970s the policies and their publicised effects had reached a stage where the government accepted the need to reconsider the explicit social priorities on which they should be based. Thus the Conservative government's White Paper 'Better Homes: the Next Priorities', issued in June 1973, followed the increasing tendency to move away from comprehensive redevelopment to more gradual renewal. This complemented their desire to cut down on public expenditure, but again it was another aspect that was not highlighted in the official explanations of policy that it is now right to redirect the priorities and emphasis of improvement policy to ensure that help is directed more purposefully to those areas where the worst housing problems are increasingly concentrated, and to those improvements which will produce the most worthwhile results (Great Britain, 1973a, para. 17.)

The Government was encouraged in its arguments by the evidence of the 1971 House Condition Survey of England and Wales, which showed the number of unfits to have fallen from 1.8 million in 1967 to 1.2 million in 1971 (7.3 per cent of the housing stock), and the 4.7 million which in 1967 had lacked basic amenities to have been reduced to 2.9 million (16.8 per cent). These figures, along with the dramatic increases in improvement grants that were approved, encouraged the Minister to put forward that dangerous, and often disappointed, proposition of being able to clear the backlog of slums by a certain date, in this case it was to be 1982 (Great Britain, 1973a, para. 14.)

The Growth of Consensus

The principles of the Conservatives' White Paper on urban renewal policy and the means of implementation that were also suggested in it were adopted by the incoming Labour administration of 1974 without major revision. The major extension of the powers of local authorities was in areas designated by them and accepted by the Minister as 'Housing Action Areas' (HAAs). In England and Wales these areas must suffer from 'housing stress' caused by a concentration of poor housing and environmental conditions; and 'social' factors, such as the numbers of elderly people, large or single-parent families and unemployed or low-paid workers, must also be taken into account (Great Britain, 1975a). The declared improvement areas usually consist of 200-400 houses and their physical upgrading is to be achieved by a slight amendment of the previous 'carrot and stick' approach to area improvement.

The 'carrot' takes the form of various preferential grants to owners of property in these areas. There are 75 per cent improvement grants up to a certain ceiling, and in cases of means-tested hardship these can be extended up to 90 per cent of approved costs. In HAAs and GIAs you can also get grants towards the costs of repairs which are done independently of any improvements. The 'stick' on the other hand consists of various powers given to local government which are not necessarily available outside these improvement areas. They include the ability for local authorities to compulsorily improve tenanted, or even in some cases owner-occupied, dwellings. The Act also allows a local authority to enforce the repayment of grants if the house is sold or not used in the way agreed during a five-year period after the grant is paid. Some HAAs will be declared GIAs after a five-year period, in which case more stress is laid on voluntary renewal, grants are lower (60 per cent) and improvement will be such as to lead to a thirty-year life for the area. The 1974 Housing Act can be seen as one of the first major manifestations of a growing consensus over urban renewal policy between the two major national parties. The evolution of housing policy since the war has been described as 'the implementation of incrementalist policies which have zig-zagged between favouring the owner-occupier on one hand and the local authority tenant on the other' (Nevitt, 1977). This remains the case in the minds of parties at a local level and even at the national levels politicians seek to emphasise their differences (Freeson, 1977; Rossi, 1977).

Yet these arguments disguise a consensus on the need to encourage owner-occupation and other forms of voluntary and private investment in order to solve our housing problems. The Conservatives now accept that there is only a limited role for private landlords to play and that privately rented housing will be replaced with new forms of 'social' (rather than 'public') ownership such as those provided by subsidised housing associations and co-operatives (Great Britain, 1973b). The Labour government has, for its part, accepted the idea of a 'property owning democracy' and the argument that it is an innately attractive and preferable form of tenure (Great Britain 1977a, para. 7.03). It is even prepared to encourage reductions in the standards to which council housing estates are built (Great Britain, 1975b).

The bipartisan approach has been even more firmly established in the consultative Green Paper on housing policy in 1977 (Great Britain, 1977b) which will probably form the basis for all our housing policies, including urban renewal, for the next decade. Indeed, it was received from Michael Heseltine, on the Tory front bench, with the view that:

A half of it is a package which abandons the more doctrinal obsessions of the left-wing of the Labour Party, and the other half embodies the policies of the Conservative Party (Hansard, 27 June 1977.)

One of this document's main concerns is the avoidance of any great disruption in the existing system of housing finance (Great Britain, 1977a, chapter 5). Thus it rejects any fundamental reforms which would either subsidise privately rented housing at a rate comparable with the council and owner-occupied sectors, or replace it completely with various forms of 'public' or 'social' ownership. The Green Paper expects that the decline in the proportion of private renting will continue in both absolute and relative terms, from 14 per cent of the total stock in England and Wales in 1976 to 8 per cent in 1986; and that this sector should be controlled through small changes in the existing system of improvement grants, rent control and security of tenure (Great Britain, 1977a). The degree of bipartisan agreement on these issues may surprise, and even dismay, the lower party echelons on both sides; but the tendency towards an enveloping consensus is clear.

This movement towards political consensus is being encouraged by the advice received from groups of professionals and civil servants who are associated with housing and housing policy. Within these groups the concept of a 'comprehensive housing service' is increasingly promoted (Housing Services Advisory Group, 1978). This idea proposes that local authorities should ensure that a wider set of housing needs should be catered for than has been the case in the past. It does not propose that this should all be done directly by the public sector, however, but that the local authority should assume a co-ordinating, policymaking and monitoring role in relation to a variety of housing agencies in the public, quasi-public (e.g. registered housing associations) and private sector.

These arguments are being accepted in official policy documents such as Department of the Environment circulars relating to the implementation of the 1974 Act (Great Britain, 1975c). The Green Paper goes further by recommending local authorities to enter the field of community planning through the new Housing Investment Programmes (HIPs) which they are being obliged to adopt. Local authorities are being asked to co-ordinate and rationalise the disparate activities of organisations such as housing associations, home-builders, building societies and residents' organisations (Great Britain, 1977b, para. 6.08).

These ideas are presented in various 'white' and 'green' papers in government circulars and in official advisory reports. They are presented as rational modifications of past practice on the basis of experience, changing conditions and the need to use limited resources efficiently. A more dispassionate analysis of the evolution of urban renewal policy must recognise that there is a wider political and economic context which is having a crucial influence on the development of policy. We have already drawn attention to the financial constraints on public expenditure which have favoured improvement policy as against clearance policy in the development of both the 1969 and 1974 Housing Acts.

On the political side one can point to the growing consensus on certain key aspects of housing policy, e.g. the acceptance of owner-occupation as the majority tenure type and of the decline of private renting. The professional housing groups (e.g. Institute of Housing, Housing Services Advisory Group) encourage this consensus by arguing against drastic changes in policy and emphasising the need for co-ordination and planning. The rhetoric which is being used in the current urban renewal policy debate is different from that which guided thinking in the 1950s and 1960s. Rather than simply accept this as an expected aspect of progress we must judge the rhetoric and the practice against the achievements and the housing situation which they must deal with.

The Current State of Urban Renewal Policy

It is now widely appreciated that the postwar slum clearance pro-grammes were an important contributing factor to the decentralisation of population and employment from the inner parts of our conurba-tions (Hall, 1973; Jones, chapter 8 in this volume). The redevelopment which followed the clearance has created large areas of postwar inner city council estates around the central business districts. As the clear-ance programmes have now come to an end there remain large areas of pre-First World War housing, intermixed with and surrounding the inner city council estates. They have been blighted in the past by the threat of clearance, by lack of investment and by insensitive planning.

Urban renewal policy in the 1970s has recognised that the mono-lithic approach of large-scale slum clearance has frequently diminished, rather than widened, 'the choice available to people in terms of the style of houses, their form of tenure and their price' (Great Britain, 1973a, para. 15). Government circulars recognise that the existing 'housing functions' of the remaining areas of older housing need to be protected, or even promoted, by government action. It is in these areas that the legislation and the ideas surrounding the 1974 Housing Act are being implemented. It is here that the flexibility of the comprehensive area approach will be tested as the HAAs and GIAs are declared, the housing associations are zoned, the building societies asked to direct their funds and the speculative builder given plots of land to build new houses for sale.

So far the improvement areas have met with only limited success; in those GIAs declared between 1969 and 1976, 35 per cent of the dwellings needing improvement have been dealt with (Great Britain 1977b, para. 10.02). But during the period 1974-7 only 8.3 per cent of the total number of improvement grants approved were in improvement areas. At the same time it is evident that the number of houses requiring major repairs (i.e. those costing over £1,000 at 1971 prices) is increasing (from 636,000 in 1973 to 911,000 in 1976) (Great Britain, 1977b, Tech. Vol. III, Table X23) and the number of improvement grants going to the private sector (including housing associations) has fallen by 63 per cent over the years 1973-7, and this is particularly so for grants providing the basic facilities alone.

Government reaction to this situation has been twofold. First, it is proposing to make certain amendments to existing procedures in relation to grants and the powers of local authorities. Repair-only grants are likely to be made more widely available for example, and there may be changes which will speed up the time which it takes compulsory improvement powers to be approved. In addition tenants will be allowed to apply for improvement grants (Great Britain, 1977a, chapter 10). However, there has been a very low take-up of most of these special grants or powers where they have been available in the past and so it is unlikely that they will make any great difference to the rate of improvement of older inner-city property.

Second, the government is redirecting the public finance which is going into urban renewal. Figure 6.2 shows that there is a cutback in government spending on urban renewal in total (at 1977 prices), but that different aspects of public expenditure related to urban renewal are going to be affected in different ways. While there are substantial cutbacks in local authority mortgage lending, municipalisation and improvement grants to private owners, housing associations are actually being given more to spend. And as Karn explains (chapter 7 in this volume), building society finance is meant to be replacing the cutbacks in local authority mortgages.

While there is some satisfaction with this state of affairs in the voluntary housing movement (it produced 22.4 per cent of subsidised improvements to private property in England and Wales in 1977 as compared with 2.1 per cent in 1973), in reality housing associations are being used to take over some of the most difficult jobs from local authorities rather than to supplement their activity. The voluntary sector is being restricted in the standards to which it can make improvements, and allowances are not being increased at a rate commensurate with the rise in building and management costs (King, 1978). It may well be that the 'voluntary' sector, which is in fact becoming a

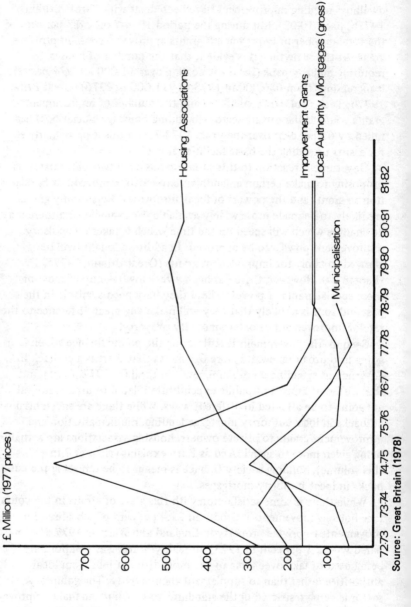

Figure 6.2: Proposed and Actual Capital Expenditure by Government (UK) on Various Aspects of Urban Renewal

£ Million (1977 prices)

Source: Great Britain (1978)

rather distant and unaccountable portion of the public sector, will be left 'holding the can' in terms of responsibility for dealing with the most acute problems in the worst housing areas in ten to twenty years' time.

What lies behind the graph in Figure 6.2 is a policy of public disinvestment in the inner city housing stock and an attempt to reduce direct government involvement in favour of the quasi-public sector of the housing associations and building societies, and increased investment by individual private households.

The Green Paper on Housing Policy completely fails to provide a rationale for this policy shift because it provides no analysis of rates of improvement against the extent of existing substandard housing and the rate of creation of more substandard housing. This is the case even though it states the objectives of urban renewal policy as being to enable 'those who live in poor quality housing to bring it up to a decent standard *as quickly as possible*' (my emphasis). The National Home Improvement Council did produce such an analysis in 1976 and their report concluded that if total new building output fell from the then current levels and if renovation rates did not rise to take up this drop then the existing state of substandard housing would not be eliminated *by the end of this century*. This is precisely what has happened since the National Home Improvement Council produced their report.

Tackling Housing Stress: The Relevance of Comprehensive Area-Based Renewal

One of the main emphases in current urban renewal programmes in the private housing sector is the one of a comprehensive area-based approach. We will, for a moment, ignore the grave limitations that are being imposed on the whole strategy due to limited public investment and political will, and consider the relevance of this type of area approach as a *technique* in its own right.

The Location and Physical Distribution of 'Housing Stress'

If a small area-based approach to urban renewal is to be appropriate then ideally it should be established that there are: (i) relatively small and (ii) distinguishable areas in which (iii) a relatively high proportion of the population suffer from 'housing stress' and that these areas contain (iv) a substantial proportion of the total number of households suffering from housing stress. Sally Holtermann, while at the Department of the Environment (Great Britain, 1975c, pp. 33-47), carried out an analysis of data from the urban enumeration district areas (mean

size of 163 households and 470 persons) used in the 1971 Census of
Great Britain. This analysis helps us to consider the above points
in relation to the distribution of 'housing stress', which is operationally
defined here as the relative deprivation of an area in terms of certain
census indicators of poor housing condition.

Holtermann compared those enumeration districts (EDs) that were
in the worst 25 per cent on any one of three indicators of poor housing
situation, while also having more than the median level of privately
rented accommodation for the whole sample of urban EDs. The three
indicators of poor housing were the lack of a bath/shower, overcrowding
(i.e. living at a density greater than 1.5 persons per room) and a lack of
the exclusive use of all basic amenities. It was found that 7.8 per cent
of the total sample of urban EDs for Great Britain were in the worst 25
per cent on all three of these indicators while also having an above-
average proportion of privately rented accommodation; this was one-
third of the number that would have resulted if these worst conditions
were always found in the same area. This does demonstrate point (ii)
above, i.e. there are distinguishable areas of housing stress.

In fact Holtermann's analysis suggests that 'housing stress' is actually
more physically concentrated than other aspects of deprivation such as
unemployment. It was also the case that EDs suffering from relatively
high housing stress tended to score high on other indicators which were
likely to be associated with other dimensions of multiple deprivation,
e.g. the 7.8 per cent of EDs mentioned above contained 31 per cent of
all people of New Commonwealth origin. This only demonstrates
that many such people live in areas with bad housing, but other studies
have suggested or demonstrated causal links between bad housing and
other aspects of deprivation (Douglas, 1964; Spencer, 1973).

The worst EDs in terms of housing stress are themselves concentrated
in certain conurbations; Inner London and Clydeside alone account for
40 per cent of those with the worst 25 per cent on the three measures
of poor housing mentioned above. This suggests that there are actually
quite sizable areas of our inner cities that would fall within such a
definition of housing stress, not just isolated and separately identifiable pockets of 300-400 houses. The Birmingham Inner Area Study
(Great Britain, 1976a, Appendix C) was particularly involved with the
Small Heath area which covered 66 EDs (excluding council estates and
redevelopment areas) and consisted of about 1,000 dwellings. When
the Census figures for the EDs were compared with those for
Holtermann's analysis of urban EDs for the whole of Great Britain, it
was discovered that 64 per cent of the Small Heath EDs came within

the worst 15 per cent nationally for the population of households suffering from overcrowding, 57 per cent within the worst 15 per cent for lack of an inside WC, and 40 per cent within the worst 15 per cent for the sharing of basic facilities.

This widespread distribution of different forms of housing stress within the inner city makes it difficult to justify drawing improvement area boundaries when differential grant rates and powers result from them (Great Britain, 1976a, p. 132). In many of our large cities then the assumption (i) above, of relatively *small* areas of housing stress cannot be made and this supports the arguments that have been made for enabling local authorities to declare much larger areas as areas of improvement potential and eligible for preferential grant levels (Great Britain, 1973c, paras. 65-7; Graham 1974).

In relation to point (iii) above, about the need to establish that a high proportion of households in the identified areas do suffer from housing stress, Holtermann's study (Great Britain, 1975c) shows that the 7.8 per cent of urban EDs with overlapping characteristics of poor housing did have large proportions of their population suffering from some elements of housing stress, i.e. 64.5 per cent lacked exclusive use of all the basic amenities, 47 per cent lacked a bath, 38 per cent lacked an inside WC, 37.5 per cent shared or lacked hot water. With respect to point (iv) above, however, the analysis also showed that these EDs contained only 22 per cent of all households lacking exclusive use of all amenities, 31 per cent of those lacking a bath, 21 per cent of those lacking an inside water closet and 25 per cent of those sharing or lacking hot water.

Thus, as with other aspects of deprivation (Donnison 1974; Townsend 1976) the *majority* of those suffering from 'housing stress' are not to be found in small geographical concentrations that are amenable to treatment by area-based deprivation strategies. This situation supports the argument for improving the procedures for directing resources to individual households in the worst housing conditions *in addition to* any area-based approach. In the case of improvement grants this could mean the introduction of means-tested 90 per cent grants for the provision of the basic amenities or higher levels of improvement rather than limiting such grants to HAAs (Great Britain 1977b, para. 10.22).

The Causes of 'Housing Stress' in the Private Sector

One further justification for a comprehensive local approach to the problems of housing stress is that its causes, or some of them, are most amenable to treatment at the local level. Certainly central government expects HAAs to concentrate 'on removing the underlying causes of housing stress in the area' (Great Britain, 1975a, para. 35). Given the physical nature of housing it is obviously true that many aspects of housing or environmental problems will require locally determined treatment, e.g. environmental improvements, of traffic problems and the redesign of the existing housing. Sensitive and imaginative local solutions will also need to be found to deal with the inevitable conflicts in opinion and objectives that will arise in any area.

When a local authority accepts the need for widespread intervention in an improvement area, and starts to introduce new social facilities such as adventure playgrounds or social club facilities for example, there are often conflicts between those who want the new facilities and those who do not. In the end the local authority has to show the wisdom of Solomon in making a decision as to what types of facilities are to be introduced, their location and as to how opposing interests can be modified. To take another example, an old-age pensioner living alone may refuse to consider even external improvements to the home that he/she lives in, an attitude which may be resented by a houseproud young couple living next door once they have been induced to spend a lot of time and money improving their own home. Such problems arise due to local circumstances specific to the area; they may well add to the 'stress' of living there and require resolution at the local or area level.

Other contributing factors to housing stress cannot be dealt with in this way, however. The author carried out a study of the impact of urban renewal policy in the private residential sector in the Cheetham Hill area of North Manchester (Mason 1977a) which suggested that one consequence of the clearance of slum housing was the encouragement of concentrations of Pakistani households in the older residential areas that were safe from clearance proposals. Like other households in the area that were faced with slum clearance they had the opportunity to move into council accommodation but they were less well-disposed to the idea of living in public housing than many British households. At the same time very few of the Pakistani households could afford to buy a second-hand suburban semi, although many of them would have liked to have done so. The result of this complex set of choices and constraints appeared to be their moving into nearby areas of pre-1920 owner-occupied housing with the help of local authority mortgages.

Although there was little overt hostility to the increasing concentration of Pakistani households in these areas it was not calculated to relieve the stresses already felt by other ethnic groups living in these areas. This was an unanticipated consequence of the local urban renewal programme, and as such was not the direct concern of the local authority at that time; indeed, it is difficult to see what the local authority could have done about it. Such consequences of local urban renewal programmes are largely determined by the context provided for them by national public policy and wider social situations such as the access that a particular group of householders has to various sources of housing finance and the attitudes they hold to particular sorts of housing.

The implications of this argument are twofold: first, it suggests that truly *comprehensive* social planning of urban renewal at the *local* level is not possible; second, the argument points to the need for local and central government to have greater control over, or effective voluntary agreements with, other major institutions in the housing system. An alternative from this latter point would be to make the urban renewal programme independent of the private financial system both at the level of the individual householder, whose housing situation was being improved, and the level of the public institutions financing the subsidy system. Such an approach would have far-reaching political as well as financial consequences, however, and is even less likely to be carried out than the effective harnessing of existing private finance.

We should also be aware of the inherent dangers of a small-area approach to deprivation in housing inhibiting any such wide-ranging analysis of the causes of housing stress. There is very often very little rigorous analysis or understanding behind the use of terms such as 'multiple' or 'urban deprivation', and the same can be said for the use of these terms as 'housing' or 'social stress' in the field of urban renewal policy (see Norris, chapter 1 in this volume). One theory that often lies behind the use of these terms is that of a 'cycle of deprivation' in which interactions between various types of deprivation which are physically concentrated in areas of bad housing produce a downward spiral or an unbreakable cycle of deprivation. Thus a Department of the Environment circular suggests that 'special categories of households' which may be concentrated in an HAA may be transferred to other areas or estates in order to ensure 'that the social stresses which lead to the declaration of the HAA would be less likely to reappear' (Great Britain 1975a, para. 42). The circular also suggests that any family ties or other close connections with the area should be respected by the 'action programme'.

We may well accept that certain types of deprivation such as physical or mental handicap may be better treated in other accommodation or other areas. Local authorities must be careful, however, not to use such advice to encourage the attribution of the cause of 'social stress' to the characteristics and personal circumstances of the inhabitants of deprived areas without reference to the condition in the wider housing 'market'. They must also be aware of the dangers of simply transferring 'problem' cases from one area or housing estate to another without actually alleviating the problems which the individuals concerned are experiencing.

Questions of Effectiveness and Efficiency

It is argued that a small-area approach to tackling urban deprivation has the potential advantage of being both more effective and more efficient in its use of human and financial resources (Holtermann, 1978). This can be argued from two points: first, the physical concentration of clients and houses will allow for easier and quicker communication between the clients themselves and with the local authority; second, it can be argued that common problems are shared or similar improvement schemes required so that the service delivery system, be it an agency service to implement improvements for owner-occupiers, or a welfare advice bureau, has a higher 'through-put' or longer 'production run' and can thus deliver the service at a cheaper unit cost. A government circular on urban renewal appeals to both these arguments:

> This area approach, integrated with other programmes designed to meet various social needs, is central to the Government's policies. It makes the best use of available resources. Residents and owners are much more likely to participate in, and to contribute to, the improvement of their homes if they are assured that their whole neighbourhood has a secure future (Great Britain, 1975c, para. 5.)

This type of reasoning ignores the fact that a concentrated local approach may actually create new demands or problems to be dealt with. The local authority may be required to reconcile different views or objectives within the area which would not otherwise have been so apparent, and its intensive impact may make for more demands for participation in decision-making by local residents than would have been the case if the urban renewal programme's resources were spread more thinly over a wider area.

Certainly HAAs are a very expensive way of implementing improvements. The Birmingham Inner Area Study estimated that HAAs as organised in that city required 13 times as many professional staff per 1,000 houses as did GIAs, and that the 1975 cost of estimated staff time per HAA house would average out at £472/year compared with £35/year for a GIA house (Great Britain, 1976b, Appendix D). It is also likely that more time will be spent on co-ordination between services and offices if a number of separate areas are declared rather than one larger one. It can be argued, of course, that the net result of all this extra work is an improved quantity or quality of service which will justify the claim to be 'the best use' of available resources; as yet, however, no rigorous or comparative cost-benefit analysis has been made (Holtermann, 1978).

We can now summarise the discussion on the relevance of the existing, officially promoted, comprehensive local approach to urban renewal in the private housing sector. The physical concentration of housing stress in the private residential areas of our cities does make the use of preferential subsidies and special powers on some sort of area basis appropriate. It can be argued, however, that the areas as at present defined are too small or that the preferential subsidies and special powers are too confined to deal with the problem (Duncan, 1974, chapter 4).

The intensive management of some small areas of housing will be necessary, and the intensive use of expensive resources including personnel worthwhile, but not necessarily as a generally applicable approach in the way currently promoted by central government. Local authorities should have more freedom to determine the size and purpose of their improvement areas. They will only be able to do that successfully if they can work within the context of a firm and comprehensive urban renewal strategy from central government which effectively co-ordinates the major national housing finance institutions. This is where the government's leadership is needed, not in making detailed guidelines for the size of local improvement areas.

The Delegation and the Dissipation of Responsibility for Urban Renewal in the Private Sector

Local authorities are being given greater responsibility for dealing with the problems of housing stress in the private sector; they have a direct responsibility through their own urban renewal programmes and an indirect responsibility through their 'local housing strategies' which the government says must go much wider than their own investment programmes (Great Britain 1977b, paras. 6.03-6.11).

The so-called 'comprehensive' involvement of local authorities in the private sector of inner city housing is increasingly a question of encouraging voluntary improvement through its provision of seed money, initiative, and a sense of confidence in the future of the areas concerned. The lack of financial backing and authoritative powers for this role results in public policy becoming dependent on co-operation and consensus between a variety of disparate organisations.

Organisations such as the registered housing associations are highly dependent on funds from local and central government and are, therefore, quite willing to fit in with the local authority's strategy. Other organisations, such as the building societies, private builders, etc., have a greater degree of financial and political independence and different sets of operating principles. They are accordingly, more difficult to tie into any comprehensive plan, as the government is finding, for example, in respect of the voluntary lending agreement with building societies (see Karn, chapter 7 in this volume). The responsibility for drawing up a comprehensive urban renewal policy is being delegated to local government, but the potential for implementing it is being dispersed among a variety of semi-public and private institutions and individuals. This corresponds with attempts to create an apolitical consensus in relation to urban renewal policy at central government level and to turn debate about it into a technical-administrative discussion.

The new comprehensive, area-based approach is, however, capable of causing internal problems in terms of administrative politics within local authorities. This is because it requires some degree of decentralisation of corporate responsibilities and is thus challenging the central tradition of local authority organisation. The requirement for inter-disciplinary area-based teams is, for example, calling into question the principle of loyalty and responsibility to a single departmental or professional head. At the same time the delegation required to effect a comprehensive area-based policy is, of course, threatening both the political and administrative hierarchies.

It is evident that these problems are now becoming problematic within the new administrative structures of area-based urban renewal teams (National Building Agency, 1977, p. 14). Internal decentralisation of local government activity to an area level can create considerable friction within the local authority structure and must be supported from the centre of the authority as studies of area management experiments have shown (Mason *et al.*, 1977b). Central government and its agents can provide advice and can disseminate experience on these questions, but that should not be its primary role.

Conclusion

Urban renewal since the Second World War, particularly in the shape of the massive slum clearance programme of the 1960s, has helped to completely reshape our cities. In the 1970s the main force of urban renewal has switched to the improvement of the existing housing stock with the emphasis on an area-based approach. There are, however, serious doubts about the effectiveness and efficiency of this strategy. The present rates of new building and renovation imply that the existing state of substandard housing will not be eliminated by the end of this century.

Part of the problem lies in the level of spatial disaggregation of the present policies, but there are also difficulties in their implementation within the present departmental structures of local authorities. Even so, copious advice from central government on the desirability of corporate management and techniques of policy analysis and planning will be no substitute for providing the resources and the direction for local housing strategies. The causes of housing stress in the private housing sector of our inner cities lie deep within the economic and social structure of our society. It is not, therefore, realistic for central government to delegate the responsibility for providing a comprehensive solution to local government. Central government must shoulder this responsibility itself; to do otherwise is to disguise a 'limited liability' approach to the relief of housing stress in the private sector under the name of a 'comprehensive housing strategy'.

References

Bowley, M. (1947) *Housing and the State*, London: George Allen and Unwin
Counter Information Services (1973) *The Recurrent Crisis of London*, London: CIS
Cullingworth, J.B. (1966) *Housing and Local Government in England and Wales*, London: George Allen and Unwin
Donnison, D. (1967) *The Government of Housing*, London: Pelican
—— (1974) 'Policies for Priority Areas', *Journal of Social Policy*, vol. 3, no. 2, pp. 127-35
Douglas, J.W.B. (1964) *The Home and the School*, London: MacGibbon and Kee
Duncan, T. (1974) *Housing Improvement Policies in England and Wales*, Centre for Urban and Regional Studies, University of Birmingham. Research Memorandum No. 28
—— and Cowan, R. (1976) *Housing Action Areas in Scotland*, Research Paper No. 3, Glasgow Planning Exchange
Freeson, R. (1977) Interview with Reg Freeson, Minister for Housing and Construction, *District Councils Review*, October

Graham, P. (1974) 'Are Action Areas a Mistake?', *Municipal and Public Services Journal*, 5 July 1974, pp. 809-11
Great Britain (1965) *The Housing Programme 1965 to 1970*, Cmnd. 2838, London: HMSO
—— (1968a) 'Housing Condition Survey, England and Wales 1967', *Economic Trends*, no. 175
—— (1968b) *Old Houses into New Homes*, Cmnd. 3602, London: HMSO
—— (1973a) *Better Homes: The Next Priorities*, Cmnd. 5339, London: HMSO
—— (1973b) *Widening the Choice: The Next Steps in Housing*, Cmnd. 5280, London, HMSO
—— (1973c) *Tenth Report from the Expenditure Committee, House Improvement Grants*, vol. I, Cmnd. 349-1, London: HMSO
—— (1975a) *Housing Act 1974: Parts IV, V, VI, Housing Action Areas, Priority Neighbourhoods, and General Improvement Areas*. Circular 14/75, Department of the Environment, London: HMSO
—— (1975b) *Housing: Needs and Action*, Circular 24/75, Department of the Environment, London: HMSO
—— (1975c) *Housing Act 1974: Renewal Strategies*, Circular 13/75, Department of the Environment, London: HMSO
—— (1976a) Department of the Environment, *Housing Policies for the Inner City*, IAS/B/11, London
—— (1976b) Department of the Environment, *The Management of Urban Renewal*, IAS/B/10, London
—— (1977a) Department of the Environment, *Housing Policy: Technical Volume Part II*, London: HMSO
—— (1977b) *Housing Policy: A Consultative Document*, Cmnd. 6851, London: HMSO
—— (1977c) *Housing and Construction Statistics*, No. 22, 2nd quarter 1977, London: HMSO
—— (1978) *The Government's Expenditure Plans, 1978-79 – 1981-82*, Cmnd. 7049, London: HMSO
Hall, Peter (1973) *The Containment of Urban England*, vols. I and II, London: George Allen and Unwin
Holtermann, Sally (1975) 'Areas of Urban Deprivation in Great Britain: An Analysis of 1971 Census Data', *Social Trends*, no. 6, pp. 33-47, London: HMSO
—— (1978) 'The Welfare Economies of Priority Area Policies', *Journal of Social Policy*, vol. 7, no. 1, pp. 23-40
Housing Services Advisory Group (1978) *Organising a Comprehensive Housing Service*, Department of the Environment: London, HMSO
King, N. (1978) Cost Limits Distortion, *Roof*, vol. 3, no. 4
Mason, Tim (1977a) *Inner City Housing and Urban Renewal Policy: A Housing Profile of Cheetham Hill, Manchester and Salford*, Research Series 23, London: Centre for Environmental Studies
——, Spencer, K., Vielba, C., Webster, B. (1977b) *Tackling Urban Deprivation : The Contribution of Area-based Management*, Institute of Local Government Studies, University of Birmingham
National Building Agency (1977) *Organisation and Staff Resources for Area Improvement*, London: NBA
National Home Improvement Council (1976) *Improvement in United Kingdom Housing – A Reappraisal*, London: NHIC
Nevitt, A.A. (1966) *Housing, Taxation and Subsidies*, London: Nelson
—— (1977) 'Housing in a Welfare State', *Urban Studies*, vol. 14, pp. 33-40

Rossi, H. (1977) 'A Policy for Housing', *District Councils Review*, October
Spencer, K. (1970) 'Older Urban Areas and Housing Improvement Policies',
   Town Planning Review, vol. 41, no. 3, pp. 250-62
—— (1973) 'Housing and Socially Deprived Families', in Holman, R.,
   Lafitte, F., Spencer, K. and Wilson, H., *Socially Deprived Families in Britain*,
   London: Bedford Square Press
Townsend, P. (1976) 'Area Deprivation Policies', *New Statesman*, pp. 169-71,
   6 August

7 LOW INCOME OWNER-OCCUPATION IN THE INNER CITY

Valerie A. Karn

The present government is committed both to the development of the inner city and the growth of home ownership. One would therefore have expected that policies to help low income owner-occupiers would have formed a very important part of government housing strategy in inner areas. Ironically, however, low income owner-occupiers and would-be buyers in the inner city consistently fail to benefit from government policies on housing finance.

This chapter attempts to document this by showing how little financial help low income owner-occupiers receive. And by taking three areas of inner Birmingham and a comparable area in Sandwell we show the impact of the present urban renewal policies on inner area buyers. The argument is not that owner-occupation is the right solution for low income families, nor that just a more equitable version of the subsidy system is appropriate. Rather the intention is to show how great an inconsistency there is between the government's stated intentions and the likely outcome of present policies. As a result, there is likely to be a fundamental conflict between the interests of owner occupiers as they see them and the implementation of current urban renewal policies, notably compulsory improvement.

Historical Development

The Growth of Owner-Occupation in the Inner City

With the encouragement of governments of both parties, owner-occupation has grown rapidly in the last thirty years. In 1947 owner-occupied houses made up only just over a quarter of all dwellings in England Wales but had grown to 43 per cent by 1960 and to 55 per cent by 1975. This growth in owner-occupation nationally has been almost exactly paralleled by growth in owner-occupation of the pre-1914 housing stock. By 1975, 58 per cent of pre-1914 houses were owner-occupied.

Of course only a proportion of this stock of pre-1914 houses was situated in the inner areas of cities, but there too the same tenure shift was in evidence; by the mid-1970s, in most inner city areas other than

in London, more than 50 per cent of the houses were owner-occupied.
In the three inner areas of Birmingham which are to be examined in
detail in this chapter the proportions were 49 per cent, 53 per cent and
57 per cent in 1971 and have risen since then. Likewise in a similar
area of Sandwell round Beeches Road, 67 per cent of households were
owner-occupiers in 1975 (Niner *et al.*, 1975, p. 16).

Table 7.1: The Stock of Pre-1914 Owner-Occupied Houses, England
and Wales, 1914-1975

	1914	1938	1960	1971	1975
Size of total pre-1914 housing stock (millions)	7.9	7.6	7.0	6.1	5.9
Size of pre-1914 owner-occupied housing stock (millions)	0.8	1.9	2.9	3.3	3.4
Pre-1914 owner-occupied stock as % of total pre-1914 stock	10	25	41	54	58
Owner-occupied stock as % of all stock	10	32	43	53	55

Source: Great Britain (1977a, p. 38, Table 1.23).

The shift towards owner-occupation in inner cities differed in character from the changes taking place in the suburbs, in that the increased
percentage of owner occupation was brought about, obviously, not by
new building, but by the demolition of the worst and oldest privately
rented property and by the sale of better privately rented housing
either to sitting tenants or to other owner-occupiers. In all, between
1914 and 1975 about 3.7 million dwellings were transferred from
private renting to owner occupation. This process had begun in the
interwar period but speeded up during the Second World War and after.
A survey by Woolf (1967) showed that in 1964 about 11 per cent of all
owner-occupiers had bought their houses as sitting tenants. The proportions
in inner areas would have been much higher.

Demolition affected owner-occupied pre-1914 houses much less
than it affected privately rented houses. Of the 1.8 million pre-1914
houses demolished between 1914 and 1975, only 300,000 (17 per cent)
were owner-occupied (Great Britain, 1977a, pp. 38-9).

Table 7.2: The Rate of Sales of Privately Rented Property into Owner-Occupation, England and Wales 1914-1975

	Sales to owner-occupiers (millions)	Sales to local authorities (millions)	Sales in each period as percentage of privately rented housing stock in :			
1914-38	1.1	—	1914	15	1938	17
1938-60	1.5	0.2	1938	23	1960	33
1960-75	1.1	—	1960	24	1975	38

Source: Great Britain (1977a, p. 38 and p. 39, Tables 1.23 and 1.24).

The Housing Stock

Owner-occupied property in the inner cities of England derives much of its distinctive character from its origins as privately rented housing built in the nineteenth century for the housing of working men and their families. The cheaper housing was usually owned in substantial blocks by large landlords. Some of the better housing was built in groups of three or four houses, one of which would often be occupied by the landlord.

This nineteenth-century terraced housing typically suffers from a number of defects. First, the original layout of the property and streets is obsolete. Densities are very high; there is little open space and there is often unattractive industrial property in the area. Where the front doors of the houses open straight on to the street, which is almost invariably the case in Manchester and fairly common in Birmingham, the streets are treeless, and hedgeless. The drab appearance is only relieved by the occupiers' efforts to brighten up doors and windows with paint.

Entry to the house itself is either into the front room or down a long, high, narrow passage. Entry to the back is usually via a tunnel shared between several houses, hence the name 'tunnel back'. The ground-floor room at the back is darkened by being in the shadow of a one- or two-storey projection, originally housing a scullery, outside toilet and sometimes a bedroom, but in improved houses a bathroom and kitchen. These projections create enormous problems for improvement because having a very high ratio of surface area to internal space, they are very difficult to heat and suffer acutely from condensation.

After the public health regulations outlawed the back-to-backs these tunnel-back houses were brought in by builders to sustain high-density building. Reaction against the 'tunnel back' ultimately came from the

Bournville Village Trust and the other model village planners who designed houses in the 'cottage style', built over a square, without back-projections (Bournville Village Trust, 1955, p. 39). The fact that this design was taken up by the Tudor Walters Committee, in their recommendations for the design of housing after the First World War, rendered the 'tunnel back' obsolete for new home design from that time (Great Britain, 1918).

Apart from these problems of the original design, the houses have experienced neglect and blight. In general the longer the houses were owned by private landlords, the more deterioration they suffered, as a result of landlords' neglect of maintenance and repairs. This had a polarising effect on the quality of property, since houses in the better streets tended to move into owner-occupation first. The worst older houses in Birmingham particularly the back-to-backs and courtyard houses, mostly continued to be rented until they were demolished in slum clearance programmes. They either stayed in the possession of private landlords or, as in Birmingham, were bought by the local authority well in advance of demolition. However, as slum clearance worked its way outwards into areas of better terraced housing built in the latter part of the nineteenth century, it became the common experience of local authorities that they found an increasing proportion of the residents were owner-occupiers. These owners resisted slum clearance.

This resistance, though only one of the factors that led to the end of a major slum clearance programme and the substitution of an improvement programme, was very crucial in determining just where the bulldozers stopped. For instance it was the owner-occupiers of George Arthur Road, Saltley in Birmingham whose campaign was instrumental in getting their road reclassified as a Housing Action Area rather than a redevelopment area. Though the houses in such areas were retained, those near the boundary where the bulldozers stopped had long been blighted by uncertainty about their future and by the sheer physical disruption caused by the proximity of vacant property, vandalism and demolition. So quite apart from the fact that their original quality was perhaps the lowest in the remaining housing stock, the houses had deteriorated badly in recent years.

All the houses, the best and the worst, however, suffered in the postwar period from the policy of concentrating on slum clearance to the exclusion of any sizable public expenditure on improvement. Improvement by private owners was almost invariably by owner-occupiers and was at the top end of the older housing stock. Landlords did few improvements or even repairs. Even the owner-occupiers, particularly the lower income buyers of the cheapest property, often only did basic or emergency repairs. Improvements were often very modest, put in outside the formal grant system which usually required them to do more work all at once than they felt able to afford.

General Improvement Areas designated under the Housing Act 1969 did little to change this pattern, for they were specifically designed for the better areas. So at the start of the new 'urban renewal policies' under the Housing Act 1974, the property was in a poor state. There was, however, a marked difference between streets at the bottom of the market where private landlords were still important, and which had often been through a period of uncertainty about slum clearance, and the areas of more substantial houses, usually referred to by estate agents as 'villa type' properties, in which the majority of houses were owner-occupied, and where many were improved properties and only the occasional badly neglected property marked the presence of a privately rented house.

The Inner City Housing Market

The Study Areas

The studies reported here were based on three inner areas of Birmingham — Saltley, Soho and Sparkhill and one area of Sandwell, Beeches Road. The interviews in Birmingham were carried out in the winter of 1974-75 and those in Sandwell in the autumn of 1973. The sample in Sandwell was 1 in 2 of all households in the area. The sample in Saltley was 1 in 3 of all people who bought their houses between 1 January 1972 and 1 January 1975. In Soho and Sparkhill the samples were 1 in 2 of such buyers. In addition, in Birmingham, an analysis was undertaken, from the local authority's records, of all council mortgage lending in those areas between 1960 and 1975.

The Beeches Road Area study was commissioned by the local authority (then West Bromwich MB) when it was in doubt as to whether the houses should be demolished or improved. Part of it, like parts of the other three areas, has subsequently been declared a Housing Action Area. The three areas in Birmingham were studied as part of an SSRC sponsored project, entitled The Operation of the Housing Market in Immigrant Areas, and were chosen to be comparable with each other in terms of housing, but having different racial characteristics. In the event it proved impossible to find any white area with housing as poor as that in the West Indian and Asian areas of Soho and Saltley. It was

therefore necessary to include the property in the southern end of
Sparkhill which was rather better than any in either Saltley or Soho.

The standard of basic internal amenities in the houses sold in
Sparkhill was higher than in those sold in the other two Birmingham
areas. In Sparkhill, 87 per cent had an inside WC and fixed bath. In
Soho 80 per cent had these amenities, whilst in Saltley only 75 per cent
had any inside WC and only 71 per cent a fixed bath. However, in
Saltley some of the houses had central heating already installed (9 per
cent). In fact in all four areas there was, within the nineteenth-century
stock of terraced houses, a considerable variety of quality of housing
in terms of both amenities and size. This variety of stock was paralleled
by quite a wide range of prices paid for houses between 1972 and
1974, anything between £1,000 and £6,000 or £7,000, though half
cost between £2,000 and £4,000.

The survey shows that despite Sparkhill having historically the
better quality housing of the three areas, it was there that most
improvements had been done since the owners bought their houses.
This is in line with the usual finding about improvement that it takes
place not where it is most needed but where the stock is already better
and the market more buoyant. In addition the majority of improvements, even the installation of a bath, were carried out without grants.

Social Characteristics of Home Purchasers

Owner-occupiers even within a single area such as Beeches Road in
Sandwell or Saltley in Birmingham are far from being a homogeneous
group. Their characteristics reflect the changing socioeconomic and
racial character of these areas and the different family types prevailing
amongst the various ethnic groups involved. There is first the scatter of
elderly or middle-aged white owner-occupiers who bought their houses
twenty or more years ago. For instance in Beeches Road a fifth of the
owner-occupiers had been living in their house twenty years or more
(Niner *et al.*, 1975, p. 79). Some of them bought their houses as sitting
tenants. Most were couples or widows living alone. Though many of
them expressed dissatisfaction with the changes taking place in the area,
the majority tended not to want to uproot and move at this stage
(Niner *et al.*, 1975, p. 54).

This group merges into that of middle-aged white couples, or in some
cases long-standing West Indian buyers, whose children are either still
at school, or are grown up but still living at home (and are therefore
categorised in Table 7.3 as large adult households.) Then there are the
newest arrivals, a mixture of small and large families and households of

adults. These are not families which have grown up in the area and are usually West Indian or, increasingly, Indian and Pakistani. Over the years this group begins to resemble the last, except that it produces large rather than small families and is Asian and West Indian rather than British and West Indian.

Table 7.3: Household Type of Existing Buyers in Beeches Road, Sandwell and New Buyers in Three Inner Areas of Birmingham

Household type	Existing buyers in Beeches Road 1973	New buyers in Saltley, Soho and Sparkhill 1972-4
	193	396*
	%	%
One person or two people under retirement age of same sex	7	7
One person or two people under retirement age of different sex		9
Small family	11	21
Large family	43	50
Large adult household	21	12
Small elderly household	19	2

* weighted sample: the sampling fractions in the three Birmingham areas were 1/3 in Saltley and 1/2 for Soho and Sparkhill. When the three areas are aggregated, the Saltley sample is weighted to the equivalent of a 1/2 sample before it is added in.

Table 7.4: Birthplace of Existing Buyers in Beeches Road, Sandwell and New Buyers in Three Inner Areas of Birmingham

Birthplace	Beeches Rd	Saltley	Soho	Sparkhill	All Birmingham Areas
	193	119	104	102	396*
	%	%	%	%	%
British Isles	36	23	13	53	29
West Indies	26	2	14	2	5
India, Pakistan and Bangladesh	33	73	69	37	63
Elsewhere	4	2	4	9	5

* Weighted sample.

It is clear then that when discussing inner city owner-occupiers, there are some major distinctions to be made between the long-standing owner-occupiers in the area, particularly elderly white people, the families who followed them into the area and finally the families who are currently buying houses there. In particular, it was found in the surveys in Birmingham, which were solely of new buyers, that, even in an area with a large proportion of West Indians like Soho, or a British and Irish area like Sparkhill, a growing proportion of buyers were Asian. In all 63 per cent of the buyers in the three Birmingham areas were Asian. Soho and Beeches Road are in many respects very alike and a comparison in Table 7.4 of existing buyers in Sandwell in 1972 with new buyers in Soho between 1972 and 1974 brings out the changing characteristics of buyers there.

These changes in the characteristics of buyers in the area do not, however, mean that individual families are 'transient'. On the contrary, in the Beeches Road Area, 78 per cent of the West Indians had lived in their house more than five years and 30 per cent more than ten years. Even of the Indians and Pakistanis, who had arrived much more recently, 49 per cent had lived in their house more than five years and 18 per cent more than ten years. So the change taking place was not one through which the area became one of transient population. Rather one stable population was being replaced by another stable population.

In interviews many white buyers say they are rejecting housing in these areas as obsolete. However they also dislike the arrival of West Indian and Asian buyers. The two factors are difficult to disentangle because Asians in particular are most heavily concentrated in the worst housing and therefore any tendency of whites not to buy into these streets cannot be attributed entirely to their attitudes to racial mix. That there is such a tendency is shown up strikingly in Table 7.5 in which the birthplace of buyers is analysed according to the proportion of Asians in the population of each Census enumeration district in Saltley, Soho and Sparkhill at the time of the 1971 Census. Thus only 10 per cent of British and Irish buyers bought houses in enumeration districts where the proportion of Asians in 1971 was 20 per cent of more; however, 42 per cent of Asians bought there. Or to put it round the other way, one can see, from the bottom half of the table, that whereas the British made up 28 per cent of all buyers, they constituted less than 10 per cent of buyers in areas where Asians made up 20 per cent or more of the population, but 35 per cent of buyers in areas where less than 5 per cent were Asian. The process clearly snowballs.

The result is that a large and growing percentage of the owner-occupiers who experience the credit difficulties and other financial problems described later in this chapter and in Karn (1978) are Asian.

Asians are most concentrated in the poorest housing, with the greatest repairs problems, the greatest difficulty in attracting mortgages and the greatest likelihood of being required to undertake compulsory improvements under Housing Action Area legislation.

Table 7.5: Distribution of Buyers 1972-4 by Ethnic Character of the Area in 1971

	Birthplace of buyers 1972-4			
	British and Irish	Indian, Pakistani and Bangladeshi	West Indian	All
Census enumeration districts with the following % of their 1971 population Asian				
	110*	240*	19*	387*
	%	%	%	%
0– 4.9	26	6	(5)	13
5– 9.9	19	10	(–)	12
10–14.9	24	14	(21)	17
15–19.9	22	29	(16)	26
20–24.9	4	13	(32)	11
25–29.9	2	12	(16)	9
30–34.9	2	6	(–)	4
35+	2	11	(11)	8
All	100	100	100	100
0– 4.9	% 58	30	2	100†
5– 9.9	% 45	49	–	100
10–14.9	% 39	52	6	100
15–19.9	% 24	68	3	100
20–24.9	% 10	73	155	100
25–29.9	% 6	82	9	100
30–34.9	% 13	88	–	100
35+	% 7	87	3	100
All	% 28	62	5	100

*Weighted sample.
† The figures do not add up to 100 because nationalities other than British, Irish, Asian and West Indian are omitted.
Source: Great Britain (1971).

Jobs, Incomes, Earners and House Prices

We have consistently referred to the buyers in inner areas with whom we are concerned as 'low income' buyers in order to distinguish them from buyers in 'gentrified' areas of the inner city (notably in London, for the phenomenon scarcely exists in Birmingham except in the surburban 'villages' of Harborne, Moseley and Kings Heath). The buyers in Beeches Road, Saltley, Sparkhill and Soho were predominantly working class. Only 5 per cent of buyers in the Birmingham areas were of professional or managerial status and only a further 6 per cent non-manual workers. Half were unskilled and semi-skilled.

Current income levels are clearly much lower for long-standing, particularly elderly, owners than for recent buyers as Table 7.6 shows. Although in the main these owners no longer have large mortgage repayments to meet, their low incomes are still of significance not just in terms of their own comfort and peace of mind but also in terms of their ability to do essential repairs and maintenance and now, their ability to do improvements and repairs within the period stipulated for Housing Action Areas. Thus the fact that one-third of all buyers in the Beeches Road Area had incomes of £25 a week or less in 1973 meant that the chances were small of much improvement taking place when it was declared a Housing Action Area.

The income levels of heads of household who bought in Saltley, Soho and Sparkhill between 1972 and 1974 were certainly lower than those of other buyers in the West Midlands at the same time. Their average income was £35 per week in 1974, while the average weekly incomes of people who obtained building society mortgages in the West Midlands in 1972, 1973 and 1974 were £42, £51 and £61 respectively (Great Britain, 1976, Table 39). It is difficult precisely to compare the two sets of income figures, because the Birmingham figures are for heads of households after tax income while the figures published for building society borrowers are for the income taken into account for the mortgage, a figure which might include all or part of the wife's income. However, because of the predominance of Asians amongst the Birmingham inner city buyers, few wives were working and so there would have been rather small additional earnings which the building society would have taken into account.

Nevertheless, while Asian wives were not often working this does not mean that Asian households were dependent on one income. In fact because of the characteristics of households, mentioned earlier, with teenage children and other male relatives often present, many households, and particularly the Asian ones, had not just one additional earner but several, as Table 7.7 indicates. The presence of additional earners in the household has an effect on the mortgage-paying capacity of Asian households which is not recognised within the formal guidelines laid down by building societies and local authorities about the desirable ratio of income to repayments. Normally only wives' incomes are taken into account.

The presence of additional earners in a household does not always mean that money is automatically available to help with house purchase. Young people may themselves be saving for their own house and may only contribute to the household the cost of their food and laundry. Asians, however, not uncommonly enter into a formal agreement between two or more men to buy the house jointly. The most common arrangement is between a father and son or between brothers or cousins. In the Birmingham areas 18 per cent of Pakistani and 8 per cent of Indian buyers were joint owners with male relatives or friends. Only 3 per cent of Pakistanis and 9 per cent of Indians were joint owners with their wives, in marked contrast to the British and West Indians, only one of whom owned jointly with another man and nearly half of whom were owners jointly with their wives. Given the number of Asian households in which there are additional male earners and the very few in which wives work, joint ownership with male relatives or friends has been a logical way to achieve better housing conditions with modest incomes. Neither the building societies nor the local authorities, however, favour this type of arrangement and will only rarely grant requests for such mortgages; though Nationwide has recently (1978) changed its policy and will, in theory, now lend to any two joint owners.

Table 7.6: Incomes of Heads of Household: Existing Owners in Beeches Road and Recent Buyers in Saltley, Soho and Sparkhill

	Existing owner-occupiers Beeches Road, Sandwell	Soho and Sparkhill buyers 1972-4
	Net Income in 1973	Net Income in Dec 1974
	172	367
	%	%
Up to £10 per week	8	
£10.01–£15.00	7	5
£15.01–£20.00	5	
£20.01–£25.00	13	5
£25.01–£30.00	19	15
£30.01–£35.00	33	24
£35.01–£40.00	14	21
£40.01–£45.00		13
£45.01+		15

Table 7.7: Numbers of Full-time Earners by Birthplace: Saltley, Soho and Sparkhill

	Indian	Pakistani	W. Indian	Irish	British	All
Sample No.	93	155	18	26	85	396
No. of full-time earners	%	%	%	%	%	%
None	2	7	(-)	(10)	8	6
1	39	37	(40)	(49)	52	42
2	39	32	(45)	(33)	34	35
3	14	14	(10)	(4)	4	11
4 or 5	6	10	(5)	(4)	2	7

Motives for Buying

Given the existence of local authority housing why do low-income people buy houses?

First, it should be said that there are strong financial incentives to become an owner-occupier in which the low income earner shares, though not to the same extent as the high income earner. The first is that there is no capital gains tax on the sale of an owner-occupied house. People's experience has been that house prices, even in the inner cities, rise, and so owner-occupation is seen as the accumulation of a tax-free capital asset. In surveys about preference for owning or renting, owners usually talk about rent being 'money down the drain' or 'you've nothing to show for it'. The Asian buyers, particularly the Pakistanis, carry this to its logical conclusion by attempting to pay off loans as fast as possible so that they own the house outright. If you receive little or no tax relief this is clearly a logical thing to do, as long as the rate of interest on a loan is more than the rate of inflation.

Secondly, owners are no longer taxed on the value of occupying their house. An owner, by investing £5,000 in a house, therefore receives an untaxed real income, on that investment, of the value of occupying the house minus his mortgage interest payments. Again inflation of house prices and of rents in the private and public sectors makes owner-occupiers more and more aware of the value of this to them, although scarcely any would perceive the benefit as anything to do with the tax system. Again paying off the mortgage early makes the asset more apparent.

Third, and linked to the previous points is the fact that owners pay historic costs for their housing. The faster incomes and house prices are inflating, the more an owner sees the difference between paying

interest on a loan, which is shrinking all the time in real terms, and
paying a local authority rent, which will, despite rent pooling, tend to
rise in a period of inflation, because of rising management and building
costs. Thus, low income owners have financial incentives to buy rather
than rent, though, as we will see later, these incentives are less than for
high income owners.

There are also a number of other non-financial incentives in the
decision to buy rather than rent. The degree to which these are emphasised by commentators on the inner city housing market depends very
much on the attitudes of those commentators towards low income
owner-occupation or even to owner-occupation itself. Some imagine
that the reason is purely negative, namely lack of access to any other
form of housing, because of the eligibility rules of local authorities
and the decline in supply of private rented housing. At the other
extreme, it is argued that the sole reason is the desire for owner-
occupation, overriding all questions of housing quality.

To polarise the argument in this way is in itself a distortion. People
arc neither totally free to choose to rent or buy, nor are they totally
prevented from exercising any choice, especially if they are willing to
accept relatively poor quality housing and/or to set aside very large
proportions of their income for buying. In the inner city housing
market, the fact that individual families can adopt different strategies
for getting into the market for self-contained housing does not alter
the fact that the range of strategies they *can* adopt is extremely limited.
While it is of interest that one type of strategy, such as joint ownership,
is more common amongst Pakistanis than other groups, and that this
fact has social consequences, it is still more important to understand, in
general terms, why such strategies should be necessary than to try to
weigh up exactly why one family rather than another has adopted it.

The crucial point is that these buyers have been seeking housing in
the inner cities at a time when the housing there has been changing
rapidly from renting to owner-occupation. Far from being able to swim
against this tide, they have been highly vulnerable to the type of pressure which has produced the switch to owning. To most of these people
buying has seemed the only means by which they can obtain self-contained accommodation relatively quickly within the inner city.

The obvious question is why owner-occupation rather than a council
tenancy? The buyers would reply that they had no choice as they
needed immediate relief from shared accommodation, not in three or
four or five years' time when they reached the top of the waiting list
(see English, chapter 5 in this volume). Some had looked for private

unfurnished rented property but could find nothing of a size and rent that was suitable. Most just did not see renting as an alternative. They wanted to feel that the house was theirs, in terms of the people they chose to have with them to occupy it, what they could do there and their security of tenure. Their unhappy experiences of private renting had made them determined not to have the interference of a landlord, whether a private landlord or a public authority.

To understand these attitudes, one has to know a little more about the people who buy houses in the inner city. First inner areas cater for a disproportionately large number of first-time buyers. In the three Birmingham areas, 76 per cent of all buyers between 1972 and 1974 were buying a house on their own for the first time. Nationally the comparable figure for buyers in each year would be about 40 per cent.

The stereotype of the first-time buyer, as for instance noted by Ineichen (1974), is the newly-married, childless couple, usually a two-earner household with relatively small savings but a respectable joint weekly income. This stereotype does not apply well to inner area first-time buyers, particularly in the cities in which a large proportion of the buyers are immigrants from Asia or the West Indies. For instance, in the three Birmingham inner areas surveyed, newlyweds constituted only 5 per cent of the total buyers and childless couples 9 per cent. The British and Irish groups had the largest number, but even then less than one-fifth were newlyweds and less than a quarter childless couples. Of all the households, 71 per cent were families with children, while 82 per cent were either families with children or large households with a mixture of children, teenagers and adults. On average there were five people in each house; 40 per cent had six or more.

Most important for their attitudes later, the overwhelming proportion of first-time buyers (75 per cent) had been previously living in rented furnished accommodation of one sort or another, usually rooms rather than self-contained flats. Adding on the proportion who were living with their parents, the figure comes to 86 per cent in furnished accommodation. The rest had been either council tenants (5 per cent) or had been in unfurnished privately rented property (5 per cent). These few were the only first-time buyers who were living in property which might be considered in any way suitable for a family. Experiences with private rented accommodation had not been happy. The delicate relationships between landlord and tenant, and tenant and tenant, had not been helped by the age and poor condition of the property, its lack of amenities and general overcrowding. People with children had found it hard to get anything suitable at all that they could afford. Before they

finally settled into their own houses, many people had long histories of
moves from one set of rented rooms to another.

We are therefore talking about families whose need of self-contained,
family accommodation was immediate and urgent and for whom a long
wait on a housing waiting list was inappropriate. In addition the nature
of the allocation system for council houses discouraged Asians in
particular from applying. Someone who goes on the council waiting list
can state their preference for living in a certain area but their likelihood
of obtaining a house in that particular area, let alone in a particular
street, is not good. A recent study of Birmingham's allocation process
has showed that only 50 per cent of families housed in 1976 obtained
the area for which they asked (Centre for Urban and Regional Studies,
1978). This means that Asians in particular feel very insecure about
obtaining housing in this way, since they stress so much the importance
of close proximity to the extended family, to friends, to Indian shops
and to opportunities for religious education.

To sum up motivations then, there was an intense urgency in the
housing situation of most buyers; renting was not an acceptable alternative which would give quick access to self-contained accommodation
at a reasonable cost. Private renting meant furnished rooms, local
authority housing meant a long wait and little choice of location. Despite the fact that most preferred to buy, to say these people 'chose'
to buy rather than rent ignores both the time they would wait for council housing and the non-availability of low-cost, self-contained, private
rented accommodation suitable for a family. The fact that these
families are so severely curtailed in their choices means that they will
buy at any cost and this leaves them wide open to exploitation.

It is not to be assumed that many of the owners, even those for
whom it was the greatest struggle financially, would have preferred to
rent; only 15 per cent said they regretted buying or had mixed
feelings. Insecure though they might appear, especially in the first few
years, they felt that owner-occupation fulfilled certain purposes. In
particular it offered relative security in terms of freedom of behaviour
in their own home, the ability to choose a house near relatives and
friends, having a cashable asset and, for those who had paid off short-
term loans, a house of 'their own' with no outstanding debt. Last, and
not least, for Asians in particular, it was felt to be a mark of status and
an achievement to report back to relatives in their home country.

While these advantages outweighed the problems they had
experienced at that time, it is still true that many of these owners were

under considerable financial strain, and this was when the level of unemployment had only just started to rise. In the next section we will
consider what impact government policy was having, and has subsequently had, upon these owners in helping them to overcome the
financial problems of low income ownership.

The Impact of Government Policies on Inner City Buyers

Despite the massive change in tenure in inner cities, the arrival of new
types of owner-occupiers in these areas and a shift of policy from
demolition to improvement, the government has not in the meantime
adapted its policies on housing finance to take the changed situation
into account. Nor has it made sure that other agencies of housing
policy, such as building societies and local authorities, are doing so.

With the demise of private renting, it has become increasingly clear
how completely the British housing system has become polarised into
two quite distinct sectors, governed by two totally different philoso-
phies. Local authority housing has been provided as a reflection of a
philosophy which stresses need rather than ability to pay. It broadly
represents the approach which sees housing as a social service. Owner-
occupation, on the other hand, represents the opposite approach, that
housing provision is best stimulated by market demand and the operation of consumer choice. The organisation and financing of each sector
reflects these differences in philosophy; local authority tenants obtain
their houses by putting their name on a housing register, competing
with other applicants on the basis of greatest housing need. Owner-
occupiers obtain their houses by borrowing money and then compete
with other buyers on the basis of their ability to pay the price of a
house.

In these two systems the low income owner-occupier occupies an
anomalous position. Having a low income, he fails to benefit fully
from the incentives to owners and not being a council tenant he fails
to benefit from subsidies available to tenants. Let us now examine
closely, with the aid of the material derived from the surveys in the
three inner areas of Birmingham, the impact of this failure of government to adapt policies and practices to the needs of lower income
buyers.

Housing Finance

The financing of house purchase in this country is largely based on
building society lending. Nationally, in 1972-4, 85 per cent of buyers
who took out loans from institutions had them from building societies

and insurance companies. A further 9 per cent received them from local authorities, making 94 per cent in all from these conventional sources (Great Britain, 1975a, Table 35.) In Saltley, Soho and Sparkhill the contrast is remarkable. There conventional mortgage lending in the same period, 1972-4, covered only 27 per cent of all buyers, 34 per cent of those with formal loans, virtually all from institutions. The other buyers with formal loans obtained them from banks, finance companies, vendors or solicitors. Some had informal loans from friends or relatives.

It is worth remembering that the survey period was one in which building societies had so much money that they scarcely knew what to do with it. If ever there were a time when they could have been expected to come down-market, this was it. But in fact, even when they did lend in these areas, building societies neglected the areas of cheapest housing. One third of building society mortgages in these areas, and even more of building society *funds*, were lent on houses which sold for £5,000 or more, though these houses constituted only 12 per cent of the total. In all, in 1972-4, building societies lent about £386,000 in the three areas, which together with £234,000 from the local authority, makes up a total of £620,000 in conventional loans, or about 25 per cent of the total price of houses bought, £2.52 million.

Table 7.8: Main Source of Finance for House Purchase 1972-4

	Buyers with formal loans				All Buyers
	Saltley	Soho	Sparkhill	All Areas	All Areas
Sample number	93	75	87	310*	396*
	%	%	%	%	%
Main Source of Finance					
Local authority	10	26	14	15	12
Building soc/Ins. co.	9	13	43	19	15
Bank	63	46	30	50	39
Fringe bank/Finance co.	16	12	10	14	11
Vendor, solicitor	2	2	2	2	2
Friend, relative					3
Cash					18

*weighted sample.

Even the loans buyers did obtain, especially those from banks and finance companies, often covered a relatively small proportion of the purchase price. For instance while 65 per cent of local authority and 60 per cent of building society mortgages covered 80 per cent or more of the purchase price, only 15 per cent of bank loans and 34 per cent of loans from finance companies did. The effect of these low percentage loans was that more than half the people who had loans covering less than 50 per cent of the price had to raise more than £1,500. Forty-one per cent of all buyers had to raise over £1,000. For many it was impossible to find enough cash to cover the down-payment so that they had to raise another loan. In all 28 per cent of the buyers were forced to take out one or more additional loans for the purchase of the house. The majority of second loans for purchase were informal ones from friends or relatives. These loans were quite apart from subsequent loans for repairs or improvements, or, even in some cases, to pay off arrears accumulated on the first mortgage.

From this very different pattern of financing for house purchase stems a whole series of financial consequences, all against the interests of low income buyers. These can be divided into, first, the terms of the mortgage and, second, the loss of subsidy. At the time of the survey the interest rates being charged on the various sorts of loans were as follows: Birmingham City 11 per cent, building societies 11 per cent, clearing banks 16 per cent and finance companies and fringe banks 24 per cent. The high interest rates of the banks and finance companies were, in addition, coupled with short loan periods. No bank loans were for more than ten years and loans from finance companies were only slightly longer.

The result of the combination of high interest rates and very short-term loans from banks and finance companies meant that monthly mortgage repayments were very high. For instance, over half those with finance company loans paid more than £50 a month, compared with 20 per cent of those with bank loans, 14 per cent of those with building society mortgages, and none with local authority mortgages. This was in spite of the fact that the actual amounts borrowed from banks and finance companies were smaller than those from building societies and the local authority. Indeed while finance companies lent only 14 per cent of all loans, they received 23 per cent of the interest payments in the first year.

The only advantages that these short-term loans have for buyers are first that the loan is available at all, second, that if one manages to meet the repayments they are soon completely paid off and, third, that there are not normally any requirements to do repairs. However, other conditions, such as penalty clauses imposed against early repayment of the loan, fall hard on those who take out loans from finance houses. Moreover finance companies are more likely than building societies or local authorities to repossess a house when the buyer falls into arrears.

The problems of inner cities then are very much those of lack of investment by the major public and private institutions. The mortgage situation illustrates this well. The low income person buying a house risks all his savings and commits his income to repay a loan on property whose future is made much more questionable by the unwillingness of building societies to risk lending in these areas, and by the dearth of local authority lending. Even when they do lend the local authorities, and even more so the building societies, tend to lend on the more improved properties. In the case of the local authority, this is partly because the cost of the repairs that it requires on poorer property cannot be met by potential buyers so they withdraw their applications.

Others knowing of this problem go straight to a bank which imposes no conditions of this sort. While the banks and finance companies were, at that time, more likely to give some sort of loan, they too reduced their own risks of financial loss by granting only low-percentage, short-term loans at high interest rates. This increased the risk to the owner by making his outgoings greater, both on that loan and possibly on an extra one to meet the down payment.

Government Responses to the Inner City Mortgage Situation

Since 1975 there have been a number of changes in the funding of house purchase in inner cities. First, since 1974-5 the clearing banks have largely withdrawn from this type of lending. Their place has only partly been taken over by the Asian clearing banks. Second, the fringe banks which were drastically affected by financial crisis in 1974-5 have only recently revived their lending. Third, the period of record lending in 1975, which as Karn (1976) showed was largely used to compensate for a temporary shortage of building society funds further up-market is now over. Local authority lending nationally since then has been cut from £786 million in 1974-5 and £443 million in 1975-6 to £157 million, including improvement loans, in 1977-8 (these figures are at 1977 survey prices). The level of lending for purchase and improvement in 1978-9 is estimated to be about £143 million (McIntosh, 1978).

Thus a scarcity of mortgage funds in 1972-4 had become a famine by 1975-8. The government's solution to this situation is based on one measure — the support lending scheme. To compensate for the cuts in council lending in 1976, it was arranged that building societies should make loans to a value of £100 million available to would-be buyers nominated by local authorities. In 1977-8 this figure was raised to £157 million, and in 1978-9 it was nearly doubled to £300 million. The aim is to use the support lending scheme to press building societies to take over the inner city lending role previously performed by local authorities.

The main reason for government's dislike of local authority lending is that it counts as public expenditure in the Public Expenditure Survey whereas the Support Lending Scheme does not. This problem of the definition of public expenditure is the main reason for the rejection of surely the most obvious solution to the mortgage problems of inner cities, namely the on-lending of building society funds by local authorities. Because of it, the tortuous procedures of nomination under the support lending scheme have been substituted.

This scheme has a number of fatal flaws as a solution to the mortgage problems of inner cities. First, the evidence is that building societies are failing to lend to the very applicants and on the very houses that the scheme is intended to help. The Department of the Environment's own (understandably confidential) survey done in September 1977 showed that out of 3,047 applicants referred by a sample of 43 authorities, only 35 per cent had had an offer made and only 19 per cent had accepted. If one excludes those whose applications were still pending the figures are 52 per cent with an offer and 28 per cent accepted.

The two major problems appear to be: (i) a reluctance to lend on property in need of improvement or repairs, or strict conditions that repairs are done in advance of completion or that a retention is made of part of the purchase price; (ii) a reluctance to lend more than 90 per cent of valuation, a policy which is made harsh by low valuations and the retentions just mentioned. In addition certain types of property are unpopular with building societies, notably houses without front gardens, leasehold property, converted flats, or property where residential and commercial uses are mixed. For all these reasons, and in spite of the fact that local authorities usually try to refer applicants who fulfil the building society criteria, the £157 million is unlikely to be taken up. The more likely figure, according to the Department of the Environment report cited by McIntosh (1978), is about £100-105 million.

Having this information has not changed government's enthusiasm for support lending. Far from it; the quota for 1978-9 has been nearly doubled to £300 million, while the ceiling for direct lending will, despite intensive lobbying by the local authorities, be only about £143 million. The impact of this cut will only exacerbate an already ludicrous situation which is particularly galling to those local authorities who, before the cuts, had a generous scheme of their own. Now the same staff are taken up with constantly referring unsuccessful applicants to building societies, only for them to lose their survey fees.

What evidence is there that government's apparent faith in support lending is justified? Williams (1977) in his review of building society lending policies in inner cities, concludes that the whole ethos of their activities is so geared to minimising risk that, though marginal changes have been made and are likely to continue, it is highly questionable whether building societies will shift their lending pattern enough to make any impact on inner cities. He quotes the chairman of Nationwide as saying,

> One does not encourage people to go to a butcher and buy bad meat, and in our view one should not encourage people to go into the older city areas and buy bad housing . . . We do not believe that it is in the interests of people to buy bad old houses that we and other building societies turn down (Williams, 1977, p. 10).

Similarly, Lambert (1976), in her study of Birmingham building societies and surveyors, quotes a building society manager who gives the same point a different emphasis, the risk to the building society rather than the risk to the buyer: 'Both individuals and property in the older areas are poorer risks. Money is always limited — then how much more sense it is to lend it on those modern houses rather than in the riskier areas' (Lambert, 1976, p. 33). In essence it appears highly unlikely that a support lending scheme based on persuasion will make building societies come sufficiently down-market to cover the properties previously mortgaged by the local authority.

The second flaw in the policy of cutting direct lending and concentrating on support lending is that, even if it were to be ultimately successful in making building societies come further down-market, no arrangements have been made to alleviate the mortgage famine which is created in the intervening years. This period of mortgage famine is likely to have such a bad effect on the housing market in inner areas and on improvement policies that the decline of inner cities will be escalated rather than halted or reversed. This in itself will make building society lending less rather than more likely.

Third, not even the most ardent supporters of the support lending scheme claim that it will cover lending down-market of even the local authorities, which in Birmingham accounted for only 16 per cent of the money lent in the three study areas during 1972-4. In order to have taken over the funding of all the main loans given in Saltley, Soho and Sparkhill during this period, the building societies would have had to have found an additional £1,115,000, approximately £372,000 a year. In addition, these loans often accounted for a small proportion of the purchase price; to cover even 85 per cent of the purchase prices of all the houses would have meant a total of £1,756,000 or £585,000 a year. These sums are only a fraction of those needed by the whole of Birmingham's inner area which incorporates over 40,000 owner-occupied houses compared with about 4,676 in the survey areas. As the funds needed would have to be withdrawn from safer properties in suburban areas, such a switch of funds is unlikely to occur through any piecemeal arrangement for individual purchasers such as the support lending scheme. It needs large amounts of earmarked funds.

Subsidies

We will turn now from the problems that inner city buyers have in obtaining credit to the support that they receive, or fail to receive, through subsidy, to help them meet their monthly repayments. Again the picture is not a favourable one. The subsidies available to owner-occupiers on the cost of buying a house are of two types.

First, they can get tax relief on the interest payments on a loan. The effect of this is to reduce the owner's taxable income by the amount of annual interest paid. Thus if he pays the standard rate of tax, he will reduce his tax bill by 34 per cent of the amount of interest paid. If he pays more than the standard rate of tax, he may have relief on even 90 per cent of all or part of the interest payments. At the other end of the scale, if deducting interest payments brings a buyer below the tax threshold, he will not receive tax relief on the whole of the interest but only on the difference between the tax threshold and his taxable income before interest payments are deducted. Those who pay no tax, even before taking interest payments into account, of course receive no tax relief. It was to give assistance to these last two categories of low income buyers that the second form of subsidy, the Option Mortgage subsidy, was introduced in 1967. This subsidy operates by giving a reduced interest rate to the borrowers and is adjusted to give subsidy at roughly the equivalent of tax relief at the standard rate.

However, there is a major distinction between the two, namely that though tax relief is available on the interest on loans for house purchase or improvement from whatever source, option mortgage is available only on building society and local authority mortgages. As we have seen in the three areas studied, the majority of buyers in the period 1972-4 did *not* have building society or local authority loans. So in inner cities where there is a lack of conventional mortgage lending, the restriction

of Option Mortgage subsidy to conventional mortgages means that
many of the lowest income buyers qualify for no subsidy at all or for
a very reduced level of subsidy. The question of how many actually
claim tax relief on bank or finance-house loans for house purchase, even
when they are entitled to it, is at present unanswered.

Quite apart from the eligibility for any subsidy at all there is the
question of the level of subsidy. First, there is the point already
mentioned that people at the tax threshold receive little subsidy.
Second, bank and finance-house loans are for short periods, usually
five or ten years. As a result subsidy is paid for only a very short period
of time. Thus someone who buys a house with a five-year loan of
£3,000 receives a total of about £365 Option Mortgage subsidy while
someone who has a loan over 25 years receives about £2,225. So the
person who borrows most receives most financial help. This would be
fair if those who borrowed most were those who needed to borrow
most, rather than the people and houses with the best credit rating.

Most important, though, is the well-documented fact that subsidy
to owner-occupiers is regressive in character, that is it rises rather than
falls as incomes and loan sizes rise. In the study period, both the Option
Mortgage and standard rate tax relief subsidy amounted to about £32 per
£1,000 borrowed at 11 per cent over 25 years. The average house price
in Saltley, Sparkhill and Soho during 1972-4 was about £3,000 which
would mean an annual subsidy of £94 on a 100 per cent loan. Compare
this with the £500 subsidy which a buyer would receive if he took out
a £16,000 mortgage and received the standard rate of tax. Even the
national average for Option Mortgages subsidy in 1974 was £188 per
mortgaged house. So not only does the subsidy system work against
those unable to obtain a conventional mortgage at all but it also gives
much smaller subsidies to those who, even with a conventional mortgage,
are able to buy only the cheaper houses.

In addition, of course, tax relief is not just paid at the standard rate
but at the highest marginal rate paid by the owner-occupiers. Therefore
the higher the person's income the greater the rate of tax relief on
interest payments. The total cost of tax relief and option mortgage in
1976-7 was £1,240 million; if tax relief above the standard rate had been
abolished there would have been a saving of £120 million. This sum is
only £16 million less than the cost of all Option Mortgage subsidy in
that year, nearly 70 per cent of the cost of all local authority mortgage
lending, and nearly twice the amount spent on improvement and
conversion grants to housing associations and private owners.

The Green Paper on Housing Policy (Great Britain, 1977b) proposes to make no change in the subsidy arrangemerits for owner-occupiers. A Conservative government is even less likely to make any change. The owner occupiers of the inner areas may well think that the government has a very contradictory approach both to owner-occupation and to housing policies in the inner cities. From the enthusiasm expressed for these two causes, they might have anticipated a lot of financial help coming their way, but current government policies show either that there is no real recognition of the way that the present form of housing finance works against inner city areas or that despite the protestations, inner cities still have little priority in mainstream housing finance policy.

In effect, the whole emphasis of mortgage lending is towards the financing of new suburban housing and away from the inner cities. In addition the subsidy system for owner-occupiers provides the greatest incentive for those who least need it, thus encouraging higher income people to move up-market, which usually means towards the suburbs. While both policies are said to release inner city housing for people with lower incomes, and certainly have had the effect of reducing pressure on inner city housing, they fail to take account of the fact that the predominant tenure is no longer private renting and, if the houses are to be occupied, they need to be sold and, if they are to be sold, there has to be credit available.

Even with credit, lower income people may need subsidy to be able to buy even the cheapest houses. So, though the movement out of the inner cities has loosened the inner city housing market, the lack of credit and the mismatch between incomes and house prices, even in deteriorated areas, means that there exist, simultaneously, homelessness, a housing shortage and an increasing number of unsaleable, vacant properties in inner cities. In other words, policies on the financing of owner-occupation have not been adjusted to deal with the new situation.

Policies concerned with the problems faced by owner-occupiers in the inner city are typically those which try to deal with the physical symptoms of obsolescence and neglect, for example via improvement and repairs grants in Housing Action Areas, rather than those which try to deal with the causes, namely disinvestment in the inner city, the disparity between incomes of low-paid workers and the costs of buying a modernised house. The final part of this chapter looks briefly at current Housing Action Area policies and shows how these, too, are often failing to help owner-occupiers because they do not take these fundamental problems adequately into account.

Housing Action Area Policies

As far as owner-occupiers are concerned there are two major differences between Housing Action Areas and the earlier improvement policies. The first is that grant levels are higher, 75 per cent of approved costs or even higher in cases of hardship. The second is that owners in HAAs are given a five-year period in which improvements must be done. Authorities begin to issue notices threatening compulsory purchase on owners who have not done their improvements about halfway through that period.

In a study undertaken by the Centre for Urban and Regional Studies of Beeches Road, before it was declared a Housing Action Area, we predicted that the level of owner-occupation would be a very significant factor in any policy for the area.

> Ownership was found to be a source of considerable satisfaction, giving a sense of achievement . . . It is arguably not legitimate to destroy this element of satisfaction under the guise of a policy aimed specifically at securing the 'well-being' of residents. Physical and social objectives would clearly be in conflict in such circumstances, and it would be up to the local council to decide which should receive priority. If large scale acquisition and changes in tenure were thought appropriate, the function of the area would change considerably (Niner *et al.*, 1975, pp. 116-17).

The circular which launched Housing Action Areas (Great Britain, 1975b) was contradictory on this issue because it stressed flexibility and sensitivity to the social character of areas while introducing measures totally concerned with the physical stock. In practice, the unresolved contradiction of the circular is becoming all too apparent on the ground. Low-income owners are proving unwilling or unable to improve and compulsory purchase orders are being issued. In Birmingham's Housing Action Areas, out of 12,000 houses scheduled for retention, only 600 had been improved by May 1978. In the first four HAAs to be declared compulsory purchase orders (CPOs) have been initiated for over 1,100 houses. It is currently believed that a large percentage of these may eventually be municipalised at a cost far greater than that of giving owners their improvements free.

About 70 per cent of the owners receiving CPO notices in Birmingham are Asians. If these CPOs go through, the effect on the Asian community is likely to be shattering. Ownership has been one of the symbols of success that Asian immigrants have most prized. They have often lived unbelievably frugally to achieve it. Now they are finding that, having survived the years of struggling with high-interest loans they may lose their homes after all at the hands of a 'well-intentioned' local authority.

If they are so anxious not to lose their houses, why then are owners not improving their property? The problem is, essentially, that the current owners could only afford to buy the houses because they were cheap and they were only cheap because they were unimproved and in a bad state of repair. Owners can no more afford to improve them than they could afford to buy a better property in the first place. Of course, grants are supposed to overcome this problem but for a number of reasons they are proving inadequate.

First, the grants cover 75 per cent not of total costs but of approved costs up to a maximum of £5,000. Currently improvements in the private sector in Birmingham are costing £7,500. The owner therefore has to find 25 per cent of £5,000 i.e. £1,250 plus £2,500, a total of £3,750. There are local authority loans to help meet this additional cost but the repayment period is only for five to fifteen years. Paying back a loan of £3,750 over fifteen years at 11 per cent costs £43, over ten years £53 a month and over five years £85 a month. Clearly for many owners such increased outgoings are out of the question, the more so because the poorest live in the most deteriorated housing in which the improvement and repair costs are greatest. These are the houses in which Asian owners predominate.

More important probably though is the problem that a house which was recently purchased for £4,000 and on which the owners have had to find £3,750 in improvement costs will not currently sell for £7,750 — but rather for about £6,000. Thus, as described elsewhere by Harrison (1977), there is a 'valuation gap' of at least £1,750 between the value of an improved house and the cost of buying and improving a similar house. If for some reason, the owner were forced to sell quickly, he would make a loss of £1,750, having to pay off mortgages and loans totalling more than the price the house would fetch. If the local authority chose not to waive its right to reclaim the grant if the house were sold within five years, the loss would be £6,750 instead. This is unlikely to happen but the prospect to buyers is appalling.

The more recently the owner bought his house, the greater the purchase price and so the greater the problem. Being the most recent buyers in most inner areas, the Asians are the worst affected. In these circumstances it would clearly be more sensible for the owner of an unimproved house to sell it and buy an improved one. But this assumes that he could afford to do so. Presumably the reason he bought the unimproved property was that it was cheaper than an improved one. In addition, there is not an endless supply of cheap older housing. In the Beeches Road study an estimate was made of the rehousing implications of demolition of the area, for residents who wanted to buy. The findings are equally relevant in relation to compulsory purchase. It was found that,

> about 15 per cent of those who would like to buy are unlikely to be able to find a house at a price they can afford, and *all* the vacancies (in West Bromwich) occurring within a year among houses costing less than £6,000 would be needed to accommodate those displaced (Niner *et al.*, 1975, p. 87).

Naturally, because there are in reality other competitors for these houses, the prices would not stay below £6,000 for long and so more than 15 per cent would be outpriced and unable to buy. An increase in the prices of older houses outside housing action areas is inevitable, just as it is inevitable that prices of unimproved properties in Housing Action Areas will drop. This may have the bonus of reducing the 'valuation gap' for new buyers, but will such buyers materialise? It seems unlikely. Buyers who know about compulsory improvement are steering clear of Housing Action Areas.

A recent survey of twenty houses for sale in the Moss Side Housing Action Area in Manchester (Massey, 1978) showed that they had been on sale on average for nine months. In the case of sixteen, the owners were trying to sell to housing associations or the council. Of the others only one had been sold. This sale had had to be financed by the owners, a finance company which had repossessed it from its previous owner. The other houses were still vacant. On none of the properties, other than the one sold, had there ever been any really serious enquiries from private buyers. The private housing market was all but dead. Though the situation may not be as bad in any of Birmingham's Housing Action Areas, a map of long-term vacancies known to the Rates Department in Birmingham shows up a heavy concentration in Housing Action Areas and to a lesser extent in the whole middle ring of nineteenth-century terraced housing (Bell, 1978).

For some owner-occupiers, of course, the chance to sell the house to the local authority and obtain a council tenancy is an opportunity they do not want to miss. Owner-occupiers are not accepted on

Birmingham's housing waiting list so anyone who buys out of despera-
tion and then regrets it is not usually given a chance to move out into
council housing. Housing Action Areas give them that chance. Similarly
elderly people may prefer to rent when they begin to find decorating
and repairs too expensive or difficult. In the Beeches Road survey about
25 per cent of owners said they would prefer to rent. Most of these
were elderly. In Sandwell, however, even these owners will not have it
all their own way. The authority there pays owners only 60 per cent of
valuation if they are to be rehoused, a practice which was roundly
condemned by the Cullingworth Committee in 1969 (Great Britain,
1969). This is yet another example of the lack of understanding of the
situation of inner city buyers and the stereotyping of owner-occupiers
as affluent.

One of the differences between improvement policies and slum
clearance is that in slum clearance everyone was moved out. In
improvement areas, tenants whose landlords have sold their houses to
the local authority or had them compulsorily purchased are likely to
be able to stay in the area. It is the owners, who were the most anxious
to stay, who are most likely to have to leave if they want to continue
to own. In Birmingham for instance eighty owner-occupiers in George
Arthur Road, who campaigned so strenuously to save their houses
from slum clearance, have now been issued with CPOs under Housing
Action Area procedures.

They will of course fight on. Slum clearance had a big role in
helping to kill off private unfurnished renting. Will compulsory
improvement play a similar role for low income owner-occupation? Or
will the political difficulties for government and local authorities of
being seen to do that, result in low income owner-occupation blocking
compulsory improvement just as it helped to end slum clearance? The
questions are important ones and very immediate.

For owner-occupiers the ultimately intolerable outcome would be if
the local authority compulsorily purchased their properties and then
failed to improve the houses itself or failed to get a housing association
to do it rapidly. This is perfectly likely. (It is also likely to be the fear
of this happening that prevents the more widespread use of CPOs.) The
rate of improvement work being done by some housing associations is
such that, if they continue at the same rate, it will take ten years or
more to improve the property that has been handed over to them,
sometimes in areas that have only a twenty year life! Meanwhile the
houses deteriorate.

Similarly Birmingham, if it municipalises many houses in the first

Housing Action Areas, and then finds itself without adequate resources to improve them, may well find itself reliving the experience of the 1960s when Birmingham Estates Department was the biggest slum landlord in Europe, as a result of what began as an enlightened policy of early acquisition of slum property but ended with appallingly delayed demolition and not even basic weatherproofing and repairs, let alone improvements. The areas were increasingly used to house the homeless and 'problem families', a process more destructive to all residents than slum clearance itself.

The rather glib assumption was made in much of the debate about slum clearance versus improvement, that the difference between slum clearance and improvement policy was that the latter enabled existing residents to stay on in their houses and that it would thus preserve the community. Current events outlined above suggest that this assumption may not prove as valid as originally thought.

Conclusion

Because of the financial difficulties of inner city owner-occupiers, the switch from private unfurnished renting to owner-occupation in the inner city has not, in many respects, conferred the benefits on owners which many proponents of owner-occupation might have expected. The houses in these areas are still of poor quality. They still need improvement and repairs but owners are often unable to afford to carry them out, even with grant aid. Probably even more important is the problem of the 'valuation gap'. The ability to take on extra financial burdens is also affected by the fact that owners have expensive loans, some from organisations which have little sympathy for those who fall into debt and little compunction in foreclosing. Though owners may be said to be accumulating a capital asset, and are certainly attracted to owner-occupation by this, doubts as to whether house values will be maintained, in the absence of conventional mortgages and with the introduction of compulsory improvement policies, also lead to doubts as to the security of the investment.

Government policies for the inner cities seem consistently to ignore the inescapable fact that the incomes of the residents are too low to meet the cost of better housing. This fact does not disappear if one introduces improvement rather than new building and current grant levels do not fill the gap. Similarly greater availability of mortgages in inner areas will not meet this problem, in the absence of an increase in the supply of cheap housing. There is no solution to inner city housing problems which is not enormously costly.

But it is perfectly possible to see what solutions there might be, if the political will were there to provide the money and to face the criticism which would surround the fact that those who benefited most would be Asian and West Indian, at least in Birmingham and other major English cities. Owners could, for instance, be given free improvements. Or municipal purchase and improvement could be guaranteed sufficient funds to be effective. Or slum clearance would be started again, forcing owners into renting. Or clearance would be coupled with replacement value compensation, so owners could buy new houses built in the area. Impossible? No, just a matter of priorities.

References

Bell, C. (1978) Unpublished findings of current research at the Centre for Urban and Regional Studies, University of Birmingham (1955) 'Bournville Village Trust 1900-1955', Birmingham: Bournville Village Trust

Centre for Urban and Regional Studies (1978) Unpublished finding of a DOE sponsored research project on race and council housing, Birmingham University

Great Britain (1918) *Local Government Board, Local Government Boards for England and Wales and Scotland*, Report of the (Tudor Walters) Committee ... appointed ... to consider questions of Building Construction with the Provision of Dwellings for the Working Classes in England and Wales and Scotland, London: HMSO

—— (1969) Ministry of Housing and Local Government, *Council Housing Purposes. Procedures and Priorities*, London: HMSO

—— (1971) Census 1971, England and Wales, unpublished enumeration district data for Birmingham

—— (1975a) Department of the Environment, *Housing and Construction Statistics*, No. 14, London: HMSO

—— (1975b) Housing Act 1974: Parts IV, V, VI, Housing Action Areas, Priority Neighbourhoods and GIAs, Circular 14/75, Department of the Environment, London: HMSO

—— (1976) Department of the Environment, *Housing and Construction Statistics*, No. 18, London: HMSO

—— (1977a) Department of the Environment, *Housing Policy Technical Volume Part 1*, London: HMSO

—— (1977b) Department of the Environment, *Housing Policy, A Consultative Document*, Cmnd. 6851, London: HMSO

Harrison, A. (1977) 'The Valuation Gap: A Danger Signal', *CES Review*, no. 2, pp. 101-3

Ineichen, B. (1974) *A Place of Our Own*, London: Housing Research Foundation

Karn, V. (1976) *Priorities for Local Authority Mortgage Lending: A Case Study of Birmingham*, Centre for Urban and Regional Studies, Research Memorandum No. 52, Birmingham University

—— (1978) 'The Financing of Owner-Occupation and its Impact on Ethnic Minorities', *New Community* vol. VI, no. 22, Winter 1977-8, pp. 49-65.

Lambert, C. (1976) *Building Societies, Surveyors and the Older Areas of Birmingham*, Centre for Urban and Regional Studies, Working Paper No. 38, Birmingham University

McIntosh, N. (1978) 'Mortgage Support Scheme Holds the Lending Lines', *Roof*, vol. 3, no. 2, pp. 44-7

Massey, R. (1978) 'The Private House Purchase Market in the Housing Action Areas of Moss Side' (unpublished paper Moss Side Urban Renewal Team), Manchester

Niner, P., Karn, V., Murie, A. and Watson, C. (1975) *The Beeches Road Area Study: A Potential Housing Action Area*, Centre for Urban and Regional Studies, Research Memorandum No. 49, Birmingham University

Williams, P. (1977) *Building Societies and the Inner City*, Centre for Urban and Regional Studies, Research Memorandum No. 54, Birmingham University

Woolf, M. (1967) *The Housing Survey in England and Wales, 1964*, Government Social Survey, London: HMSO

8 POPULATION DECLINE IN CITIES

Colin Jones

There is at present great concern about the future of cities; many are facing physical decay and economic decline together with falling populations. The latest population estimates for each major British city and conurbation suggest a continuation of this process (Great Britain, 1977a). Cities not only in Britain but also in the United States have reacted to this population crisis with schemes to attract back owner-occupiers from their suburban rings. In this chapter we look at the historical growth and decline of present day cities and the processes which have shaped them. In particular we focus on the detailed evidence available from Liverpool and more especially from Glasgow.

Urban Development

Cities

The nineteenth century saw a huge growth in the population of Great Britain; it rose from 10.5 million in 1801 to 37 million in 1901. Accompanying this rise the industrial revolution led to a general movement of population from the country into the cities. Manchester, perhaps a symbol of this new age, increased its population nearly six times in the sixty years prior to 1831 when its population was 142,000. In the previous decade alone the city's population had risen by 42 per cent. Fifty years later it had gained another 200,000 people so that its population stood at 341,000 (Briggs, 1968).

Henry George (1884) wrote,

So across the Tweed, while London, Liverpool, Leeds and Manchester have grown, the village life of 'merrie' England is all but extinct. Two thirds of the entire population is crowded into cities

Nothing more clearly shows the unhealthiness of present social tendencies than the steadily increasing concentration of population in great cities.

The density and populations of the nine largest towns in Britain in 1881 are shown in Table 8.1. The implications of these density statistics can be shown by consideration of Glasgow in more detail. Although not

Table 8.1: Population and Densities of the Major Cities in 1881

	Population 1881	Density (persons per acre)
London	3,831,719	51
Liverpool	554,073	106
Glasgow	511,532	84
Birmingham	402,314	48
Manchester	341,173	80
Leeds	310,483	15
Sheffield	285,619	15
Edinburgh	228,190	55
Bristol	207,522	47

Source: Russell (1885).

the most densely populated of these, on average there were two persons to every room in the city. According to the 1871 Census, 41 per cent of all Glasgow families lived in one room and a further 37 per cent in two rooms. Such was the pressure on housing that 23 per cent of all families took in lodgers, including 1 in 5 of those families living in one room. There were even inner city wards with population densities of more than 300 persons to the acre including Gorbals (350) and Calton (388).

These were the peak recorded densities within the city; after 1871 the population of the inner city began to decline, initially as the result of slum clearance under the 1866 City of Glasgow Improvement Trust Act and the growth of the business area, but subsequently as a result of changes in transport technology. The first section of the Glasgow tramway opened in 1872; prior to this date, although there were some horse-drawn omnibus services, the principal means by which the people moved about the city was by walking.

This development brought areas of the city within access of the working classes for the first time and more importantly enabled a reduction in the time of the journey to work. This in turn enabled the working classes to seek homes at progressively further distances from the city. The initial fares were 1d per mile and this was eventually reduced to ½d when the tramway was municipalised in 1893. In that year it carried 54 million passengers and by the turn of the century when it was electrified Glasgow boasted the best tramway in the world. Indeed by 1904 it had 79 miles of track and the number of passengers had increased to 189 million annually (Oakley, 1962).

A similar pattern could be seen in other British cities. Trams were first introduced in Birkenhead in 1860 and they spread through provincial cities; services began in Liverpool in 1869, London in 1870,

Birmingham in 1872 and Manchester in 1877. By the end of the century 61 local authorities owned tramways and a further 89 were operated by private enterprise. It was the advent of cheap and efficient public transport (Bett and Gillham, 1962).

At the same time suburban railways were also contributing to this movement. Their influence, however, was more indirect up until the close of the century. The railway companies were in the main reluctant to offer concessionary fares to commuters or workmen to enable them to take advantage of the facilities. During the period 1860-1900 the suburban railway was predominantly used by the middle classes and rail journeys by the working classes were reserved for holidays and occasional excursions if at all.

While it is likely that the development of suburbs in general preceded the provision of railway services by a decade or two, their impact is described by a contemporary observer of Manchester (quoted by Kellett, 1969, p. 358) who noted,

A large proportion of the middle class, the clerks, warehousemen and others seize upon the new suburbs vacating their houses in town, which are most frequently absorbed for shop and business purposes or sub-divided and sub-let, until the dwelling which has served for one household contains as many families as it did persons.

The suburban railway was drawing off the 'well-to-do' leaving the working classes in the inner areas of terraced houses.

The Victorian period then had seen great changes in British cities and an essentially rural country transposed into an urban-dominated society. During the latter half of the century while cities continued to grow, densities in the inner parts of the cities began to fall as the introduction of mass transport wrought a revolution in spatial structure.

In the subsequent period up to the Second World War, core cities continued to grow and many annexed surrounding land in the 1920s and 1930s to enable this expansion. The major exception was London (LCC) which began to decline at the turn of the century and has had a net loss of population in every subsequent decade. The other major cities were to follow in these footsteps; Glasgow, Liverpool and Manchester all probably reached their population peaks at the beginning of hostilities in 1939. Only Birmingham of the largest five cities, as Table 8.2 shows, significantly increased its population between 1931 and 1951, while Glasgow's was largely static and Manchester and Liverpool lost approximately just over 40,000 people. Undoubtedly war damage

Table 8.2: Population Trends in the Major Cities

	1921	1931	1951	1961	1966	1971
(Inner) London	4,484,523	4,397,003	3,347,982	3,198,145	2,999,990	2,772,131
Glasgow CC	1,034,174	1,088,461	1,089,767	1,055,017	976,540	897,483
Birmingham CB	922,167	1,002,603	1,112,685	1,110,683	1,064,220	1,014,670
Liverpool CB	805,412	856,072	788,659	745,750	691,380	610,113
Manchester CB	735,665	766,311	703,082	661,791	598,640	543,650
Leeds CB	463,152	482,827	505,219	510,676	504,630	496,009
Newcastle upon Tyne CB	277,033	286,260	291,724	269,678	249,240	222,209

Source: Great Britain (1951, 1971b and 1977b).

took its toll in these cities, and the worst affected, London, emerged from the turmoil with a million less people within its boundaries. However, the smaller cities of Leeds and Newcastle continued to grow.

Since 1951 all these core cities have experienced net losses in population, although in the cases of Birmingham and Leeds these losses have been relatively small. Leeds indeed even registered a marginal increase during the decade up to 1961. But the general pattern is one of population decline with Manchester and Newcastle experiencing the fastest relative decline in the period 1951-66 with an average net reduction of 1 per cent per annum. 1966 provides a significant landmark in this decline for after that date the process shows a marked acceleration. Glasgow and Liverpool both lost an astonishing total of 80,000 people in the subsequent five years, 8 and 12 per cent of their respective populations. Similar relative reductions occurred in Manchester and Newcastle, 9 and 11 per cent respectively. Again Leeds did not follow the general pattern for although it did experience a sudden drop in population this amounted to only 1 per cent of its 1966 total.

In this brief analysis of urban change we have made no attempt to standardise for the changing administrative boundaries of cities. Consequently comparisons between cities will be influenced by the timing of annexations of land which will also tend to mask the decentralisation process. It is, however, apparent that the irresistible rise of the city has been reversed. London had reached its population summit at the beginning of this century, the older cities in the late 1930s and the more modern cities such as Birmingham began to lose population in the 1950s. This process of population decline shows a dramatic acceleration during the late 1960s, the latest period for which definite statistics are available.

Conurbations

If the nineteenth century saw the growth of urban society, the twentiet twentieth century has seen the development of the conurbations as cities and their surrounding towns coalesced. Today about one-third of Britain's population lives in one of the seven major conurbations. This is in part the result of changing transport technologies; in the first years of this century tramway systems of different towns grew to meet each other, the motor bus was introduced in the 1920s eventually to supersede the tram and finally there was the development of the family car during the late 1950s and 1960s.

As the populations of the core cities grew so naturally did those of their respective conurbations, but despite the onset of population decline in the central cities most conurbations continued to grow until the early 1960s. These changes in spatial structure have been mapped by Hall *et al.* (1973) and are illustrated by Table 8.3. During the decade

Table 8.3: Pattern of Population Change 1951 to 1966

	1951-61 '000's			1961-6 '000's		
	Core	Ring*	Net	Core	Ring*	Net
Birmingham	+47.4	+324.9	RD**	-73.4	+78.8	AD
Leeds	+5.4	+16.9	RD	-25.1	+54.0	AD
London	-280.6	+324.9	ADt	-610.7	+78.8	Decline
Liverpool	-74.1	+103.4	AD	-187.5	+129.4	Decline
Manchester	-38.0	+91.2	AD	-124.4	+63.0	Decline
Newcastle	-24.3	+60.9	AD	-65.3	+54.6	Decline

*the contiguous administrative areas sending 15 per cent of their resident population to their respective core.
**relative decentralisation
tabsolute decentralisation

Source: Hall *et al.* (1973).

Table 8.4: Populations of Core Cities as a percentage of their respective Conurbation Totals 1951-71

	1951	1961	1966	1971
Glasgow CC	62.0	58.3	55.3	52.0
Birmingham CB	49.7	47.3	44.8	42.8
Liverpool CB	57.1	53.9	51.7	48.3
Manchester CB	29.0	26.8	24.9	22.8
Newcastle upon Tyne CB	34.9	31.5	30.0	27.6

Source: Great Britain (1977b).

1951 to 1961, London, Manchester, Liverpool and Newcastle all experienced absolute decentralisation with the suburban ring increasing its population by more than the amount the core was losing. After that date although the suburbs were still expanding there was an overall population downturn in these urban areas. Meanwhile Birmingham and Leeds and their surrounding areas were also subject to decentralisation but were still increasing their overall populations up to 1966. However, since then the West Midlands conurbation has shown a slight decline and West Yorkshire a marginal increase in their populations.

The impact of these processes on the structure of conurbations can be seen in Table 8.4. With the core cities declining in population at a much faster rate than their respective conurbations as a whole, their relative dominance has been eroded. This is most notable for south-east Lancashire and Tyneside whose core cities suffered a more than 20 per cent relative decline in population during the twenty-year period 1951-71. Glasgow experienced the largest percentage decline in absolute terms, from 62 per cent to 52 per cent of the population of Central Clydeside.

American Experience

Urbanisation in the United States occurred later than in Britain. It proceeded at a relatively slow pace before the Civil War before quickening during the period of rapid industrialisation in the latter part of the nineteenth century. Set to this background Chicago expanded its population nearly twentyfold between 1860 and 1910. The proportion of the population living in an urban environment has increased during every decade from 1790 to the present day. By 1970, 73.5 per cent of the country's population was living in either cities or towns with populations of more than 2,500.

However, there has undoubtedly been a decline in the populations of the central parts of the older metropolitan areas since 1950. Rasmusson (1973) shows that of the eighteen older conurbations that had a central city with a population exceeding 250,000 in 1910 only three — Los Angeles, Milwaukee and New Orleans — increased their core populations in the two decades following 1950. And if Los Angeles, which gained over 900,000, is excluded there is an average 8 per cent decline in the populations of these central cities. Meanwhile each conurbation as a whole without exception continued to grow.

From a different perspective Mills (1972) examines the changes in urban structure by a study of population density functions over time in a range of different cities. The differences in the estimated gradient coefficients enable him to make observations on the rate of suburbanisation. His major conclusions are that the process was at its most rapid during the period 1880-1920, when there was rapid urban growth, and between 1948 and 1954 following a pause during the depression of the 1930s and the Second World War. Since then the process has decelerated but is still continuing.

Hence the American experience is remarkably similar to that experienced by Britain with the older central cities beginning to lose population after the Second World War. However, their conurbations have yet to begin to shed population as in Britain, but this may be purely the result of differing definitions of administrative boundaries.

Implications of Population Decline

One major worry particularly of the local authorities in question has
been the selective nature of the recent migration from the core cities.
More than a quarter of net out-migrants from both Glasgow and
Liverpool were aged in the range 25 to 34 years. Indeed the overall age
structures of these net out-migrants and the consequent age distributions in 1971 are, as Table 8.5 indicates, remarkably similar for both
cities.

The impact on the age structure of these cities was inevitably a
higher proportion of older persons. A recent review of urban trends by
Liverpool MD Planning Department (1977) shows that during the
decade 1961-71 the retired population of the city, both males and
females, rose from 13 to 16.2 per cent of the total. In the same inter-
censal period the proportion of the city's population within the 25 to
54 years age group fell significantly. This group accounted for 60 per
cent of the drop in both male and female populations. The
consequences are an increasing proportion of economically dependent
people in the city. This is balanced by a decline of 24.3 per cent in the
number of females of childbearing age during the same period, compared with the city's overall population decline of 18.3 per cent. But
even this fact is also a cause for concern with its long-term implications
for educational facilities.

Just as the net-migrants have tended to be younger than the
remaining population so they have also been concentrated in particular
socio-economic groups. As the development of suburban railways
enabled the 'well to do' to leave the Victorian cities similarly the
migrants from the cities in the 1960s included relatively few unskilled
and semi-skilled workers. More than one-fifth of the net migration from
Glasgow between 1966 and 1971 was accounted for by managers, professionals and other self-employed, more than double their proportion of
the population in 1966. A similar pattern was found in Liverpool and
other cities. Part of the cause of this selective migration was the overspill process which led to a preponderance of foremen, supervisors and
skilled manual workers being rehoused by formal agreements. During
the period 1959-71 this group amounted to more than half of all the
households rehoused in this way.

The impact of this migration on the socio-economic structure of
cities is masked by the general upgrading of the work force and social
mobility. Semi-skilled and unskilled manual workers declined in
numbers in each conurbation as indeed they did in the remainder of the
country. Similarly the number of managers and professionals and other self

Table 8.5: Age Structure of Net Out-Migrants from Liverpool and
Glasgow 1966-71

	Liverpool		Glasgow	
	1971	1966-71	1971	1966-71
Age Groups	Population	Net Out-Migrants	Population	Net Out-Migrants
	(%)	(%)	(%)	(%)
5-9 years	9.3	14.3	9.7	12.5
10-14	9.1	8.8	9.5	8.1
15-19	8.8	5.4	8.9	4.9
20-24	9.2	10.1	8.8	10.7
25-34	11.5	28.7	11.9	28.4
35-39	5.9	6.8	5.8	6.7
40-49	12.8	9.7	12.8	10.0
50-64	19.4	9.7	19.4	11.5
65+	14.0	6.5	13.2	7.4

(Note that percentages are calculated by ignoring those aged under 5 years at the
time of the Census.)
Source: Great Britain (1971a and 1971b).

Table 8.6: Percentage Change in the Economically Active Male
Populations of Merseyside and Central Clydeside 1961-71

Socio-economic Group	Liverpool	Merseyside	Glasgow*	Central Clydeside	Britain outside conurbations
Managers and professionals (1, 2, 3, 4, 13)	-18.2	-4.3	+0.4	+21.9	+26.7
Other self-employed (12, 14)	-15.9	-4.4	+5.5	+11.7	+24.1
Skilled manual (8, 9)	-25.6	-16.7	-14.4	-19.5	+0.4
Other non-manual (5, 6)	-19.4	-13.1	-15.9	-13.4	+14.9
Service, semi-skilled manual and agricultural (7, 10, 15)	-24.1	-14.2	-16.4	-19.7	-17.1
Unskilled manual (11)	-32.0	-26.0	-11.7	-14.0	-6.4
All	-24.3	-14.5	-13.0	-12.4	+2.8

*The figures for Glasgow only are for the period 1966-71 as the relevant break-
down is not available for the city in 1961.
The appropriate Census groupings are shown in brackets.
Source: Great Britain (1961a, 1971a, 1971b and 1977b).

employed increased in every conurbation except Merseyside and Tyne-side. And as Table 8.6 shows in Central Clydeside, despite an overall reduction of 12 per cent in its male force, there was an increase of more than one-fifth in the number of managers and professionals. However, Glasgow like Liverpool did not experience the same rate of upgrading as its conurbation. Even so the polarisation of socio-economic groups between the core cities and their suburban rings is not as great as suggested by the migration patterns.

Unfortunately, too, the loss of population is not spread uniformly throughout central cities. The consequences can be seen if we focus on the east end of Glasgow, an area singled out for special attention by the government in the form of the Glasgow Eastern Area Renewal (GEAR) project. The administrative area of GEAR, an area by no means unique in Glasgow, in August 1976 contained 315 acres of vacant land (Glasgow DC, 1976a). Yet in 1871 Calton, which is part of this area, was the most densely occupied ward in Glasgow. The population exodus fuelled by urban renewal in this part of the city has been staggering. Between 1951 and 1971 the area covered by the project lost approximately 63,000 people, nearly 37 per cent of its 1951 popula-tion. Even so the area suffered a further devastating fall in its popula-tion from 82,000 in 1971 to 45,000 in 1978.

A recent sample survey of the GEAR area in 1977-8 undertaken by the Scottish Development Agency (1978) reveals that despite the low residential densities caused by the amount of industry and the large amount of vacant land, 40 per cent of all households are living in two rooms or less and 85 per cent in three rooms or less (excluding bath-room and hall). This statistic rises to 94 per cent in one ward. In addition 22.2 per cent of households living in the inner six wards of the project area have no inside bath or shower. Similarly in this inner area 10 per cent of households lack an inside toilet.

In general the picture is one of a very stable if diminishing com-munity; 81 per cent of households contained a member who had lived in the east end for 25 years, and as many as 44 per cent had lived there for 50 years or more. The high mobility out and the low level of migration in has taken its toll with the resultant ageing population; 20 per cent are retired and only 23 per cent are children under 16 years of age compared with the city's average of 28 per cent. Many are living on very low incomes, 50 per cent receiving less than £1,750 and 79 per cent less than £3,375. This is in the main caused by the large numbers living on pensions and the relatively high level of unemployment — 20 per cent of economically active males are registered as such.

The major matters of concern for the population are dominated by the level of crime and violence and the appearance of the area but the main needs of the area are seen as shops, followed by facilities for the children, entertainments and sports. Statistics are inadequate fully to describe the problems of these areas, the Final Report of the Liverpool Inner Area Study (Great Britain, 1977c, p. 47) puts the matter more vividly:

In 1975, eleven per cent of land in the study area was lying vacant, much of it the cleared sites of terraced houses. For those who have to live with the day to day reality of large, rubble-strewn sites the impact is immediate, unsavoury and depressing. Packs of half wild dogs scavenge among bags of abandoned household refuse. Pools of water collect where badly filled cellars have subsided. Children build fires with cardboard cartons and the abandoned timber from demolished houses and play among the piles of brick, rubble and broken glass. Half bricks provide a ready and almost endless supply of ammunition for the frequent destruction of the windows of surrounding houses. Mattresses, furniture, gas cookers, prams and even cars that have outlived their usefulness are dumped. There is a pervading smell of old town gas from the partly buried gas pipes or demolished houses and the stopped off gas mains. It cannot be surprising that nearby residents faced with five to ten years of dereliction, feel abandoned by an impersonal and uncaring bureaucracy.

But the problems of these communities, even if in part created by the local authority, also cause problems for the council. Just as shopping centres become economically unviable with the resultant closures as their local markets disappear in rubble so there are also problems with falling school rolls. The need to continue to provide a basic level of local services on an area basis which is now far from optimum while at the same time receiving no additional revenue may cause strains on the city's finances. Although in Scotland this factor has recently been added to the formula which determines the rate support grant from central government to each local authority the matter remains contentious.

Possible Causes of Population Decline

Transport Technology

One major factor in the process of urban change which we have stressed is the influence of new transport technologies in enabling people to live at greater and greater distances from their work and the city centre. The introduction of a new mode of travel and the subsequent suburbanisation has almost in all cases been associated with an increase in urban population. As urban growth inevitably leads to suburbanisation, it is worth examining the impact of a change of transport technology in isolation.

Consider a model of a city on a uniform plain with only one centre, where all employment and purchases are concentrated. Each household makes a fixed number of trips to this centre every week. If we also assume that travel costs are the same in all directions, locations can be specified by distance only. To simplify matters further, taxes and prices of all other goods other than housing and transport are regarded as spatially invariant.

In such a schema a household will seek to maximise its satisfaction or utility subject to a budget constraint. More formally, the utility function may be written

$$U = U(x, q, k)$$

where

q = consumption of housing
x = money expenditure on all goods except housing and transport
k = distance, as a proxy for the consumption of travel which is assumed to be proportional to it.

The budget constraint is

$$y = x + p(k) \cdot q + k.t$$

where

p = price per unit of housing, a function of distance
t = cost per unit distance of travel to the centre per week
y = household income.

From such a model it is possible to derive that in equilibrium, Equation (1) holds and hence the price of housing declines with distance from the city centre.

$$p = -\frac{1}{q} t \qquad (1)$$

Households then trade off increased travelling costs against a low unit price of housing at the periphery. Thus people in the suburbs will consume a large amount of housing at a lower unit price relative to those near the city centre who will consume less housing but at a higher unit price.

The introduction of say a new more flexible mode of travel will only alter the system if it reduces unit travel costs (t). Such a reduction would lead to a new long-run equilibrium with, as Equation (1) shows, a more gentle price distance gradient (P) emerging. Translated into more pictorial terms this means that the quantity of housing produced at distant locations will increase with an equivalent decline near the centre. A reduction in unit intra-urban travel costs will therefore result in increased suburbanisation.

Of course the picture drawn by this simple model will be somewhat more complicated by the introduction of suburban sub-centres and public sector housing but the general pattern remains. Similarly the model assumes that long-term equilibrium exists. While such an event in our dynamic urban system seems rather unlikely the model does furnish some insight into the process of urban growth. Indeed this is confirmed by considering the introduction of the family car to Britain during a period of overall relative stability in the populations of the conurbations.

In 1954 there were 3,173,000 cars in the United Kingdom; by 1964 this had more than doubled to 8,436,000 (Great Britain, 1970) when there were 7.1 persons for every car. A decade later in 1974, the level of car ownership had nearly doubled again; there were only 4 persons for every car (Great Britain, 1975). Today, according to the 1975-6 Travel Survey, three-quarters of travel mileage is now undertaken by car or van (Great Britain, 1977d). This continuous growth of car usage can only be explained by a relative reduction of costs bringing it within the financial means of the average family. At the same time, as we have seen in Tables 8.3 and 8.4, there has been a strong decentralisation trend from the core city to the surrounding ring of the conurbation. While it is difficult to attribute the extent of this suburbanisation to any one factor it is clear that the rise of the motor car is a major contributor.

The Location of Employment

Another possible explanation is that the loss of employment in the central parts of our cities (see Dicken and Lloyd, chapter 2 in this volume) has led to population movement away in search of new job opportunities. There is necessarily a fairly close relationship between the distributions of employment and population and in fact the trends of both in our major cities and conurbations have been very similar. Cameron and Evans (1973) show that despite the development of large office blocks in city centres, employment was decentralising between 1961 and 1966 and that this pattern was true for nearly every individual industry in all conurbations. This process has numerous components — the relative decline and deaths of firms in the central cores, industrial plant migration to the suburbs to further expansion or to take advantage of changing production technologies which are more land extensive, and the incentives of regional policy.

The interaction of the parallel decentralising movements of employment and population is difficult to assess. It is impossible for instance to distinguish the components of regional policy which encourage both industry and families to move to new towns rather than to the central areas of our conurbations. Hall *et al.* (1973, p. 251) have considered this question and conclude,

It is clear that the outward movement of people is older and more strongly rooted than the outward movement of jobs, and this was certainly the pattern of the 1950s. But since 1961 the pattern has become more complex.

Warnes (1975), too, broadly agrees that there is a lag between the decentralisation of population and that of employment. This is also confirmed by Mills (1972) in his comparison of employment and residential density functions over time in the United States. He finds that the movement of people to the suburbs has attracted manufacturing employment to the suburbs rather than vice versa.

Slum Clearance and Overspill Policy

As we noted earlier slum clearance began in Glasgow in the 1870s. Similar developments occurred at the same time in other cities and so slum clearance has been with us for more than a century. However, as English *et al.* (1976) note, it was not until 1930 with the Housing Act of that year that central government turned its attention to redevelopment. The first real slum clearance drive was inaugurated in 1933 and by 1939 266,000 dwellings had been demolished.

Resumption of slum clearance was out of the question in the

immediate postwar period; there was a desperate shortage of accommodation and even a slum house was better than being homeless. It was
not until the late 1950s that slum clearance restarted in earnest. As the
true extent of bad housing became apparent (Mason, chapter 6 in this
volume) the programme gained momentum in the late 1960s reaching a
plateau of approximately 70,000 demolitions a year in England and
Wales. It continued at this rate until the approach of the 1974 Housing
Act which changed the main thrust of urban renewal to one of improvement.

The upsurge of slum clearance in the 1960s was seen most dramatically in the major cities. By 1970 Glasgow was demolishing three times
as many slums as it had done in 1965. Birmingham doubled its demolition programme to 4,000 slum houses a year in 1965. Similarly
Manchester moved from clearing about 1,350 houses in 1961 and 1962
to 4,000 per annum from 1963 onwards. Only Leeds with a clearance
programme of 2,000 houses a year throughout the decade did not follow
the same pattern. It was not planned to rehouse all the displaced
families within each city's boundaries. Local authorities sought the
solution to their congestion problems in overspill either by building
estates in neighbouring districts within their conurbation or through
formal agreements with new towns.

In 1966 Liverpool Corporation approved a clearance programme of
33,000 slum dwellings over the subsequent six years. In order to meet
the demands generated by this programme, municipal housing had to be
built at Cantril Farm and Halewood, both outside the city's boundary.
As a consequence of this policy by 1973 more than a quarter of the
city's public housing was on overspill estates. In addition many families
undertook more long distance migration to the new and expanded
towns of Runcorn, Skelmersdale, Widnes, Ellesmere Port and Winsford.

The impact on the city was devastating; between 1966 and 1969
15,600 dwellings were demolished in the inner areas of the city but
only 3,800 dwellings were built on the cleared land. According to a
study by the City Planning Department (1975), for the city as a whole
there was a net loss of approximately 12,100 occupied houses between
January 1967 and December 1971. During this period while 18,380
houses were cleared and the number of dwellings vacant on sites
compulsorily purchased and awaiting demolition in December 1971
exceeded the equivalent number in January 1967 by 6,200, only
10,650 municipal and 1,840 private dwellings were built. The city's
clearance programme as Stones (1972) argued had totally outstripped
its capacity to rebuild. However, by now the worst slums were gone and

a council reassessment led to a reduction in the target of the original clearance programme and the introduction of an improvement strategy.

These policies not surprisingly were reflected in the population of the city; the net outflow from Liverpool increased from 65,000 people in the five years up to 1966 to 82,650 persons in the following five. The most important destinations for this population movement were the new and expanding towns which accounted for 18 per cent of the net outflow between 1961 and 1971. In fact their importance naturally grew in the latter half of the decade with the expansion of overspill. Whereas 9 per cent of net migration out between 1961 and 1966 went to these towns, in the subsequent five years they received more than a quarter of the net outflow.

Redevelopment in Glasgow caused similar problems; during the decade 1961-71 it led to a net loss of 27,000 dwellings within the city. In fact each year since 1966 there has been a deficit between the number of council houses built and the numbers of houses closed or demolished. These deficits were as many as 5,000 houses or more in 1967 and 1970, and again in 1972. There has hence been a great dependence on overspill housing to alleviate the consequent strains on the city. The overspill strategy was conceived soon after the Second World War as a response to the high densities still existing at that time but it was not translated into practice until the early 1960s. At first the proportion of households displaced by clearance who were rehoused under overspill agreements was quite small but after a change in the regulations the numbers gradually increased. In 1970 just over half of all overspill families had been urgent cases, i.e. had come directly from either unfit or overcrowded houses or were homeless. A further 38 per cent were former council tenants.

Between 1961 and 1971, 19,000 families, an estimated 65,000 people, left the city under formal overspill agreements. Assuming none of these returned to Glasgow, Farmer and Smith (1975) estimate this would amount to about 27.7 per cent of the net migration from the city. This figure rises to 32.1 if those moving to East Kilbride without official encouragement are added to the total. If we assume the 3,000 families who relinquished their tenancies between 1961 and 1971 in the new towns fed by Glasgow returned to the city, the contributions of these formal overspill agreements still account for 22.2 per cent of the net exodus.

The impact of slum clearance on the conurbations has been described by Morton (1974). The conurbations of West Yorkshire, South-East Lancashire and Central Clydeside all cleared more homes than were replaced by local authorities during the period 1968 to 1972. As slum clearance continued into the early 1970s at a steady rate of 65,000-70,000 houses in England and Wales and the council house building programme fell by one-third from its maximum of more than 140,000 houses to less than 100,000 by 1973, so the West Midlands was also facing a similar deficit in 1972. The surpluses in Merseyside and Tyneside were also reduced with the latter just in balance in 1972. However, with the move towards improvement rather than clearance in 1974 these deficits are probably no longer significant.

Thus slum clearance particularly in the late 1960s created a unique upheaval in our cities while at the same time there was a dramatic fall in their populations. Much of this fall can be attributed to the consequent formal overspill to new towns and surrounding districts. But slum clearance did not only occur in the central core cities but also in the older parts of the conurbations. By the early 1970s, with a reduction in our national building programme the numbers of houses being demolished, in all but one of the provincial conurbations, were outstripping the totals being built by local authorities.

Demand for Home Ownership

Another possible cause of the movement out is the classic English if not British dream of owning a 'semi' in suburbia with a garden where the children can play. This desire and the relative lack of opportunities within cities to buy a home is arguably a major component of the decentralisation movement. In addition the general raising of living standards also leads to a demand for better houses which are more readily available at the periphery.

This view is endorsed by the low levels of owner-occupation in central cities; in 1971 for instance 32 per cent of households in Liverpool were owner-occupiers compared with a national average of more than 50 per cent. In Glasgow the tenure distribution is dominated by the public sector with 61.2 per cent of households living in public housing in 1971. Just 25.1 per cent owned their own home compared with a Scottish average of 33 per cent. The District Council's 1977 Housing Plan projects a decline in this proportion with the implementation of the city's urban renewal programme (Glasgow DC, 1977a).

The recent Green Paper, 'Housing Policy: A Consultative Document' (Great Britain, 1977a) has identified the lack of choice between tenures in inner urban areas as a major problem. It suggests as partial solutions measures to assist first-time purchasers and the building of houses for sale by local authorities. Most cities have sought to stem the flow of out-migration by considering the latter solution. Already Liverpool DC has built 194 houses in Anfield which have been sold under leasehold agreements. Other similar developments are in the pipeline. In Glasgow, the Scottish Special Housing Association, a public agency, has been directed to provide approximately 1,000 houses for sale in the GEAR area through new construction or by the conversion of existing properties. Overall the ultimate aim of the city is to bring the level of home ownership up to the Scottish average; to achieve this goal the sale of council houses has also been canvassed but as yet has not been implemented.

To examine the role of the demand for home ownership in the process of suburbanisation it is important to look at the dynamics of the housing market. During 1975 we know from the Register of Sasines, the land registry in Scotland, that there were almost 7,000 housing transactions in Glasgow, nearly half of which were financed by building societies and almost one-fifth by the local authority's mortgage scheme. The average price of a house in the city bought with a building society mortgage was £6,434 compared with £3,100 for a house funded with a local authority mortgage during 1974-6.

A survey of the records of the District Council's mortgage scheme over the period 1975-6 reveals that the vast majority, 87 per cent, of these mortgagors are in fact first-time purchasers who have in the main lived in Glasgow for more than five years. These borrowers are also predominantly under 30 years of age, with three-quarters of them single, engaged couples or married couples without children. All these households then are at the very beginning of the family life cycle and many are setting up a household for the first time; indeed over half of even the childless couples were living with relatives prior to buying their home.

It would appear that in Glasgow there is no significant movement of established households out of the local authority sector into owner occupation. Less than 5 per cent of these mortgagors were themselves previously local authority tenants. The equivalent figure for building societies nationally is 9 per cent of all first-time purchasers (Building Societies Association, 1976, Table 5). However, as over one-third of these borrowers were staying with relatives who were living in the public sector, it can be said that two out of every five of these households originated from the public sector. The demand for home ownership is therefore stemming from the 'children' of local authority tenants rather than the tenants themselves.

If there is this apparently restricted movement of established households between these tenures, it is instructive to consider how the possible flows within and between tenures relate to the migration process out of the city. In particular it is necessary to trace the moves out of the public sector which amounted to 8,263 in 1974 (Glasgow DC, 1977b, p. 15). During the period 1971 to 1974 the net outflow of the population is estimated to have been 26,000 per people per year.

Few of the moves from the public sector will have been absorbed into the Glasgow home ownership market. It is estimated that the number of moves in this sector in 1974 totalled 5,400 and about 1,300 of these movers were households buying a home for the first time through Glasgow DC's mortgage scheme; only about 60 of them were former local authority tenants. The Strathclyde Household Survey also estimates in 1976 that there were only 8,100 home owners in Glasgow who originally lived in the public sector. Equally although the turnover in privately rented accommodation is not known, the small size of this sector, estimated to be 42,593 in 1975 (Glasgow DC, 1977a) suggests that it too is unlikely to be enough to account for many of these moves from public housing. Again the Strathclyde Household Survey estimates there were just 3,600 private tenants in 1976 who were originally in the public sector (Strathclyde RC, 1977, Table 3.5D).

A proportion of the moves out of local authority housing will be related to old age, either through death or the tenant going to live with relatives or in an old people's home. Bentley and Poyntz (1978) have estimated that about one-third of relets in Plymouth are caused in this way. 1974 also saw a record number of abscondences from council tenancies amounting to 2,258 with a further 844 tenants evicted (Glasgow DC, 1976b, p. 89). Very few of these tenants are likely to have moved into the owner-occupied sector, a large proportion will have moved in with relatives in the short term or left the city. Meanwhile of the 1,496 households rehoused under formal overspill agreements in that year, 649 were in fact local authority tenants (Glasgow DC, 1977b, p. 23).

Thus we conclude that there are no obvious indications of a demand for home ownership within Glasgow by established households in local authority housing. Indeed it would seem that the order of 6,500 of the 8,263 moves from the public sector can definitely not be attributed to the desire to buy a home. However, there does appear to be a large demand for home ownership stemming from the offspring of public authority tenants. This is also confirmed by the District Council's survey on attitudes to the sale of council houses which found the greater interest in the idea from the householders' children than from the tenants (Glasgow DC, 1977c).

The major components of population decline from Glasgow at this time are therefore new households buying a home on the periphery, households moving within the owner-occupied sector to the suburbs, households moving from public housing to rented housing elsewhere and people moving to the new towns. Much of the motivation for these movements can be seen as the search for better housing in the form of a new house or a house with a garden. Credence to this argument is given by the fact that a large proportion of the overspill migration to East Kilbride and Cumbernauld has not been forced moves from clearance areas but households opting for the better housing, almost entirely all rented, in the new towns. The increased job opportunities may also have been a factor but Deakin and Ungerson (1977) found in a survey of migrants to new towns from inner London that the main reasons for moving were the better housing conditions and the improved physical environment with only 10.5 per cent mentioning the attraction of the jobs available. The role of employment in the overspill migration process would appear to be of only minor importance with the dominant force the desire for better housing.

If the demand for home ownership *per se* and the restricted choice within Glasgow was a major factor in the suburban migration process one would expect to see some evidence of the latent demand from public tenants in the form of a significant movement into owner-occupation particularly at the cheaper end of the market financed by local authority mortgages. However, only 5 per cent of mortgagors under this scheme are former local authority tenants and more generally there is no sign of such a movement.

Instead the picture is more complicated with large numbers of the offspring of public tenants setting up a household for the first time and forsaking the tenure of their parents for home ownership. Although we cannot be certain why there is such a movement it must be closely related to the substitutes available to these new households. In Glasgow this undoubtedly means the public sector, but as English (chapter 5 in this volume) notes the price of the better housing is the length of time on the waiting list. The choice then is between unpopular housing curiously in the 'peripheral' schemes or buying one's own home, in reality a choice between different qualities of housing (and expenditures). The same logic applies to those new households who are moving out and buying homes on the edge of the conurbation (see Karn, chapter 7 in this volume).

So while the statistics suggest there is no movement of any substance out of council housing into home ownership, it would also appear that the movement out to the periphery either through buying a home for the first time or through moving out within the owner-occupied market can largely be explained by the desire for better housing. Therefore the role of the demand for home ownership *per se* in this process seems to be of only minor importance.

Conclusions and Policy Implications

Since the birth of cities as we know them today the suburbanisation process has been continually with us. Up until the Second World War in British cities this decentralisation was also associated with population growth and led to the creation of conurbations. Since then decline has set in and by the beginning of the 1960s all the major cities and most of the conurbations were losing population. This process dramatically accelerated in the late 1960s. The selective nature of this recent fall in population has caused serious problems, particularly in its impact on local communities.

The major factors in the decline of the cities' populations have been the reduction in suburban travel costs, slum clearance and overspill policy, and the desire for better housing, in part the result of increased incomes. It does not, however seem likely that suburban travel costs are likely to fall significantly in the future, they are most likely to remain relatively stable or even rise as the world runs out of oil. Possible policies which might radically alter the present price structure and reduce commuting costs are the widespread building of urban motorways and expressways, the introduction of free public transport and a reduction in central parking fees. Large-scale slum clearance and overspill was the major cause of the decline in population between 1966 and 1971 but is now effectively over for the foreseeable future. Even if wholesale slum clearance is necessary again it would seem likely that sufficient land is available within the cities to make a return to overspill extremely unlikely.

Many cities have seen the salvation to their population crisis in increasing the opportunities for home ownership within their boundaries. The evidence in Glasgow suggests that while there is a demand for home ownership by certain groups it is motivated in part by the desire for good housing and that this is only available to them in the private sector. The building of houses for sale within the city will undoubtedly help to stem the migration of newly married young couples to the periphery. But as long as houses continue to be built for sale on the edge of conurbations the price differentials will need to be sufficient to attract people to the inner city sites.

The sale of council houses on the other hand, given the nature of the flows between tenures certainly in Glasgow, will do virtually nothing to stem suburban migration since established local authority tenants are only minor contributors to the process. In fact if the demand for home ownership for significant sections of the community is partly created by the lack of access to good quality council housing, it makes more sense not to think in terms of selling off the public sector or even building houses for sale but to consider changes in the allocation mechanisms to local authority housing. This is particularly true for Glasgow as it now faces an apparent surplus of council houses.

In conclusion it would appear that at least two of the major forces which have influenced the decline of population from cities, reduced travel costs and overspill policies, are likely to be of negligible importance in the future. The future demand for better housing remains more imponderable as it is very dependent on supply, incomes and public policy. While it has been impossible to assess precisely the impact of all three factors it seems likely that the rate of recent population decline will slow down.

Caveats to this conclusion must be made; although it is unlikely that transport technology will advance significantly in the near future it is possible that because of lags in reaction, the impact of the motor age is not yet totally complete. In addition it is conceivable that the changes in the recent past have set in motion an unstoppable decentralisation movement, a bandwagon, which will continue long after the original causes have disappeared. Whatever the likelihood of these hypotheses, the era of the central city dominating its hinterland is undoubtedly over; the cities of the Victorians, like their seaside piers, are lingering artifacts, and the pains of change remain.

References

Bentley, R. and Poyntz, C. (1978) 'Forecasting Council Dwelling Relets', *Urban Studies*, vol. 15, pp. 215-20
Bett, W.H. and Gillham, J.C. (1962) *Great British Tramway Networks*, London: The Light Railway Transport League
Briggs, A. (1968) *Victorian Cities*, Harmondsworth: Penguin.
Building Societies Association (1976) *Facts and Figures No. 6.*
Cameron, G.C. and Evans, A. (1973) 'The British Conurbation Centres', *Regional Studies*, vol. 7, pp. 47-55

Chalmers, A.K. (1916) *Health and Housing*, London: The Medical Officer

Deakin, N. and Ungerson, C. (1977) *Leaving London: Planned Mobility and the Inner City*, London: Heinemann

English, J., Madigan, R. and Norman, P. (1976) *Slum Clearance: The Social and Administrative Context in England and Wales*, London: Croom Helm

Farmer, E. and Smith, R. (1975) 'Overspill Theory: A Metropolitan Case Study', *Urban Studies*, vol. 12, pp. 151-68

George, H. (1884) *Social Problems*, London: Kegan Paul, Trench

Glasgow DC (1976a) Planning Department, *East End Project, Survey Information – 1*

—— (1976b) Housing Management Department, *Annual Report 1975*

—— (1977a) *Housing Plan, No. 1.*

—— (1977b) Housing Management Department, *Annual Report 1976*

—— (1977c) *The Sale of Council Houses*

—— (1951) *Census 1951, England and Wales: Report on Greater London and Five Other Conurbations*, London: HMSO

—— (1961a) *Census, 1961, England and Wales*, London: HMSO

—— (1961b) *Census 1961, Scotland*, Edinburgh: HMSO

—— (1966a) *Sample Census 1966, England and Wales* London: HMSO

—— (1966b) *Sample Census 1966, Scotland*, Edinburgh: HMSO

—— (1970) Central Statistical Office, *Abstract of Regional Statistics, No. 6*, London: HMSO

—— (1971a) *Census, 1971, England and Wales*, London: HMSO

—— (1971b) *Census, 1971, Scotland*, Edinburgh: HMSO

—— (1975) Central Statistical Office, *Abstract of Regional Statistics, No. 11*, London: HMSO

—— (1977a) Office of Population Censuses and Surveys, *Population Estimates: 1975 revised, 1976 provincial*, London: HMSO

—— (1977b) Department of Employment, *Employment in Metropolitan Areas*, London

—— (1977c) Department of Environment, *Change or Decay: Final Report of the Liverpool Inner Area Study*, London: HMSO

—— (1977d) Central Statistical Office, *Regional Statistics, No. 13*, London: HMSO

Great Britain (1977e) *Housing Policy: A Consultative Document*, Cmnd. 6851, London: HMSO

Hall, P. Thomas, R., Gracy, H. and Drewett, R. (1973) *The Containment of Urban England*, London: George Allen and Unwin

Kellett, J.R. (1969) *The Impact of Railways on Victorian Cities*,

London: Routledge and Kegan Paul

Liverpool MD (1975) Planning Department, *The Changing Social and Housing Structure of Liverpool*

—— (1977) Planning Department, *City in Transition*

Mills, E.S. (1972) *Studies in the Structure of the Urban Economy*, Baltimore: Johns Hopkins Press

Morton, J. (1974) 'Slum Clearance', *New Society*, vol. 28, p. 74

Oakley, C.A. (1962) *The Last Tram*, Glasgow: Corporation of City of Glasgow

Rasmusson, D.W. (1973) *Urban Economics*, New York: Harper and Row

Russell, J.B. (1885) *The Vital Statistics of Glasgow*, Glasgow: Corporation of City of Glasgow

Scottish Development Agency (1978) *Preliminary Results of GEAR Household Survey*, Glasgow: Unpublished mimeo

Stones, A. (1972) 'Slum Clearance – Now!', *Official Architecture and Planning*, vol. 35, no. 2

Strathclyde Regional Council (1977) Department of Physical Planning, *Household Survey 1976*

Warnes, A.W. (1975) *The Decentralisation of Employment from the Larger English Cities*, London: Centre for Environmental Studies

NOTES ON CONTRIBUTORS

Glen Bramley is a lecturer at the School for Advanced Urban Studies, Bristol University. He was formerly the economist on the Lambeth Inner Area Study project.

Peter Dicken and *Peter E. Lloyd* are senior lecturers in the School of Geography, Manchester University. They are authors of a number of articles on the components of industrial change and are joint authors of *Location in Space* (Harper Row 1972.)

John English is a lecturer in social policy at Trent Polytechnic. He was formerly a lecturer in the Department of Social and Economic Research, University of Glasgow. He is joint author of *Slum Clearance: the Social and Administrative Context in England and Wales* (Croom Helm, 1976).

Valerie Karn is a lecturer in housing policy at the Centre for Urban and Regional Studies, University of Birmingham. She is a member of the Department of Environment's Housing Services Advisory Group, and winner of Oddfellows Social Concern Book Prize for 1977.

Alan McGregor is a lecturer in labour economics in the Department of Social and Economic Research, University of Glasgow. He is the author of a number of articles on unemployment and labour market aspects of urban deprivation.

Tim Mason works as research officer for Merseyside Improved Houses. He has previously worked at the Institute of Local Government Studies, Birmingham University and has carried out a study of urban renewal policy with the help of the Centre for Environmental Studies.

Geoff Norris is at present a Senior Research Officer with Newcastle City Council. He was formerly a lecturer in the Department of Social and Economic Research, University of Glasgow.

INDEX